Laurent Cantet

MANCHESTER
1824

Manchester University Press

Laurent Cantet

Martin O'Shaughnessy

Manchester University Press

Published by Manchester University Press
Altrincham Street, Manchester M1 7JA
www.manchesteruniversitypress.co.uk

British Library Cataloguing-in-Publication Data
A catalogue record for this book is available from the British Library

Library of Congress Cataloguing-in-Publication Data applied for

ISBN 978 0 7190 9150 6 hardback

ISBN 978 1 5261 2302 2 paperback

First published in hardback 2015

This edition first published 2018

Typeset by Out of House Publishing
Printed by TJ International, Padstow, Cornwall

To Kay, Gloria, Ana, John and Michael

Contents

LIST OF PLATES   *page* viii
SERIES EDITORS' FOREWORD   ix
ACKNOWLEDGEMENTS   xi

Introduction   1

1   **A director and his methods**   3

2   **Early applications**   30

3   **The work diptych**   56

4   **Going global, heading south**   96

5   **Between Republican walls**   124

6   **Before and after the political**   153

Conclusion   180

AFTERWORD. RETURNING TO CUBA   183
FILMOGRAPHY   186
FURTHER READING   189
INDEX   191

List of plates

1   The father, the son and the rest: socialising the primal
    scene (*Ressources humaines*, 2000)   *page* 90
2   The consciousness before it meets the world (*Entre les
    murs*, 2008)   90
3   The hero (far right) is part, yet not part, of the group (*Jeux
    de plage*, 1995)   91
4   Breaking free or losing oneself (*Les Sanguinaires*, 1997)   91
5   The text of muteness or the silent voice of the voiceless
    (*Ressources humaines*, 2000)   92
6   Mutual surveillance: the glass as plane of encounter and
    separation (*L'Emploi du temps*, 2001)   92
7   The 'innocence' of the tourist gaze: taking possession of
    the beach (*Vers le sud*, 2006)   93
8   Inequality in the spaces of leisure: the mute eloquence of
    the image (*Vers le sud*, 2006)   93
9   Cinemascope: the distance between people (*Entre les murs*,
    2008)   94
10 The unstructured, egalitarian space of the school-yard
    (*Entre les murs*, 2008)   94
11 The public shaming of Buttinger: turning the car into a site
    of struggle (*Foxfire*, 2012)   94
12 From vamp to ingénue: Violet's use of the masquerade
    (*Foxfire*, 2012)   95
13 The non-mirroring of gendered identities (*Foxfire*, 2012)   95

Series editors' foreword

To an anglophone audience, the combination of the words 'French' and 'cinema' evokes a particular kind of film: elegant and wordy, sexy but serious – an image as dependent upon national stereotypes as is that of the crudely commercial Hollywood blockbuster, which is not to say that either image is without foundation. Over the past two decades, this generalised sense of a significant relationship between French identity and film has been explored in scholarly books and articles, and has entered the curriculum at university level and, in Britain, at A-level. The study of film as art-form and (to a lesser extent) as industry has become a popular and widespread element of French studies, and French cinema has acquired an important place within film studies. Meanwhile, the growth in multi-screen and 'art-house' cinemas, together with the development of the video industry, has led to the greater availability of foreign-language films to an English-speaking audience. Responding to these developments, this series is designed for students and teachers seeking information and accessible but rigorous critical study of French cinema, and for the enthusiastic film-goer who wants to know more.

The adoption of a director-based approach raises questions about auteurism. A series that categorises films not according to period or to genre (for example), but to the person who directed them, runs the risk of espousing a romantic view of film as the product of solitary inspiration. On this model, the critic's role might seem to be that of discovering continuities, revealing a necessarily coherent set of themes and motifs that correspond to the particular genius of the individual. This is not our aim: the auteur perspective on film, itself most clearly articulated in France in the early 1950s, will be interrogated in certain volumes of the series, and, throughout, the director will be treated as one highly significant element in a complex process of film production and reception that includes socio-economic and political determinants, the work of a large and highly skilled team of artists and technicians, the mechanisms of production and distribution, and the complex and multiply determined responses of spectators.

The work of some of the directors in the series is already well known outside France; that of others is less so – the aim is both to provide informative and original English-language studies of established figures, and to extend the range of French directors known to anglophone students of cinema. We intend the series to contribute to the promotion of the formal and informal study of French films, and to the pleasure of those who watch them.

DIANA HOLMES
ROBERT INGRAM

Acknowledgements

My great thanks go to Diana Holmes and Robert Ingram for their support, advice and encouragement. I am tremendously grateful too to Matthew Frost and his colleagues at Manchester University Press for their patience and helpfulness. Thanks are also due to Robert Whitelock for all his work on the manuscript and to Rob Wilkinson for his deft handling of the production process. More specific thanks are owed to friends and colleagues with whom I discussed specific Cantet works and whose ideas and comments undoubtedly helped shape this book: John Marks at Nottingham University, with whom I have discussed Cantet on many occasions; Gary Needham at Nottingham Trent University, who is a mine of information on all things film-related; Winifred Woodhull from the University of California San Diego, who gave so generously of her time and insights; all the participants, and especially the two organisers, Rosemarie Scullion and Nathalie Rachlin, at the wonderful colloquium in La Bretesche in 2012, where so many ideas were exchanged. Thanks finally to the Arts and Humanities Research Council and to Nottingham Trent University for providing the sabbatical time that allowed me to research and write this book.

Introduction

Laurent Cantet is one of France's leading contemporary directors although he has only made a relatively modest number of films. If the undoubted high point of his career to date was the award of the Palme d'Or at the sixty-first Cannes film festival in 2008 to his *Entre les murs* (*The Class*), it was not his first critical success. It came on the back of the Don Quixote award given to *L'Emploi du temps* (*Time Out*) at the Venice film festival in 2001, the French *César* for best first film and other prizes given to *Ressources humaines* (*Human Resources*) also in 2001, and the Jean Vigo prize for best short film given to his *Tous à la manif* in 1995. These awards together underlined Cantet's French reputation and growing international stature, something that certainly helped him obtain backing for his multilingual Franco-Canadian *Vers le sud* (*Heading South*; 2006[1]) with its stars (Charlotte Rampling and Karen Young), and the recent *Foxfire: Confessions of a Girl Gang* (2012), which hit the festival circuit in September 2012 – another Franco-Canadian co-production. A filmmaker whose stature and international appeal feeds off festival and critical success, Cantet bears many of the hallmarks of the international *auteur*. Yet there is also something different about his films, something related to but not entirely dependent on his general preference for low-budget work with amateur actors. At Cannes in 2008, he was accompanied not by stellar, glamorous performers, but by the group of school-children with whom he had shot *Entre les murs* and who had been allowed a far-from-passive voice in the way the

---

1 I have preferred to give the release date rather than year of production for the films.

film developed. This was an international *auteur* film that marked out the director's determination to make films in a certain way, despite industry expectations.

Part of Cantet's importance undoubtedly lies in the compelling relevance and intelligence of his output, his determination to probe and bring to the surface key social evolutions and fault-lines of our time: from the changing world of work, through the challenges facing the French Republican school and the inequalities of globalised consumption, to gender oppression and emergent forms of rebellion. But another equally central part of his importance lies in how he makes films (his 'method'), with his egalitarian commitment to allowing different voices to be heard and participate actively in the production of his work. At a time when inequality seems to be rising inexorably and when many struggle to have any meaningful voice, this commitment is a vital one. In the end, what makes Cantet such an interesting figure is this double timeliness of his film-making, his ability to speak to his period in ways so suited to it. While this book will provide a rounded analysis of Cantet's work, an exploration and explanation of this double timeliness lies at its core. Although the book can be perused in different ways, and the chapters can be read reasonably independently from each other, the first chapter, with its discussion of Cantet's way of making films, provides a vital prelude to what follows.

1

A director and his methods

Cantet was born in 1961 in the small town of Melle in the Poitou-Charentes region. His parents were teachers. His cinematic vocation began to emerge when he studied photography at Marseille University and started to assemble photographs to make short pictorial stories. At the same time, he bought a digital camera, a piece of equipment that was becoming an affordable consumer item at the time, and started to make short films with friends. Then, moving decisively towards cinema, he took the entrance examination at the prestigious Institut des Hautes Etudes Cinématographiques (IDHEC) in Paris and passed, against his expectations. There he would learn his trade and round out his cinematic education by working on his and friends' films and watching numerous other films with the same people. After graduation in 1986, he worked in television and made *Un été à Beyrouth* (France 3, 1990), a half-hour film about the Lebanese civil war as seen through the eyes of a child. He would go on to be the assistant of the famous documentary-maker, Marcel Ophüls, on his *Veillée d'armes* (1994), a film about the reporting of the 1992 siege of Sarajevo. Along with friends from IDHEC like Dominik Moll and Robin Campillo, he would join Sérénade, a small production company founded by Vincent Dietschy, another of the group, in 1991. Sérénade was driven by a collaborative spirit: returning to the kind of collective working that had characterised their IDHEC days, its participants would read each other's scripts and work on each other's films, interchanging roles in the process. Cantet made two short films with Sérénade, *Tous à la manif* and *Jeux de plage*, and was the cinematographer on Dietschy's *Cette nuit* (1998) and Gilles Marchand's short, *Joyeux Noël* (1994). Marchand would in turn co-write *Tous à la manif* and *Ressources humaines*. This way of working with friends is nothing exceptional within French cinema: for example, Arnaud Desplechin and Matthieu Kassovitz, very different directors in many ways, are both known for doing likewise. But the way in which Cantet routinely asks long-standing acquaintances either to co-write or to comment on his work suggests that he embodies a type of authorship that is anything but narrowly personal. This is something to which we will return.

After the demise of Sérénade in 1998, the next stage in Cantet's career began when he was contacted by Caroline Benjo of Haut et Court, the Paris-based production company. Benjo and her co-producer Carole Scotta had earlier suggested to Arte, the Franco-German cultural television channel, that they should put together a series of ten films called *2000 vu par* ... (*2000 seen by* ...) to mark the upcoming millennium. They agreed with Pierre Chevalier, the commissioning producer from Arte, that the films would last about an hour, cost 4 or 5 million francs, with Arte contributing 2.3 million, and generally be made by promising new directors.[1] People like Walter Salles and Abderrahmane Sissako were recruited alongside American director Hal Hartley, at that time the best known of the group. Benjo turned to Cantet because she had been impressed by his short films. Cantet's contribution to the series was called *Les Sanguinaires* and told the story of a group of friends who take their children to an almost uninhabited island to escape the hype surrounding the millennial festivities. The film was aired on Arte in November 1998 and also shown at a number of festivals including Venice but did not achieve a general cinematic release, not least because of its unsuitable length (Lebtahi and Gillet, 2005: 142).

Pierre Chevalier is an important figure in French television and film and has produced several notable series of made-for-television films, including *2000 vu par* ... and *Tous les garçons et les filles de leur âge* (*All the Boys and Girls of Their Age*). Obliged by legislation to invest in film, television has become one of the main cash-cows of French cinema. This relationship is often seen negatively, with television perceived to exercise a conservative influence on film and to push directors towards pre-formatted works suitable for a mass audience (Le Club des 13, 2008: 78, 93–102). Going against the grain, Chevalier has

1 For an account of the series by the producers, see Nicklaus (2002).

shown the capacity to encourage some of the best and most imaginative directors, and to support films with a distinct social or critical dimension.[2] His encounter with Cantet was undoubtedly an important one for the latter, since Chevalier would again turn to the still relatively inexperienced film-maker when putting together another new series of television films called *Au travail* (*At work*). The outcome of this second collaboration was *Ressources humaines*, Cantet's film about a management trainee doing a placement in the provincial factory where his father has always worked. Like some of Chevalier's other productions, notably Robert Guédiguian's *Marius et Jeanette* (1997), the film achieved both television screening and cinematic distribution, thus blurring the lines between the two media in a way that was not to everybody's taste. It went out on television on 14 January 2000 and was released in cinemas the next day. It had a television audience of 1,715, 320 and was seen by 219,434 cinema spectators (Gillet and Lebtahi, 2005: 142). Addressing the introduction of the thirty-five-hour working week by the Socialist Government, the film served as a catalyst for public debate. It marked Cantet out as a politically committed director at a time when French cinema more broadly was moving back towards political involvement after years of disengagement. Shown at New York's Museum of Modern Art (MOMA), and at the Thessaloniki, Torino, Sundance and San Sebastian film festivals, it also saw Cantet's international profile begin to develop.

Written with Campillo, now his established co-writer and another IDHEC comrade, Cantet's next film, *L'Emploi du temps*, tells the story of a high-flying management consultant who hides his redundancy from friends and family. The film draws on real-life events in the shape of the celebrated Romand affair, the case of an apparently successful professional who was in fact unemployed and murdered his family when his deception was discovered. It thus shared two obvious things with *Ressources humaines*: it focused on the world of work and bore a relationship to contemporary events, although in this case with a less obvious connection to political debates. Yet, where it was very different is that it was a cinematic production from the start and confirmed Cantet's growing status as a film- rather than a television-director. Its style was rather more poetic and did far more

---

2 Chevalier has worked, for example, with Claire Denis, Erick Zonca, Philippe Garrel, André Téchiné, Robert Guédiguian and Patrick Chéreau.

to express its hero's evolving subjective state than the much flatter realism of the earlier film. It also relied more on professional actors: while *Ressources humaines* had deployed a nearly entirely amateur cast, *L'Emploi du temps'* two leads, Aurélien Recoing and Karen Viard, were well known stage and screen performers.

Taking what one might call a midway position between these two films, Cantet's next work, *Vers le sud* would self-consciously play off star and amateur performers – Charlotte Rampling and Karen Young on the one hand, Haitian unknowns on the other –, as it sought to render the asymmetrical interaction of prosperous, white tourists and the young black men with whom they sought romance and sexual satisfaction. On the surface at least, the film represented several new departures for Cantet. Firstly, it moved his film-making away from France. Secondly, mixing English, French and Creole, it was a multi-lingual film. Thirdly, although again co-written with Campillo, it was an adaptation, albeit a very free one, of a pre-existing literary text – *La Chair du maître* (*The Master's Flesh*; 1997) by the Haitian novelist, Dany Laferrière – a work whose loosely articulated stories probe the erotically charged interface of race, power, class and sex (Laferrière, 2000). Finally, by situating itself in the 1970s, at the time of the brutally corrupt Baby Doc Duvalier regime, it apparently took Cantet away from the immediately contemporary period that had seemed his preferred terrain. However, at a deeper level, it might be seen as confirming certain key aspects of Cantet's film-making. Firstly, as we will later see, the historical distance is more apparent than real, and the film speaks eloquently to the current moment. Secondly, although an adaptation might seem a less personal project, the source work was chosen precisely because Cantet recognised some of his own preoccupations in it, notably the complex intersection of the personal and the social, the affective and the political.

Entre les murs would see a double return home. It took the director very much back to France and questions about French society. It also returned him to his preferred practices in terms of how it was made. Like *Tous à la manif* or *Ressources humaines*, its shooting, with an all-amateur cast, was preceded by a long period of casting and workshopping during which the script, an adaptation of François Bégaudeau's successful novel of the same title (2006), was tested and refined. Cantet's satisfaction with this way of working confirmed his sense of what his directorial 'method' should be. His second experience of working in a foreign setting with *Foxfire: Confessions of a Girl Gang* (hereafter *Foxfire*) would be very different from *Vers le sud*. This time there would be no star performers. Instead, he carefully selected his cast (mainly of teenage girls) during a winter spent in Toronto. Casting would give way to two weeks of intense workshopping when, true to his preferences, Cantet had the young women try out ideas from the script, allowing them to inflect its evolution (Mangeot, 2012: 10).

Foxfire seemed to confirm Cantet's recent preference for adapting literary works, in this case Joyce Carol Oates's hit 1993 novel *Foxfire: Confessions of a Girl Gang*. Like *Vers le sud*, the film also moved the director back in time – in this case to the small-town America of the 1950s – although with Canada standing in for the USA in the same way as San Domingo largely stands in for Haiti in *Vers le sud*. However, the film's theme, the revolt of a gang of girls against the misogynist values and attitudes surrounding them, had the same contemporary relevance as the exploration of neo-colonialism in *Vers le sud* (Mangeot, 2012: 11).

After *Foxfire*, varying his approach by moving away from direct adaptation of an existing text, Cantet collaborated with Cuban novelist, Leon Padura, to produce the script of his latest film, *Return to Ithaca* (2014). Cantet had got to know Padura when working on his segment of the multi-director work *7 Days in Havana* (2012), a film to which he contributed the final, Sunday, section. Made in Spanish, the latter two works would confirm the increasingly international nature of Cantet's authorship.

Alongside his film-making, Cantet has maintained a long-standing commitment to France's illegal migrant workers, the *sans-papiers*. The *sans-papiers* came forcefully to French public attention in 1996 when a group of them who had been occupying a Parisian church were forcibly expelled. A short film supporting them was released by a film-makers' collective and shown at many cinemas around France. It ended with an appeal for public support signed by many film industry figures, including Cantet. The director's support for the *sans-papiers* (and that of the collective) was reaffirmed in 2007 with the making and national release of another very short film, *Laissez-les grandir ici*,[3] a work co-sponsored by the Réseau Education Sans

---

3 *Let Them Grow up Here.*

Frontières (RESF),[4] an organisation of which Cantet is a high-profile member. More recently still, in 2010, Cantet's commitment to the *sans-papiers* was again visible when he first turned out to stand with and speak up for a group of migrants threatened with expulsion from a building that they had been occupying in the rue du Regard in Paris, and then took a leading role in making a three-and-a-half-minute film defending their broader cause.[5] While Cantet's support for migrant workers and their children might seem narrow in its focus and humanitarian in its intentions, he is clearly very aware of the political issues at stake. In an interview given to communist daily, *L'Humanité*, on 24 February 2010, he first commented on how companies use migrant workers' vulnerable status to drive down wages, and secondly noted how the migrants embodied a precariousness that increasingly threatened French society in general. They were effectively the advance guard of a broader struggle.[6] Cantet's filmmaking and his commitment to the *sans-papiers* converged doubly at the time of *Entre les murs*. The film, as we will see, figures the story of a Chinese pupil whose mother is threatened with expulsion from France. At the same time, the real-life mother of one of its actors, Boubakar, was discovered also to be without papers. Cantet became her sponsor in her application for regularisation.[7]

Cantet's method

At around the time of *Entre les murs*, Cantet would repeatedly refer to his 'method' – that is, his preferred way of making a film (Rigoulet, 2008; Burdeau and Thirion, 2008). As discussed above, this involved a long period for casting a largely amateur cast, then a period of workshopping when the script and situations were refined in collaboration with the performers and, finally, the kind of shooting that was flexible enough to allow for this spontaneity and inventiveness to be kept alive. In some ways, the use of amateurs might seem similar to that adopted by other leading contemporary directors like the Dardenne

---

4 Network for an Education without Frontiers.
5 The film was called *On bosse ici! On vit ici! On reste ici! (We Work Here! We Live Here! We Are Staying Here!).*
6 See Fache (2010).
7 See Bonal (2008).

brothers or Bruno Dumont, who seek to make a break with conventional commercial film-making while opening their films to the rawness of the real. Yet, there is something specific and important about what Cantet does. The Dardennes, for example, use amateurs in an essentially Bressonian way: that is, following the method established so famously by Robert Bresson, the great post-war French director, they use amateurs as blank canvases upon whose surfaces performances, as purely external manifestations, can be painted through obsessive rehearsal of gestures and movements (Bresson, 1997). The external nature of these performances leads us, as spectators, to deduce an interiority that escapes our observation. In the process, characters, although socially disempowered, are granted a resistance to the spectatorial gaze and a certain independence from their creators. Yet, this relative empowerment of the *characters* depends on the curtailment of the initiative exercised by the actors who are denied the ability to internalise and interpret their role. Cantet's use of amateurs is very different. He deliberately chooses people to play not themselves but someone with a similar social role: the woman trade unionist in *Ressources humaines* is a real trade unionist, the boss a manager, the sacked father a worker forced into early retirement, and so on.[8] The casting starts from the presupposition that each character is an expert in his or her own role. When discussing *Entre les murs*, for example, Cantet said of his amateur cast, 'Aussi bien les élèves que les profs, ils ont une expertise de leur vie dont j'avais besoin pour écrire le film' (Burdeau and Thirion, 2008: 16).[9] Rather than being asked to erase their subjectivity, his performers are encouraged to

8 The father is played by Jean-Claude Vallod, who, just before shooting, was made to take early retirement from the Comédie Française, France's most prestigious theatre company, where he worked as an electrician. The representative of the Confédération générale du travail (CGT) trade union confederation is played by Danielle Mélador, a woman who had been the chief accountant at a clothing manufacturer. Upon being made redundant, Mélador herself had become a representative of the unemployed within the CGT. Didier Emile-Woldemard, the character who plays Alain, the worker on the next machine to the father, had experienced a range of short-term, temporary contracts before taking on a part in the film. Lucien Longueville, who plays the part of the boss, was the real boss of a small iron-casting company (Lemahieu, 2000).

9 'Just like the teachers, the pupils have a knowledge of their life which I needed to draw on to write the film.' (All translations are my own unless otherwise indicated.)

enter into active discussion of their character's behaviour and to draw upon their experience to inform the part. This is one reason for the films' long gestation. The period of casting and workshopping is a time when director and cast enter into dialogue and shape characters and situations. Cantet comments, 'Le casting est une manière de mettre à l'épreuve ce qui est écrit, en proposant des situations, en voyant ce que cela peut devenir. En retour, ces improvisations viennent s'intégrer dans le scénario écrit. Je ne sais jamais exactement à quel moment le scénario est fini' (Burdeau and Thirion, 2008: 11).[10] Because Cantet uses amateur performers to gain access to areas of experience closed off to him, his films might seem to resemble documentaries. However, because the cast are playing, not themselves, but someone whose social role is close to theirs, they are free to develop their role more fully. Cantet describes his work with the cast of *Entre les murs* in just this way: 'Ils étaient protégés par leur personnages et pouvaient se lâcher davantage que dans un documentaire où chaque mot peut se retourner contre vous' (Burdeau and Thirion, 2008: 17).[11]

In the post-1968 period, one of the key tasks that emerged as a pre-condition for political advance was a breaking down of the rigid separation of roles that separated intellectual from manual labour or decision-taking from execution of decisions. Because existing hierarchies were hard-wired into the definition of social roles and places, progress could only occur when people moved outside their position and hierarchical specialisation began to be broken down. Applied to cinema, this implied that directorial prerogatives and specialist, technical knowledge had to be democratised, so that workers, say, would no longer be merely the objects filmed but also the subjects filming.[12] Some such loosening of roles, albeit without the broader radical political context, would seem to be at work in Cantet's filmmaking, where, far from being merely untutored performers,

---

10 'Casting is a way of testing out what is written by suggesting situations and seeing what emerges from them. In return, these improvisations find their way back into the written script. I never know precisely when the script is finished.'

11 'They were protected by their characters and could be more open than in a documentary where each word can come back to haunt you.'

12 The most famous film in which this occurred was the legendary Medvedkin group film *Classe de lutte* (1969).

amateur actors are seen as sources of expertise and able partners in the production of the script and in the process of documentation. If the Dardennes' response to the disempowerment of those at the bottom is to build resistances into their characters, Cantet takes a distinct and much more dialogical route grounded in his faith in people's ability to reflect upon their own lives. One might say that he is seeking his resistance in a different place: that is, in the encounter between his and his co-writers' initial ideas and the thoughts and experiences of others.

This desire to engage with others, with the recognition of the limitations of his own position that it implies, is also one of the principle explanations for Cantet's recourse to adaptation of novels in *Vers le sud*, *Entre les murs*, and *Foxfire*. It might seem paradoxical that a director so obviously drawn to investigate others' lives and to the real should turn to literary works, allowing successive mediating layers (the original text, the adapted screenplay) to come between him and what was filmed. However, knowing that his own experience of Haiti, school-teaching or the lives of adolescent girls is strictly limited, Cantet recognises the need to turn to others. His authorship is a knowingly self-restricting one that brings other viewpoints within the films to probe and to compensate for its own limitations. As he told a journalist, 'ça me paraît intéressant d'être dépassé par le dispositif qu'on met en place' (Rigoulet, 2001: 42).[13] To the extent that his films are able to open themselves up to others' voices without controlling them, one might say that they are polyphonic, in the sense that Mikhail Bakhtin gives to that word.

For Bakhtin, any instance of speech or writing is inevitably dialogic; that is, it enters into dialogue with utterances that precede it and anticipates those that may follow. Never independent in its existence, it builds into itself its relationship to the multiplicity of ambient voices. Within this broader dialogic context, the novel has a special place owing to its unique capacity to internalise the discourses around itself. However, as Bakhtin also notes, not all novels internalise their imbrication in a heteroglot environment in the same way. Most subordinate the play of voices to an authorial voice, thus cementing the centrality of the latter and the values and judgements

13 '[I]t's interesting when the system one has put in place escapes from one's control.'

it bears. Only some writers, and, for Bakhtin, Dostoevsky is the key example, are able to restrain authorial control enough to allow other voices enduring autonomy so that, not simply dialogic, the novel becomes polyphonic, an egalitarian interweaving of viewpoints that is never resolved into some hierarchical fixity (Morris, 1994: 88–122; Holquist, 1981: 348–9).[14] What I will suggest in later chapters is that Cantet's cinema strives for a similar polyphonic quality. In a period when the inequality of voices has been driven to new extremes and many have become politically inaudible, this commitment to vocal equality is a key dimension of the films' politics.

Cantet's fictional universe and self-effacing authorship

If Cantet's 'method' has been much discussed by him and others, his way of approaching a story and constructing a narrative, another *methodical* part of his film-making, is less widely analysed. In the pages that follow, I will discuss key recurrent elements of his films: his use of what one might call the family romance to explore the inter-face of the personal and the social; his recourse to shame to probe the tension between individuals and groups; his probing of conservative and progressive utopias with their promises of social harmony; his exploration of space and the power dynamics embedded within it; his capacity to combine realism and melodrama as a way to drive social fault-lines to the surface. The argument that I will begin here and develop throughout the book in relation to these elements will be a twofold one. I will argue, firstly, that their recurrent presence constitutes what one might call an authorial signature. I will suggest, secondly, that they come together to constitute something like a tool kit that allows Cantet to open up the contexts with which the films engage without imposing a specific content on them. This, I will suggest, helps explain why he can be very present in his films without drowning out other voices. In other words, there is a consist-ency between his method, as explored in the previous section, and

---

14 Developed over a period of time and in different works, Bakhtin's use of key terms inevitably shifts. For the sake of simplicity, I have limited myself to the core opposition between 'dialogism' and 'polyphony'.

his methodical but self-effacing story construction. Both allow other voices to be heard.

Socialising the family romance

Cantet's films often centre on broadly Oedipal dramas. This is clearly the case with his two shorts, *Tous à la manif* and *Jeux de plage*, both of which are built around father–son relationships. It applies equally to his work 'diptych', for both *Ressources humaines* and *L'Emploi du temps* have a father–son pairing near the heart of their narrative. However, it also applies more loosely to films like *Entre les murs*, *Vers le sud* and *Foxfire*. In *Entre les murs*, someone whom one could consider a surrogate parent, a teacher, is shown interacting with young people on the threshold of the adult world. In *Vers le sud*, a group of mature women have romantic and sexual relationships with young men and adolescents young enough to be their sons. In *Foxfire*, a group of young women revolt against the sexist and misogynist attitudes that surround them as embodied in older male figures. The specific form taken by the drama varies, but there is something constant enough to be a distinct pattern. However, while he is undoubtedly interested in the familial, Cantet is anything but an intimist director purely drawn to the psyche or the domestic interior. Rather, he is someone who likes to work at the threshold of the personal and the social, the private and the public. His 'Oedipal' dramas always open onto broader dynamics.

Although it is not my intention to take this book in a psycho-analytical direction, there is a short but important text by Freud that is relevant here. It is called 'Family romances' and begins thus:

> The liberation of an individual, as he grows up, from the authority of his parents is one of the most necessary although one of the most painful results brought about by the course of his development. It is quite essential that the liberation should occur and it may be presumed that it has been to some extent achieved by everyone who has achieved a normal state. Indeed, the whole progress of society rests upon the opposition between successive generations.
>
> (Freud, 1959: 237)

What is interesting about this opening, apart from its assumption that the individual is male, is the way that it feels compelled to open the question of the family romance onto much broader socio-historical processes ('the whole progress of society'). It is as if the Freudian family romance struggles to remain within its own frame despite the author's intent. The same struggle makes itself felt throughout the text. Freud talks about how, experiencing the feeling that he is not receiving his due share of his parents' love, often because of sibling rivals, the child fantasises that he (she?) is a step-child or adopted. Developing a low opinion of his parents, he imagines that he is the offspring of others who 'as a rule, are of higher social standing' (Freud, 1959: 239) The romance thus opens onto questions of social hierarchy and class before Freud once again ties it back into the family unit, as if the broader social dynamics evoked were simply an expression of something more intrinsically narrow. This is what Freud writes as he moves to the end of his text:

> If we examine in detail the commonest of these imaginative romances, the replacement of both parents or of the father alone by grander people, we find that these new and aristocratic parents are equipped with attributes that are derived entirely from real recollections of the actual and humble ones; so that the child is not getting rid of his father but exalting him. Indeed the whole effort at replacing the real father by a superior one is only an expression of the child's longing for the happy, vanished days when his father seemed to him the noblest and strongest of men and his mother the dearest and loveliest of women.
>
> (Freud, 1959: 241)

The convergences with Cantet are clear. At least two of his films, for example, have heroes who turn to what could be seen as better, surrogate fathers. The boss who takes the hero under his wing in *Ressources humaines* is part of the higher social group to which the hero initially aspires while the smuggler of counterfeit goods who brings the hero into his organisation in *L'Emploi du temps* is a more protective father than the hero's sterner, biological father. However, while in Freud's case, the opening of the family romance onto broader socio-historical contexts is resisted, for Cantet, it is a given. The films' families and their Oedipal relationships are always knowingly tied to external questions such as class, power or ethnicity.

The classic Freudian Oedipal drama has a cast of three: the father, the mother and the young son. The son's awakening desire for the mother draws him into direct rivalry with the much more powerful father and generates the fear of castration. Rather than challenge the father, the son chooses to identify with him and accepts the need to change the object of his desire and to postpone its realisation. Being social, Cantet's Oedipal dramas are less tightly circumscribed. Thus, for example, in *Ressources humaines*, rather than simply being a powerful figure, the father, as a subordinate, working-class male is already exposed to a form of social castration, a position made worse by the impending sacking that comes to the surface during the film. His desire, a social rather than a sexual one, is that his son should enjoy the power and prestige that he himself was unable to know. The delayed gratification that the Freudian narrative associates with the son is thus linked instead to the working-class father because of the latter's position as a minor, someone unable to take his own decisions, in the workplace. The son, although he does not know it at first, is in an impossible position. To the extent that he identifies with his father, he takes on the latter's social humiliation. To the extent that he identifies with the boss, as a paternal substitute, he participates in the biological father's symbolic castration. The elements of the Oedipal drama all seem to be there, but the story has lost its neat containment, its clear definition of roles and the possibility of any successful resolution at individual or family level. At the same time, it has shed its atemporal quality and become associated with a specific and precisely detailed socio-historical context related not simply to capitalist class relations but also to the way in which the recent availability of mass further and higher education and the declining place of industry in western societies have made it difficult and undesirable for the children of industrial workers to follow in their parents' footsteps (Beaud and Pialoux, 1999: 161–278).

Closely associated with the Freudian Oedipal complex is what is called the primal scene, the moment when the traumatised but fascinated young child accidentally witnesses or perhaps imagines the sexual act between two adults, typically but not necessarily the parents, misperceiving it as a violence done to the mother. Uninterested in such moments of sexualised trauma, Cantet's cinema nonetheless tends to work towards the production of what one might call social primal scenes when something that should normally remain hidden is driven to the surface and witnessed by one person or more. Staying with *Ressources humaines*, we might note that there are at least two such scenes in it, one near the beginning, one at the end. In the first one, the hero enters not the parental bedroom, but another off-limits space, the factory, for the first time. After walking past different machines, he eventually comes to the one where his father works. The latter s proud explanation of his productivity is cut short when the foreman appears and humiliates him, telling him he cannot keep up with the pace. An embarrassed witness, the son is confronted with something he had not wished to see, the socially dominated position of the working class. At the same time, another worker looks on, observing both the father's shaming and the son's profound unease. Like the sexual primal scene, this social one is associated with violence and trauma. Unlike that scene, however, it is both a public and a private one where the family cast are joined by extra-familial actors who open it onto the social. The scene is mirrored by another late in the film when, during the strike, the son harangues the father for carrying on working and having passed on his class shame. The son throws the components that the father has been making onto the floor only to see the latter scrabble around picking them up. It is a moment of excruciating cruelty and embarrassment. It would be bad enough were it private, but it is observed by striking workers and the woman trade unionist. Like other Cantetian primal scenes, it ties together the familial and the social, refusing any self-enclosure of the former, yet also showing what is at stake emotionally and in terms of individual identity in the latter.

The individual and the group: shame and the utopian ideal

Shame is an important feeling running through Cantet's films. It occurs when characters feel the eyes of others upon them in a way that questions their sense of themselves and their place in relation to the group or the broader world. In his famous *Being and Nothingness*, the great existentialist philosopher Jean-Paul Sartre discusses shame in just this way as something that occurs when one is exposed to the gaze of the other. He notes that, while shame is an intimate relationship of the self with the self, it is also always, in its primary structure, shame before somebody. It occurs when, 'I am ashamed of myself as I appear to the other' (Sartre, 1969: 222). It thus generates a radically different self-awareness: although the reflexive self of the ego has an awareness of the self as an object, the self of immediate consciousness, caught up within embodied sensation and action, cannot experience the self from outside in this way. However, when caught in a shameful or embarrassing situation, this unreflective consciousness becomes aware of its own existence in the world and its status as an object for others, not in terms of a distanced intellectual observation but as an immediate feeling of being watched. Just as importantly, shame forces the subject to engage with the existence of the other as a subject. As long as the other is experienced as an object, the self remains sovereign in a world centred upon it and organised by its gaze. At the moment of shame, however, the look of the other is outside my control and forces me to recognize the other's subject status, placing me in a world that is simultaneously the world I know and a world foreign to me. This moment is traumatic. Sartre in fact describes it in terms of a double haemorrhaging. He writes, 'the world flows out of the world and I flow outside myself' (Sartre, 1969: 261). In short, shame generates a sense of the world looking back at the subject; 'to apprehend myself as seen is, in fact, to apprehend myself as seen *in the world* and from the standpoint of the world' (Sartre, 1969: 263, original emphasis).

Shame recurs in Cantet's work because it is produced when the main protagonist is confronted by the sense that neither (s)he nor the world are as (s)he sees them. It generates both vertigo (the Sartrean haemorrhaging of the world one thought one knew) and knowledge and potential acceptance as characters are forced to confront themselves and their places in the world as they appear to other people. Moments of shame thus bring to the surface the deeper underlying tensions among individuals and groups that run through the films. The famous closing line of his *Ressources humaines*, 'elle est où, ta place?' ('where is your place?') could stand as an epigram to Cantet's whole output. His films repeatedly show people seeking to negotiate their relationship with the groups that come between them and broader social structures. In this encounter, the values, viewpoint and position of the individuals concerned are typically questioned and challenged by those of the group. Thus, for example, in *Entre les murs*, the class challenge the philosophy of their teacher, bringing out its blind spots and forcing him to question how he sees himself and his role.

Sara Ahmed suggests that a double idealisation is important to the sense of being shamed. For the other's look to matter to me, she notes, I will tend to have idealised him or her. At the same time, the other might be assumed to be 'like me', and to share my ideals. So shame can bring together an ideal other with an idealised version of self. When we are ashamed, it is because we have failed to approximate to an ideal (Ahmed, 2004: 105–6). This sense that shame arises when an ideal is challenged underscores how shame exists as a counterpoint to something more utopian. It is unsurprising therefore that, complementing their focus on shame, Cantet's films typically revolve around individual and collective utopias. From the early shorts onwards, the characters' idealised sense of themselves and the social order will be probed in the encounter with the group. If the group is where the utopian ideal could potentially take flesh, the encounter with others, and the shame that may come with it, test its viability. In any case, of course, the ideal may be a conformist one. Thus, for example, the North American women in *Vers le sud* have an idealised vision of Haiti and are wilfully blind to certain harsh realities. Far from being radical, their outlook is a conservative one rooted in a history of regressive representations that paint the Caribbean island as an unspoilt paradise. This potential for conservatism does not necessarily make the utopias politically less interesting. Traditionally, conservative thought opposes its own defence of what exists to the unrealistic and potentially tyrannical utopias of radical thought. While Cantet's films are aware of the blind spots of the latter, they also challenge the role *conservative* utopias play in sustaining belief in the current order.

Looks and spaces

Cantet's films often start with characters about to awaken to or enter into the world. *Ressources humaines* opens with the hero sitting on a high-speed train looking out of the window as he approaches his home town. This image of a character moving through the world effortlessly and looking commandingly upon something of which he is not part has something utopian about it. The rest of the film, as we will see, and in keeping with our discussion above, will challenge this sense of separation, command and mobility. *L'Emploi du temps* begins with its hero asleep in his vehicle in the car park of a motorway service station. As the sequence progresses, he will increasingly come into contact with a world initially held at bay by his car's windscreen.

Entre les murs begins with a close-up of the hero at a cafe counter, drinking his coffee as he prepares to re-enter the world of school, meet new colleagues and re-encounter his now slightly older class at the beginning of another school year. *Vers le sud* begins with an airport scene. After figuring a brief discussion between a hotel manager and a Haitian mother (of which more later), it shows the arrival of Brenda (Karen Young), an American tourist, as she enters – or re-enters, as we later discover – a space that is foreign to her but that initially seems there for her tourist gaze. Of course, the arrival of an outsider in a space or a group is too generalised a narrative trope to be specific to Cantet. It is nonetheless interesting that the films tend to foreground the encounter between a character and the world as if they were setting out to challenge the sovereignty of the individual mind and gaze, along the lines we have been discussing above. It is also worth noting how, in several cases, characters are in fact *re-entering* a world (Haiti, the school, the home town) after a period away. They start with an assumption that they know a space and their place within it, an assumption that will gradually be unpicked. The predominant movement of Cantet's films is away from certainty rather than towards it.

A key part of the characters' developing encounter with the world around them is the experience of spatial unevenness. As James Williams underscores in his perceptive analysis, 'space is never just space in Cantet: it is always already codified, apportioned, distributed, even segregated' (Williams, 2013: 147). Because Cantetian space is not a smooth surface, but one marked by multiple hierarchies and boundaries, movement through it necessarily throws divisions and power relations into visibility. Thresholds are both frontiers – one space having different rules to another – and passages – all spaces being part of something larger than themselves and being socially and institutionally permeable to the outside. The importance of Cantetian space becomes evident in a work like *Vers le sud*, much of whose narrative revolves around spatial contrasts and transitions both within the tourist resort and between the resort and the broader Haitian reality. As characters move between spaces and shift their behaviour accordingly, they drive hidden constraints and boundaries into visibility. The beach, for example, seems a place of freedom and playfulness where black and white can mingle freely. Things change when characters move into the resort bar or restaurant where the

Haitians are only welcome as employees. They change again when the characters move outside the resort where the tourists find local colour but the Haitians face dangers. The film's complex social, sexual and racial dynamics only become legible when laid out across this uneven spatial terrain.

In some of the films, movements in and out of domestic space are important and can serve to underscore and open out the underlying Oedipal dynamics. In *Ressources humaines*, for example, the relationships between father and son are very different in the family house and in the workplace. When the hero moves back into the family home he finds that his old bedroom is now set aside for his nephews in a way that reminds us of his status as a child in the house but also suggests that he cannot simply resume his old role. Within the house, the father is an assertive presence and is happy to tell his son how to behave on arrival at work. Within the factory, on the other hand, he is in a subaltern position while his son is aligned with management. At the same time, the son's passage through the factory is far from frictionless. Initially, he is not allowed to enter the workshop. Certain doors will later be shut upon him and office blinds will be drawn to exclude his eyes in a way that draws attention both to power dynamics and to the existence of barriers that might not appear as such on the surface. Movements through space thus underscore broader social inequalities and shifting interpersonal dynamics.

Because spatial contrasts are so important, windows can play an important role in the films' visual economy. Those on vehicles like cars or trains seem to emphasise a character's apparent autonomy and self-containment, their ability to hold the world at bay. Windows on buildings allow characters to look into spaces from outside and those inside to look out. They make manifest, in the material fabric of the on-screen universe, the sense described above that the world, or a group within the world, can return the gaze of an onlooker and subject him or her to judgement according to the norms governing that space. There is, for example, a very telling sequence late in *L'Emploi du temps* in which Vincent (Aurélien Recoing), the hero, confronts Jeffrey (Nigel Palmer), an ex-colleague who has taken too close an interest in his unemployment, outside the workplace they used to share. Other employees of the company come to the window to look at the confrontation. The scene underlines Vincent's location outside the world of work. It also underscores how he is exposed not simply to the private disapproval of his erstwhile friend but also to a more general scrutiny, the frontiers between the personal and the public clearly being permeable. Vincent's look upon the workplace underscores his sense of alienation from its constraints. Its look back upon him emphasizes the weight of social expectation that bears upon him.

Realism and melodrama

If one were to seek to assign Cantet's cinema to a category, one would probably be drawn initially to social realism or neo-realism. With their social themes, exploration of social divisions and generally realist aesthetic, they clearly converge with social realism. More specifically, with their use of real locations, repeated recourse to amateur actors and the rootedness of at least some of them in the contemporary, they seem closer to received understandings of neo-realism. Yet, there are also important aspects of them which seem to ally them at least as much with melodrama.

Melodrama is a notoriously elusive object (Mercer and Shingler, 2004: 4). If, in its broadest sense, we tie it to a narrative style that eschews the flatness of the everyday and the mundane and seeks out the spectacular, the emotionally raw and the Manichaean collision, then much cinema, including action cinema, could be labelled melodramatic. Yet, used in such a way, the term becomes so general as to lose any critical purchase. It is better to use it more narrowly to talk about films that focus on interpersonal and domestic relations, and within which, precisely because emotions and conflicts cannot issue into external action, tension must find other forms of expression. In one of the classic texts on melodrama, Thomas Elsaesser evokes exactly this dimension, noting how, within the domestic melodrama:

> the social pressures are such, the frame of respectability so sharply defined that the range of 'strong' actions is limited ... The tellingly impotent gesture, the social gaffe, the hysterical outburst replaces any more directly liberating or self-annihilating action, and the cathartic violence of a shoot-out or a chase becomes an inner violence, often one which the characters turn against themselves. (Elsaesser, 1987: 56)

The typically domestic frame of melodrama is also underscored by Chuck Kleinhans, who suggests that it is not simply something intrinsic to the genre but links more broadly to the way capitalism splits the work of production and reproduction so that 'people's personal needs are restricted to the sphere of the family, of personal life, and yet the family cannot meet the demands of being all that the rest of society is not' (Kleinhans, 1991: 200). Working in the interpersonal and familial domain, the melodrama deals with frustrations that cannot be properly addressed in that narrowed framework. One potential consequence of this is that it may seem to propose purely private solutions to public problems by showing characters who find all they need for happiness (or misery) in the domestic sphere. However, it may also be that melodrama opens a space in which broader contradictions can be explored. By bringing them into private space and tying them to strong emotional states, it allows them to find an expression that they might not find elsewhere. This is the case, for example, in classic melodramas such as those of Douglas Sirk, which have occupied such a central place in discussions of the genre. Sirk's *All that Heaven Allows* (1955), for example, uses a romance between a middle-class woman and a younger, working-class man to explore the rigid gender and class dynamics of 1950s America, while his *Imitation of Life* (1959), with its story of a young, ambitious white-looking woman in denial of her black mother, uses the parent–child relationship to engage with the racial and class dynamics of the same period. What might seem purely private miseries are used to lay bare how broader social structures affect individuals and their relationships. Something similar might be said about Rainer Werner Fassbinder's *Ali: Fear Eats the Soul* (1974), a film, loosely inspired by Sirk's *All that Heaven Allows*, that uses the relationship between an older German cleaning woman and a Turkish migrant worker to open up some of the fault-lines in German society, showing how they not only impact on groups but penetrate private life and divide individuals against themselves.

Sirk's work has also proved paradigmatic for discussion of melodrama because of how it underscores the importance of non-verbal elements within the genre. Given melodrama's socially constrained environment, tensions and deeply held feelings tend not to be explicitly conveyed through dialogue but are displaced into performance, *mise en scène* or sound. In Sirk's films this comes through in elements like costume, decor and screen composition. In *All that Heaven Allows*, for example, the heroine's emotional entrapment becomes tangible because of how she is hemmed in by the expensive trappings of her bourgeois home or caught by frames within frames (as when she stands at a window looking out of her house). A sexuality that she must hide comes to the surface in the red dress she puts on, shocking her children, who expect their widowed mother to dress in a more restrained manner. The way that melodrama displaces emotion into visual elements is also discussed at length by Peter Brooks, whose famous study, although about theatre and the novel, has played a central role in discussions of the cinematic genre. Looking at melodrama's origins in non-verbal theatrical forms, Brooks describes what he calls the genre's 'text of muteness', its recourse to gesture, mime or the expressive tableau to bring ethical clarity to an otherwise morally opaque world (Brooks, 1976: 56–80). This same search for clarity explains its turn to Manichaean characterisation and constant recourse to heightened situations and dramatic moments that can drive the truth to the surface.

There are some clear reasons why we might align Cantet with melodrama but also reasons we might hesitate to do so. We might begin by noting that what we have described as his 'primal scenes' have clear melodramatic qualities in their capacity to concentrate unspoken feelings and force them into view. We might observe more generally how Cantet's films are typically traversed by repressed tensions that are made explicit as the films proceed. Like the works of Sirk and Fassbinder, Cantet's films operate at the frontier of the private and the public and use the former as an arena wherein the divisions of the latter and their human consequences can be made manifest. Indeed, two of Cantet's works have echoes of particular Sirkean melodramas: despite its clear surface differences, there is something of *Imitation of Life* in *Ressources humaines*. Sirk's story of a child who denies her ethnic origins and her mother to assert her belonging in white society is less different than it might appear from Cantet's story of an upwardly mobile son's alienation from his working-class background and father. There is also something of *All that Heaven Allows* (and of Fassbinder's *Ali: Fear Eats the Soul*) in *Vers le sud*, with the former film's story of a middle-class woman falling for her younger gardener having its echoes in Cantet's tale of middle-class white women with young Haitian lovers. Beyond these particular resonances, Cantet's Oedipal dramas are also very much in the tradition of what one might call male melodramas: films like Elia Kazan's *East of Eden* (1955) or George Stevens's *Giant* (1956), with their focus on father–son relationships and the difficulty faced by the son in adopting the patriarchal role.[15] Given these convergences, it is unsurprising that a focus on shame and its capacity to probe social pressures unites Cantet and his illustrious predecessors.

I have suggested elsewhere that there are clear reasons for a broader melodramatic turn in recent French social realist film. The impressive production of committed cinema that followed the radical surge of 1968 was able to draw on an elaborated leftist dramaturgy of socio-political struggle that came with an established script, favoured locations such as the factory and its forecourt, and a familiar cast (bosses, French and immigrant workers, trade unionists, representatives of the State and of political parties). This dramaturgy has been unpicked. The radical left has largely fallen silent or been marginalised. Old industrial bastions of worker militancy have been closed. Production has been outsourced or moved overseas. The workers, once seen as the heroes of a progressive history, have to a considerable degree become invisible or consigned to the past. Globalising capital, for the moment at least, seems to have won. Injustices have not, of course, vanished and indeed have worsened, as wealth has been redistributed upwards and the post-Second World War social settlement and the Welfare State have come under sustained assault. Yet there is no longer a powerful radical voice to name wrongs and frame social suffering and struggle. It is within this context that the turn to melodrama to restore a lost socio-political eloquence makes clear sense (O'Shaughnessy, 2007: 36–55 and 131–59).

Brooks locates melodrama's origins in the nineteenth-century world that followed the French Revolution. The pre-Revolutionary world was one with an apparently stable aristocratic and divine order where the meaning and value of people and things seemed to be legible on the surface. The Revolution swept away these certainties and produced a morally opaque world. Melodrama's Manichaean oppositions, drive to ethical clarity and text of muteness served to

15 For an insightful discussion of two of Cantet's films as male melodramas, see Higbee (2004).

bring moral legibility back to the surface (Brooks, 1976: 1–80). The turn to melodrama in recent French and Belgian film (I am thinking of the Dardennes here), comes in response to the similarly traumatic loss of clarity that I have described. This melodramatic turn is not, of course, a uniform phenomenon. What can be found, however, across a range of film-makers is recourse to certain strategies typically associated with melodrama: the use of individual, interpersonal and familial stories to amplify the impact of broader, unspoken social divisions and oppressions; inter-generational narratives that bring out a radical disruption of the transmission of roles and traditions; narratives with heightened moments that force tensions to the surface; the loss of a language of struggle and the concomitant rise of bodily attitudes, gestures and collisions as a mute locus of expressiveness (O'Shaughnessy, 2007: 131–59). Despite the strong voice that comes through in his film-making, Cantet clearly has his place within this broader picture.

The melodramatic turn in his films and those of his contemporaries is tempered but not negated by the drive to social realism. Realism and melodrama cannot be opposed as two mutually exclusive modes but can exist, as Peter Brooks shows when discussing canonical realist novelists like Honoré de Balzac or Henry James, in complex and productive tension (Brooks, 1976: 14–23). The same tension can of course be found in Italian neo-realism where André Bazin, the great French film theorist and critic, identified, with obvious frustration, melodramatic elements (Bazin, 1990: 275). In Cantet's works, the drive to the real as manifested in the engagement with contemporary issues and the use of amateur actors and location shooting is similarly balanced by the predilection for Oedipal and familial dramas and the search for moments of heightened expressiveness. The interaction is a complex one, however. Melodramatic strategies offer a way to make the real speak to us by driving what is hidden to the surface but realism militates against some of the expressive armoury of melodrama. Sirkean melodrama famously uses lighting and colour to express the unspoken. Social realist film, and Cantet is no exception here, tends towards an understated, naturalist visual style. It would therefore be a mistake to expect to find all the classic elements of Hollywood melodrama in Cantet's films. It should also be underscored how the melodramatic drive to clarity is counterbalanced in Cantet's films by a refusal to provide answers. While the films do indeed drive unseen divisions to the surface, they also leave us with questioning rather than certainty.

Conclusion

This chapter has led us into Cantet's work by examining the nature of what one might call his two methods: his way both of organising the shooting of his films and of constructing their narratives. The former, as we noted, has two main characteristics: a preference for working with an amateur or partly amateur cast in real locations and a dialogic way of generating scripts through interaction with his favoured collaborators, amateur actors and pre-existing texts. The latter is more complex. As we have seen, it revolves around working at a series of intersections: between the family romance and the broader society; between the individual and the group; between the melodramatic and the realist; between the pre-determined and the unplanned. It has two consequences that pull in apparently opposite directions. If it engages with the contemporary real in a way that forces unseen fault-lines into visibility, it does so in a way that ultimately challenges certainties rather than leading to them.

Cantet's two 'methods' come together in two important and interconnected ways. They converge, firstly, in a procedural sense; that is, they both start with a way of doing things before they approach a specific task or topic. What this means is that, while there is enough consistency in Cantet's films for us to see them as a coherent but developing body of work, this is not something that excludes openness to other voices. On the contrary, Cantet's methods are designed to allow just such a quality, both when preparing a shooting and within the films themselves. The 'methods' converge, secondly and interrelatedly, in what one might call their interrogative thrust. In terms of their genesis, Cantet's films are, to a considerable extent, investigations that allow him to explore areas with which he is not directly familiar. In the same way, within the films themselves, there is typically also a process of questioning whereby a character (or group of characters) enters a milieu but is obliged by the encounter with the looks of others to rethink his or her values. To this extent, Cantet's characters are doubles of the director himself.

Two things often associated with political cinema that seem absent from Cantet's works are reflexivity and distanciation. Because an essential part of political film might be considered to reside in its ability to think its place within cinema more generally and in relation to earlier or alternative models of committed film more particularly, it tends to be expected to reflect on its own practices. A classic example of this would be the way in which Godard's *Tout va bien* (1972) begins by listing all the different costs that have been involved in its production as a way of forcing us to think about the material conditions of cinema's existence and their consequences for the kind of film that gets made. By so doing, the film also distances the spectator from its story rather than encouraging the usual absorption. It clearly aims to produce a critical spectatorship rather than an emotionally involved one. On the surface, there is nothing similar in Cantet's work. Yet there is nonetheless a type of reflexivity and distanciation implicitly incorporated within his films. Because they foreground the interchange of looks within their own visual organisation, and because they make it difficult to align with one particular look, each look showing up the blind spots of the other, they force us to think hard about how we should view what is shown. When we watch *Vers le sud*, for example, we are certainly drawn to sympathize with the way the female leads defy social prejudices about older women's sexuality. But we are also distanced from them by their unawareness of the neo-colonial situation they find themselves in. We are sucked in and pushed back at the same time, become unsure of where to view the film from and question the nature of our own spectatorship. Frank's closing question to the black worker in *Ressources humaines*, 'elle est où, ta place?', also speaks to us.[16] The films are political in the way they force us to challenge our own position with respect to the situation they help us discover.

References

Ahmed, S. (2004), *The Cultural Politics of Emotion*, New York, Routledge.
Bazin, A. (1990), *Qu'est-ce que le cinéma?*, Paris, Editions du Cerf.

16 The more usual French spelling of the character's name is Franck. The film's credits use the English spelling. I have taken my lead from them.

Beaud, S. and Pialoux, M. (1999), *Retour sur la condition ouvrière*, Paris, Fayard.

Bonal, C. (2008), 'Enfant star, parents sans-papiers', *Liberation société*, www.liberation.fr/societe/2008/05/27/enfant-star-parents-sans-papiers_15611 (accessed 17 September 2014).

Bresson, R. (1997), *Notes on the Cinematographer*, trans. J. Griffin, Copenhagen, Green Integer.

Brooks, P. (1976), *The Melodramatic Imagination: Balzac, Henry James, Melodrama and the Mode of Excess*, New Haven and London, Yale University Press.

Burdeau, E. and Thirion, A. (2008), 'Entretien avec Laurent Cantet', *Cahiers du cinéma*, 637 (September), 10–18.

Club des 13, Le (2008), *Le Milieu n'est plus un pont mais une faille: Le Club des 13, rapport de synthèse*, Paris, Stock.

Elsaesser, T. (1987), 'Tales of sound and fury: observations on the family melodrama', in C. Gledhill, ed., *Home Is Where the Heart Is: Studies in Melodrama and the Woman's Film*, London, British Film Institute, 43–74.

Fache, A. (2010), Laurent Cantet: 'Les travailleurs sans-papiers sontà [sic] l'avant-poste du combat social', www.humanite.fr/node/490864 (accessed 17 September 2014).

Freud, S. (1959), 'Family romances', in Freud, *The Standard Edition of the Complete Psychological Works of Sigmund Freud*, Vol. IX: *(1906–1908)*, ed. and trans. J. Strachey with A. Freud, London, The Hogarth Press, 237–41.

Higbee, W. (2004), '"Elle est où, ta place?" The socialist-realist melodramas of Laurent Cantet: *Ressources humaines* (2000) and *Emploi du temps* (2001)', *French Cultural Studies*, 15:3, 235–50.

Holquist, M., ed. (1981), *The Dialogic Imagination: Four Essays by M. M. Bakhtin*, trans. C. Emerson and M. Holquist, Austin, University of Texas Press.

Kleinhans, C. (1991), 'Notes on melodrama and the family under capitalism', in M. Landy, ed., *Imitations of Life: A Reader on Film and Television Melodrama*, Detroit, MI, Wayne State University, 197–204.

Laferrière, D. (2000), *La Chair du maître*, Paris, Le Serpent à Plumes.

Lebtahi, Y. and Roussel-Gillet, I. (2005), *Pour une méthode d'investigation du cinéma de Laurent Cantet: Les déplacés, vertiges de soi*, Paris, L'Harmattan.

Lemahieu, T. (2000), 'A la vie comme à l'écran et retour: Que mettent les acteurs non professionnels en jeu dans leurs rôles?', *L'Humanité*, 15 January, www.humanite.fr/node/220544 (accessed 22 December 2014).

Mangeot, P. (2012), 'Entretien avec Laurent Cantet', in the *Foxfire* press-book, downloadable at www.hautetcourt.com/film/fiche/191, 6–19 (accessed 11 April 2014).

Mercer, J. and Shingler, M. (2004), *Melodrama: Genre, Style, Sensibility*, London, Wallflower.

Morris, P. (1994), *The Bakhtin Reader: Selected Writings of Bakhtin, Medvedev, Voloshinov*, London, Edward Arnold.

Nicklaus, O. (2002), 'Carole Scotta et Caroline Benjo: Bien vu', www.lesinrocks.com/2002/07/17/cinema/actualite-cinema/carole-scotta-et-caroline-benjo-bien-vu-11113592/ (accessed 7 April 2014).

O'Shaughnessy, M. (2007), *The New Face of Political Cinema*, Oxford, Berghahn.

Rigoulet, L. (2001), 'Sur les pas de Laurent Cantet: Réalisateur de *L'Emploi du temps*. Les vertiges du mensonge', *Télérama*, 17 November, 40–4.

Rigoulet, L. (2008), 'La méthode Cantet', *Telerama*, 25–6 September, www.telerama.fr/cinema/la-methode-cantet-1,34030.php?xtatc=INT-41; and www.telerama.fr/cinema/la-methode-cantet-2-2-le-travail-avec-les-acteurs,34031.php?xtatc=INT-41 (accessed 5 September 2014).

Sartre, J.-P. (1969), *Being and Nothingness: An Essay on Phenomenological Ontology*, trans. H. Barnes, London, Routledge.

Williams, J. (2013), *Space and Being in Contemporary French Cinema*, Manchester and New York, Manchester University Press.

2

Early applications

What becomes quickly apparent when one watches Cantet's early films, *Tous à la manif*, *Jeux de plage* and *Les Sanguinaires*, is how many key elements of his now well established way of making films were already in place. The first of the three, *Tous à la manif*, is seen by the director himself as the moment when he discovered his 'method', his way of casting, scripting, rehearsing and shooting a film. Taken together, and despite their differences, the three films also underscore just how much he also had a clear sense of how he liked to construct his stories from early in his career. They converge in how they foreground the problematic relationship between the individual and the group. Two of the three, *Tous à la manif* and *Jeux de plage*, have a classic Oedipal drama at their centre, while the third, *Les Sanguinaires*, plays more loosely on generational differences. All three foreground the typical Cantetian collision between the utopian and the real. Two of the three, *Tous à la manif* and *Les Sanguinaires*, also underscore Cantet's predilection for developing his stories of groups at the point where they intersect with much broader societal or political dramas: the former stages its father–son interaction in a cafe frequented by *lycéens* who are preparing to strike against the rightist Balladur Government's *loi quinquennale*, or five-year law, and its negative consequences for young people; the latter tracks the drama of a small group who have taken themselves to an island just off the coast of Corsica to avoid the mass celebrations marking the turn of the millennium in 2000. The three films are typical of Cantet in the importance they attach to spatial and temporal dynamics and thresholds, notably those between the domestic and the public, childhood and adulthood, and the everyday and the exceptional. The way that all three focus on moments when the underlying tensions of relationships are driven to the surface underscore how much the director's affinity with melodrama was there at the outset. Finally, all three bring out the dual nature of his films, the way they are built around a basic dramatic frame that tends towards the universal and existential (the person seeking their place in the world, the tension between individual and group) but is also able to open itself up to the concrete specificity of the socio-politically or spatially located narrative. Because they embody so many elements that will be built on in the later works, they can be seen as rehearsals for what is to come. Trying out certain situations and a very specific way of knitting the interpersonal and the social, they give us precious insights into the workings of the better-known films.

Tous à la manif

The short films on which budding directors cut their teeth are very much the poor cousins of full-length fictions and struggle even more than many of the latter for public visibility. They might achieve some attention through France's art cinema circuit, still much the most vibrant in Europe despite the pressures on it. They might make it to air via Arte, the Franco-German cultural channel, or Canal +, the pay-TV station that is committed to supporting cinema. They might, finally, achieve recognition at one or more of the festivals that provide an alternative outlet for so many films. It was at one of the latter, the seventeenth Clermont-Ferrand short film festival in 1995, that *Tous à la manif* brought Cantet to the attention of prominent critic Gérard Lefort, of left-of-centre newspaper *Libération*. Lefort was typically scathing about much of what was seen at the festival: too many calling-card films – lifeless, over-polished works with nothing worth saying. However, some films, particularly *Tous à la manif*, did stand out. Here was a film that was not simply about an inward-looking, self-satisfied world but one that was open to the real – a film that managed to incorporate spontaneity but within which everything was carefully thought through, with each shot playing an important and necessary role. The use of sound was equally admirable with what Lefort described as its sonic depth of field ('profondeur de son'), allowing the egalitarian mingling of the voices of the film's cafe owner and his son and the rebellious students who frequent their establishment. The film's melancholic mood cut against the facile, advert-like optimism of too many other works (Lefort, 1995).

One is struck by Lefort's prescient identification of what would become key features of Cantet's works, notably the ability to allow spontaneous voices to be heard within a very calculated framework and to engage with real events and struggles but also open up a distance from them. Cantet himself would have no doubt about the film's importance in his development, particularly with respect to his preferred way of developing a story over a period of time through workshopping with amateur actors:

> *Tous à la manif* avait été une expérience marquante, le début d'une méthode. J'ai l'impression de toujours chercher à retrouver cela ... j'ai travaillé avec les jeunes pendant plusieurs mois avant de tourner. Je les avais rencontrés, on avait commencé à improviser autour de situations que je leur proposais. Il a fallu les essayer une première fois, les laisser en jachère quelques semaines, puis les reprendre.[1]

Cantet does not specify the contribution of the students he worked with, beyond their ability to bring their own experience to bear on what was written and to inform the script. What is clear, however, is how much their voices do come through in the film, bringing their experiences of anti-Government mobilisations into it in a way that allows it to anchor itself in a context.

The students in the film are seen at the moment when they decide to strike. There is no classic expository scene explaining the reasons for the strike or precisely what is at stake. Instead, we are plunged into the thick of the impromptu debates, the rehearsals of slogans and the drawing of posters as they overspill into the cafe, the film's main location. The students are protesting about tuition fees, a two-speed education system and university selection. A word glimpsed on a poster suggests that the main source of their discontent is the *loi quinquennale* of 1993, a law about job creation,

---

1 *'Tous à la manif* had been an important experience, the beginnings of a method. I feel like I've always been searching to repeat it ... I worked with the young people for several months before shooting began. I had met them and we'd begun to improvise around situations I'd suggested to them. We had to try them out once, leave them to rest for a few weeks, then take them up again' (Burdeau and Thirion, 2008: 11).

work and professional training.[2] The part of the law that French students were particularly exercised about was the Contrat d'Insertion Professionnelle (CIP), a type of labour contract that would have given young people a diminishing proportion of the minimum wage – the salaire minimum interprofessionnel de croissance (SMIC) – according to their age: effectively, the younger they were, the less they would get. Those who had passed their *bac* and completed a further two years of study would still only be entitled to 80 per cent of the minimum wage. In a context of sustained high unemployment, this measure effectively sought to get young people into work by treating them as cheap labour in a way that angered them, but also threatened other workers whose wages would be undercut. Students, especially *lycéens*, took to the streets in mass protests that forced the Government to suspend and eventually withdraw the CIP. Papering over the embarrassment of its retreat, the right-of-centre Balladur Government undertook a mass consultation of young people in an attempt to defuse their anger and to give them a sense that their opinions counted while strategically bypassing any intermediary bodies that might speak for them.[3]

Only fragments of this bigger picture come through in the film although there is enough there for someone reasonably well informed to connect what is seen to real events. What we hear more of are the debates among the students themselves about how they should be organised. There are those, on the one hand, connected to particular leftist organisations, who talk of the need for order and discipline. There are those, on the other hand, who worry about the protest being co-opted. Some students seem to be treating their action above all as a carnivalesque interruption of normal routines. Others stress the hard work involved in organising a demonstration. One of the

2 The film also makes reference to two other strike actions, both discussed between the cafe owner father and one of the striking students. One is an Air France strike: presumably the very angry protest of Air France ground staff late in 1993. The other is by employees of the Régie Autonome des Transports Parisiens (RATP), the Paris transport authority. The RATP workers mobilised along with other workers against the *loi quinquennale* in 1994.

3 Those familiar with *Ressources humaines* may well suspect that this use of a consultation to neutralise opposition found its way into that later film in the guise of the survey of workers' opinions carried out by the hero, a survey meant to by-pass trade unions and to give workers a false sense that their opinions were taken into account.

students is seen making posters. Later, along with the cafe owner's son, he is shown tearing up an old table-cloth to make banners. A news report seen on the cafe's television gives us a glimpse of the students gathered together in a lecture theatre for one of the *co-ordinations*, assemblies characterised by direct democracy, that have been such a feature of recent protests in France. The students seem to be a body with many different voices but also an at least temporarily cohesive group. In almost the last shot of the film we see their disappearing backs, as, grouped together chanting slogans, they head off in high spirits to join the larger demonstration.

We might seem to be seeing something akin to a classic piece of committed cinema, perhaps from the period after 1968, with the classic debates over organisation and spontaneity, party discipline and direct democracy. To some extent, the film feels like a documentary. With the astonishingly fresh performances from amateur actors clearly drawing on their own experiences, it gives the impression of tracking real events, not least because of how the often mobile camera shifts from one group or person to the next as if trying to record something unfolding at that moment. Yet, what disrupts this impression, what makes the film so typically Cantetian, is the presence of a rival and obviously fictional focus, the unfolding story of the cafe owner and his son, Serge – a story also going through its own partly similar and partly very different moment of crisis.

This double-centred nature of the film is signalled very efficiently and clearly in the opening shots. The first shot, over Serge's shoulder as he plays on a slot machine and has a drink, aligns us with the young man's vision, foregrounding the individual consciousness as Cantet's openings tend to. Yet, disrupting this impression of the sovereign individual, the next shot, which pans to follow Serge as he leaves the cafe, also introduces the father, a figure only partly seen through the hatch of the cafe kitchen as he tells his son how many croissants and how much bread to buy. The son's consciousness is now placed in a social and familial setting in which, far from sovereign, it is doubly subordinated, as son and waiter. The next shot further complicates matters. Picking up Serge through the door as he returns with the bread and croissants, it pans to reveal the tightly grouped students who now fill the cafe. The soundtrack is filled with the hubbub of voices. One of the students helps himself to a croissant from the bag prompting Serge's father to ask if he would do the same thing at home, a stereotypical comment of the older generation to the young which constructs the students as a playful group able to disrupt norms. As Serge moves into shot, he is placed among the students, aligned with them in terms of age, but separated from them by his role as waiter, something signalled by the food he is bringing and his white shirt. His father stands by the counter in the white barman's jacket he will wear throughout.

If *Tous à la manif* seems to condense many essential elements of Cantet's dramaturgy, then these opening shots take that condensation still further. Beginning with the individual's consciousness, they have first moved out to a familial relationship before bringing in a larger group. To the extent that the editing together of the three shots connects them into a unit, their succession might seem to be a straightforward refutation of any sense that the individual consciousness or the family are self-contained. To the extent that the editing separates the three shots, it would seem to preserve at least a partial autonomy for the questions that each shot seems to pose about subjectivity, one's place in the family and relationships within a broader social group. Many of the essential dynamics of Cantet's film-making can be located in the partial separation and partial connection of these three questions. While his films refuse the self-enclosure of the individual or the inter-personal, they also refuse to fold them back into the social. It is the gap and the tension between the three instances that opens a space for both drama and politics. Rather than simply being defined by his or her situation within the family or the larger group, the individual's place is open to question.

The interconnectedness of different levels of interaction is also worked out, in typical Cantet fashion, across the spatial layout of the film, which is organised in terms of concentric spaces, each *partially* open to the outside. The first, most private space is the cafe's kitchen: this is the only area entirely reserved for Serge and his father. It is also where they will have their most important discussion. The second space, behind the cafe counter, is normally reserved for bar staff, but is penetrated at one stage by the students, no respecters of norms or boundaries. Beyond the counter lies the public space of the cafe, and, beyond that, the street. Opposite the cafe, across the junction where it is located, is the *lycée* from which the students periodically issue. Each space has its norms and associations but none is self-enclosed or mono-functional. The kitchen and the area behind the bar are simultaneously spaces of work and of domesticity, not least because the barman and the waiter are also father and son. The public area of the cafe is a place of leisure and relaxation (for some); a workplace (for others); and,what one might call an agora, a site of public debate (open to all but not necessarily on equal terms).[4] The street is similarly a space for routine circulation and the more exceptional mobilisations such as marches and demonstrations that we see in the film. Tensions are produced and worked through across this complex, uneven spatiality.

Spatial relations are not static however. They need to be seen dynamically and particularly in terms of the opposition between the routine and the exceptional. There is a temporality built into the cafe itself around the working day, meals, coffee breaks, opening and closing. But this regularity is disrupted by the far less orderly temporality of the strike, the impromptu debate and the march, moments when routines are suspended and when spatio-temporal barriers and boundaries are challenged and reworked. If the film's tensions are expressed spatially, they are also driven to the surface by the collision of these two temporalities.

The film's melodramatic core unfolds and takes on meaning in this spatio-temporal frame. The plot is a classic one of paternal heritage: will the son follow in the father's footsteps and have a pre-programmed life, or will he break out and find something different? The father is not an authoritarian monster: he is over-protective but also seeks to pass on his practical skills to his son, as in the lovely little scene when he shows the latter how to position cups and glasses on a tray so that it will not tip over when carried. This transmission of gestures between generations points to a routine and social roles that self-replicate over time. Yet, as we have seen, the cafe is open to the world. The *lycée* opposite it and the students that spill into it are constant reminders that young people do not necessarily follow in their parents' footsteps but can find a different, upwardly mobile path through education. At the same time, through the strike action and their taking of public voice – and the way both overflow into the cafe – the students remind the son that authority and order can be challenged and routines disrupted.

4 The cafe has been a key location for political discussion in French history. The role of certain cafes at the time of the Revolution is legendary.

Relationships between the son and the students are cordial. They treat him as if he were *almost* one of their number, with the whole drama of the film residing in the probing of this 'almost'. The second scene of the film sees a telling interaction between Serge and three female students. As he cleans a window from the outside, they sit inside, teasing him through glass that suggests, as it will so often in Cantet, proximity and separation. It is also a typical Cantetian moment in that, making Serge very much the object of the gaze, it reminds us how the individual's look on the world is answered by the look of the group on the individual thereby made aware of his or her objectification in the eyes of others. Embarrassed by being so viewed, Serge leaves his cleaning and comes inside to serve the girls, his presence at their table being conveyed to us by the sight of his hands and his tray, physical reminders of his waiter's status. As he stands there, they knowingly discuss the sexual experience one of them has had the previous night with a young man. When the again embarrassed Serge has left the table, his father comes forward to scold the girls. The film then cuts to the younger man looking on from behind the bar, further embarrassed by his father's over-protective intervention. Though he is so close to the girls in age, we now see that Serge is separated from them by status, experience and the autonomy that they have and that he, as a worker in his father's cafe, so obviously lacks. In a manner that anticipates many key scenes in his later films, Cantet has used an apparently anodyne interaction to force social fault-lines into visibility.

The visual organisation of the remainder of the film will underscore what we have learnt. There are moments that emphasise Serge's separation from the students. Some of these are produced by cuts from actions or discussions involving the latter to shots of him looking on, a witness, not a participant: for example, we see him watching two young men as they animatedly discuss the strike's organisation; later, we see him standing on the pavement outside the cafe as the young people walk out of their *lycée*. Other scenes bring him into the student group but then marginalise him. At the end of the first of the two days narrated by the film, for example, we see him and his father sit down with a group of students who have insisted on staying later than normal. The father takes centre stage as he gets a female student to attempt a familiar trick with a glass of beer and a banknote. Serge watches from the edge of the group, distinctly in the shade of his more confident father. Other scenes emphasize his difference by showing him moving among the students wearing his waiter's white shirt and carrying his drinks tray, his proximity to them only serving to bring out his separation.

However, the film does not simply pin Serge in his place. The students are an anarchic force and the strike a utopian moment when voice is taken and boundaries challenged. At an early stage, one of the students calls Serge over to ask his advice on two posters he has made. The two are brought together in a single shot, and Serge engages in discussion and becomes part of something larger. Later, in a crowded shot, when the students are having an animated, impromptu debate about how their action is organised, Serge puts down his tray, picks up a megaphone from the floor and takes control of the situation. When his father tells them that they have no right to hold a meeting in the cafe and that the police will soon arrive, Serge, still with megaphone in hand, retorts, 'on emmerde les flics' ('to hell with the police'), simultaneously stepping out of his role, challenging paternal and State authority, and loudly asserting his right of public speech. He draws loud applause from the student group. Now it is the father's turn to find himself isolated in a shot. An annoyed but sheepish figure, he is framed behind the bar, looking out towards the others. Yet, a few seconds later, just as he seems to have merged into the group, Serge loudly distances himself from the strike when pressured to voice his opinions. Their issues of bosses and workers are no concern of his, he says. He will still be stuck in his current position when he is fifty while they will have moved on. All eyes are on him again, but in a way that underscores his separation. When the students depart to join the demonstration at the end of the film, he is left watching them recede into the distance, despite having been invited to go with them. His father puts a hand on his shoulder and ushers him back into the cafe. The last shot of the film shows the two cleaning tables and stacking chairs, drawn back into the time of routine and fixed roles, as the off-screen sound of the students' chanting recedes and the period of disruption comes to a close.

There is a temptation to read the film through the opposing lenses of two of the most important French intellectuals of recent times, Pierre Bourdieu and Jacques Rancière. The former's work, as expressed in his writings on education and especially on social distinction, is often cited to explain how, having internalised social subordination, the dominated not only struggle to challenge it but become inadvertently complicit in it. The notion of *habitus* is central to this understanding. *Habitus*, as deployed by Bourdieu, is used to describe the acquired sensibilities, judgements and dispositions through which people internalise their relationship to the social world, not simply as mental habits, but also through routinised gestures and behaviours. The *habitus* of the dominated means that they effectively live their embodied relationship to the world in a way that reinforces their subordination. In such circumstances, it might seem that only external intervention in the form of the sociologist's expert knowledge can break the grip of *habitus*, force domination into visibility and make people aware of the reality of their situation (see, for example, Bourdieu, 1984). Rancière's starting point is radically opposed. He begins from the presumption of the equality of voices and the existence of one, shared, human intelligence. The subordinated, as he sees it, are always aware of and able to speak about their subordination. What therefore needs examination is not how they have internalised their dominated role but why only some people's voices count and are deemed capable of judgements on issues beyond what relates to their immediate social function. Rancière distinguishes between, on the one hand, what he calls the police order and, on the other, the political. The former evokes the existing distribution of roles, places and rights to public speech, and the mechanisms that hold these in place. The latter arises when, challenging the police order, those normally deprived of a say in the allocation of roles and places assert their equality as speaking beings. Bourdieu emphasises all that ties people to their social role. Rancière is interested precisely in those moments when people step outside it (Rancière, 1995, especially 19–67). There is no way to reconcile the pair. Rancière considers that Bourdieu undermines the emancipatory aspiration they share precisely because he denies people's ability to speak unaided of their situation. By setting up a hierarchy between the superior knowledge of the sociologist and the lack of knowledge of those under study, he reinstates the very hierarchy he sought to challenge (Pelletier, 2009).

When one initially looks at *Tous à la manif*, one might judge that it implicitly embraces a Bourdieusian social critique. It works to bring unseen social barriers into visibility, as Bourdieu himself did, and shows how difficult it is for someone to step outside their established social place. Serge's subordinate role as waiter is inscribed in his clothes, posture and gestures, his lack of self-confidence, and his circumscribed spatial universe. He is a prisoner, one might say, of his *habitus*, of all those ingrained attitudes and embodied practices that tie someone to a social location. Yet, this is not where the film leaves things. As we have noted, it works to open a gap between Serge and his social role from its very opening shot when it established his existence as a consciousness before putting him into a more tightly defined context. It also stresses, as we saw, how, never simply able to capture or define somebody or exclude alternative possibilities, boundaries are porous and social roles can be taken off, as when Serge puts down his tray, picks up the megaphone and takes voice. This latter gesture, one might suggest, is far more Rancierian than Bourdieusian. In Rancière's terms, it is precisely at moments like these when people step outside their allocated roles and contest their silencing that an authentic politics arises. In the end, Serge is not unaware of his situation. On the contrary, it is because he knows that he cannot break out of it that the film's conclusion is quietly tragic.

As we noted earlier, when the Balladur Government faced mass protest from young people in early 1994, it sought to disarm revolt by circulating a questionnaire, the *Consultation Nationale des Jeunes*, to the 8.4 million French people aged between fifteen and twenty-five. Of the nearly 1.6 million who sent back replies, 50 per cent, an astonishing number, said that they struggled to find a place for themselves in French society.[5] The way Serge also strives to find his place is thus entirely of its moment, in a way that reminds us just how much Cantet feeds off and into the issues of his time. There is, of course, nothing intrinsically radical about seeking a place in the social order. As long as such a quest simply implies finding an opening within the status quo, it is in fact conservative. It is only when one's search leads to a more general questioning of the allocation of places and roles that it can become truly radical. What Cantet does in *Tous à la manif* is to set Serge's individual revolt in the context of a broader contestation in a way that probes the limits of each. If Serge cannot find a way to align himself with the students' struggle against authority, his revolt may be strictly limited. If the students, on the

5 For an account of responses to the consultation, see Biais and Faure (1994).

other hand, cannot find a way to include him, their challenge to the status quo may also be less radical than it seems. This question is implicitly put by the film's title, *Tous à la manif*. The last shot of the film shows that *tous* does not include everybody.

Jeux de plage

Jeux de plage was Cantet's second film but one he tends to talk about much less than *Tous à la manif*. In some ways, because it works at the intersection of father–son and individual–group relations, it seems exactly on the same territory. What it lacks, and presumably what makes Cantet refer back to it less, is the further intersection with a contemporary issue. This absence may in some ways make it feel like a sketch for a Cantet film rather than a fully developed project. In other ways, and what makes it of interest, is the insight it gives into how the director constructs his films, something that comes through all the more clearly because of the relative paring down of the story.

Jeux de plage was filmed in Cassis, a beautiful Mediterranean resort town, situated on the coast between Marseille, where Cantet had studied, and La Ciotat, the place where the Lumière brothers' legendary *L'Arrivée d'un train dans la gare de la Ciotat* (1895), one of the first ever films, was shot. Explaining why he had been attracted by Cassis, Cantet said he had wanted to film the sea but was also drawn to the kitsch element of the holiday resort. The film cost about FF 350,000 to make, quite a large sum for a short, but was able to draw on the selective aid fund of the Centre National de la Cinématographie (CNC), the State body that deals with cinema funding and regulation in France. Its genesis was typical of a Cantet work. The director met a teacher who ran a cinema class in a *lycée* and cast some of his pupils in the film, with the other young people, apart from the young hero, being children of friends, or friends of those same children. Shooting took only two weeks but was preceded, in typical fashion, by a long period of rehearsals, during which Cantet would lay out the general shape of sequences, providing a framework within which the cast could improvise. The film's father, Denis – played by Jean Lespert, an experienced theatrical performer – was, at the time, the only professional, although the young male lead, Jalil Lespert, would go on to become a well-known screen actor and work in two other Cantet films.[6] When Cantet cast the elder Lespert, he explained to him how his film was about the difficult relationship between a father and a son: Jean commented that he understood the situation all too well because of his relationship with his own seventeen-year-old. Cantet invited both to audition in a way that allowed them, also in typical Cantet fashion, to draw on their experience to fill the roles. The father–son relationship would provide the film with its melodramatic core. The mixing of melodrama and documentary elements might seem less in evidence in this film than in other Cantet works. It is nonetheless still there but without the usual political edge: real festivities in Cassis (the fireworks and the dance in the square) were woven into the fiction.[7]

If the central character of *Tous à la manif* is obviously the son, that of *Jeux de plage* is more the father, Denis, as the first shot of the film signals. It picks him up as, naked to the waist, muscles straining, he carries two buckets of water up a steep slope to a cabin overlooking the sea. As he climbs, we see two swimmers in the distance and some yachts in the idyllic Mediterranean scenery. There is already something out of place about him: in an environment made for leisure, he is determined to work. The next shot introduces a second character, his wife, to the drama – her relaxed posture, reading in a deckchair, further making him stand out. The third shot emphasises her point of view by showing her in the foreground as she looks towards him. When he invites her to admire his 'worker's' body, she responds that he will not be able either to walk that evening or to work for three days. Denis is annoyed that Eric, his son, has not offered to help. The fourth shot of the film is a long tracking shot framing Denis through his car window as he drives alongside Eric, apologising for having upset him and trying to persuade him to accept a lift. The two bodies, both naked to the waist, are aligned so that Denis's rather stringy muscles contrast with Eric's lean, toned body. Succeeding shots will pick up Eric as he cuts across the rocks to go into town, appears in the town square among a group of children playing, and then reappears

6 Jalil is spelt Djallil in the credits of the first two Cantet films in which he performed.

7 Details concerning the production and shooting are taken from Chauville (1997).

as part of a festive group of young adults with a woman riding on his shoulders.

Like *Tous à la manif*, the film begins with the isolated male before inserting him into a burgeoning set of social relationships. In the process, and in characteristic Cantetian fashion, the character's look upon the world and upon himself has been challenged by other looks, something initially signalled by the wife's refusal to be impressed by Denis's physique as he had wanted. The film establishes a potential parallelism between father and son by framing them side by side and showing both as individuals against a natural setting before placing them in a broader context. Yet there, to some extent, the parallelism seems to end. Not only is Eric more handsome and more athletic, he slides effortlessly into the youthful group. Indeed his trajectory seems to be a model Oedipal journey: moving away from his parents, he goes out into the world, finds a different woman and, at the same time, integrates into a broader social setting. The process is too easy, of course. In what will become an increasingly uneasy narrative, Denis follows Eric into town and effectively spies on him.

We pick up the action in a beachside bar. Eric and his friends sit in a large group around a table, talking and joking together. The mood changes when a bottle of champagne arrives at the table. Knowing who has sent it, Eric looks back over his shoulder towards the bar, his worried look and implied feelings now different from those of the pleasantly surprised group. He goes to the front of the bar and uses the microphone to thank the person who has bought the champagne for his generosity and *discretion*, a clear attempt to persuade Denis to stay in the background. Having come to the front, Eric now finds himself pressured to do a Karaoke song. Rescuing him, Denis steps forward and performs a rather sheepish version of Serge Gainsbourg's classic, sensual and romantic song, 'L'eau à la bouche'. As in *Tous à la manif*, the father's attempt to protect the son (or displace him from the limelight), only generates further embarrassment. While the rest of the young people look on with amusement, Eric looks down or glowers, far from at one with those around him. Nothing is said openly but all is conveyed, in classic melodramatic fashion, by the interaction of looks and the orientations and postures of bodies. The action resumes in the early hours when we see Eric and the girl whom he had earlier carried on his shoulders as they embrace romantically on the rocks by the sea. Another couple from the group come into shot and the foursome descend to a secluded, idyllic cove where the others await. They all swim in the sea. One girl strips naked and the others laughingly follow suit. However, one of them says that she has seen someone watching them. Eric and his girlfriend climb out of the sea, dress and embrace again on the rocks. As Eric uncovers his girlfriend's breast, she covers up, worried that they may be being watched: she has seen the older man from the bar, a rather ridiculous figure, hiding in the trees. The rest of the group catch sight of Denis, and the young men pursue and capture him. They decide he should strip as punishment. Before he can finish doing so, Eric pushes him off the rocks and into the sea and blurts out that the man is his father. Now, the group's eyes turn from Denis to him and his latent sense of shame and embarrassment is driven into full view. He jumps into the sea after his father. We see him help Denis out of the water before the latter in turn helps him. The two sit together on the rocks. If we expect a moment of inter-generational reconciliation, we do not get it. Denis explains how beautiful he had found the couple formed by Eric and his girlfriend. He adds that people of twenty cannot see the world in the same way as those of fifty. Eric replies that these things do not interest him and departs, leaving Denis as alone as at the start.

Jeux de plage is profoundly melodramatic in its focus on family dynamics and its use of the interplay of bodies and looks to drive unspoken tensions into visibility. It is also melodramatic in its narrative arc. The opening hints at latent tensions and unspoken feelings. The sequence in the town shows these tensions and feelings more openly expressed but in a way that is still hidden from public eyes. The final sequence on the shore pushes things to their limit: Eric's inability to shake off Denis; his difference from the group because of the ties he bears within himself; the perversion of Denis's desires, but also his vulnerability. All these things are driven to the surface by the end of the film. A similar trajectory will characterise other later and better-known Cantet films such as *Ressources humaines*.

Tous à la manif stages its melodrama in a single location. Its hero's inability to break with his father finds spatial expression in the way his life revolves around the father's cafe. *Jeux de plage* has a more expansive spatial economy. The young man's ability to leave the family's holiday home and set off along the coast to town suggests that he has managed to break out in a way that the hero of *Tous à la manif* could never manage. In *Tous à la manif*, the young man never achieves real communion with the striking students. In *Jeux de plage*, there seem to be fewer barriers to full integration. The film stages utopian moments of fusion in the festive streets of the holiday town and the Karaoke bar and on the natural space of the shore, where the young people seem able to invent their own rules and shed constraints. Yet the way Denis catches up with Eric not once but twice – in the town, then by the sea – shows that family ties and broader social attitudes are not so easily cast off. This is the lesson of the moment in the film when the son's girlfriend covers her breast. What had seemed a moment of innocence and new beginnings in an idyllic natural setting is now overshadowed by the need to hide from probing, paternal eyes.

Part of what the film dramatises is this impossibility of leaving one's past and personal ties behind. The way in which the father's bodily presence and his prying eyes seem impossible to avoid are a physical manifestation of a more symbolic truth, that one always carries one's parents and what they represent with oneself. Another part of what the film explores is the complexity of relationships between parent and child, father and son. What initially seems to be a desire for companionship on Denis's part turns out to be something more complex and perverse, combining a refusal to let Eric grow up with a vicarious enjoyment of his experiences. The initial juxtaposition of Denis's ageing body with Eric's youthful frame suggests latent rivalry, and a father's awareness that the son may now be living those things that he can no longer experience. However, it also suggests Denis's vulnerability. His later proclamation of admiration for the beauty of the couple his son establishes is coloured by voyeurism and potential jealousy but also a sense of lost youth. The scene on the beach is a kind of inverted primal scene. When Denis spies on the son in a moment of intimacy, he is the one who is symbolically castrated, a state given public expression by the way in which he is forced to begin stripping and reveal his ageing body by the young men.

Denis is perverse and vulnerable, monstrous and protective. We are unsure how to view him. To the degree that camera positioning and sympathy for his vulnerability align us with him, we find ourselves viewing the world through a voyeur's eyes. To the degree that we feel close to the son, we find ourselves aligned with his growing shame and embarrassment as he feels himself and his father exposed to the look of the group. We cringe when Denis performs at the Karaoke and squirm when he spies on the naked swimmers. We might choose to align ourselves with the festive group, yet their gaze is a limited one. They only see Denis as a pervert who needs some form of punishment. They fail to see the complexity of the situation. Each viewpoint casts the limitations of others into view. In truth, of course, and not least because the camera is often detached from any individual or collective look, we never identify completely with any position. Nor, however, are we allowed to be completely detached. We understand too much of people's situations simply to judge them from afar. We are torn and challenged and thus made to question our own position with respect to what we see. This is a typical Cantetian stance.

Although *Jeux de plage* is less obviously rooted in its present than *Tous à la manif* and the later films, it can be seen as at least gesturing towards an important transition. Initially, the father is cast in a traditionally repressive role. Like the father in *Tous à la manif*, Denis expects his son to work with him rather than relax, even though they are on holiday. As the film progresses, however, and in his wish to stay close to Eric, Denis changes his position and encourages Eric to enjoy himself and seek sensual pleasure. When he spies on the young people on the shore, he completely abandons the traditional role of the censorious father and becomes something far more permissive and perverse. Accompanying the film's movement from labour to leisure, this shift in the paternal function looks forward to more developed narratives of transition in the later work. It anticipates, in particular, the consumerist abandonment of restraint and the associated confusion in inter-generational relations we will see in *Vers le sud*.

Les Sanguinaires

Les Sanguinaires tells the story of a group of Parisian friends who agree to escape to an island to avoid the millennium celebrations of 2000. At sixty-eight minutes long, it is a more substantial piece than either of the shorts we have just discussed. It draws on established actors to a greater extent than the other two films: Frédéric Pierrot, who plays François, the male lead, is a prominent screen actor, while Marc Adjadj, who plays François's friend, Pierre, is a theatrical director and screen actor of long standing. Cantet's close collaborator and the film's screenwriter, Gilles Marchand, plays Didier, another of the group. Other performers, notably the adolescents and children in the film, are amateurs. Cantet's daughter, Marie, is one of the four younger children. Jalil Lespert, who had been such a revelation in *Jeux de plage*, plays the role of Stéphane, the young man contracted to look after the Parisians. Because of the commitments of some of the performers, and contrary to his preferred practice, Cantet was unable to gather his cast a long time in advance. Shooting was nonetheless a time of intense contact with the cast and crew based at the isolated island building that was one of the film's main locations.[8] The film was set and filmed on the largest of the Sanguinaire islands, which are located just off the coast of Corsica, near the port of Ajaccio.

Cantet recognised that this story had a strong personal dimension. In his dislike of public festivities and difficulty slotting into the group, the film's hero was not unlike the director himself. Similarly, the way the former sought to flee the millennial celebrations was parallel to the director's own response when he was commissioned to make a film marking the event: if he undoubtedly put his heart into the work, he took it in decidedly non-festive and indeed rather sombre directions.[9]

The title sequence suggests the film may offer something more conventional. It shows what looks like stock footage of New Year celebrations in New York, Italy and two unidentifiable locations. However, like in its two predecessors, the narrative proper begins by showing the main character alone, this time using a series of shots rather than a single long take. We see his face, the back of his head, his hands typing and his computer monitor, as, using both telephone and email, he communicates with clients and friends. Very elegantly dressed, working in what seems to be his own travel agency, he is telling a client that all flights to New York are booked and no-one is likely to cancel. At the same time, he is writing a note promising his friends an escape to a 'paradise' where, away from the global media event, the processions and the countdown, all that they will have is 'calm and fresh air'. In some ways, beginning with the individual before moving out to the group, this opening is like that of the other two

8   For an account of the shooting, see Nicklaus (1997).
9   See anon. (n.d.).

films. In other ways, it is very different, for this particular individual, although physically isolated, is multiply connected, via telephone and internet and his travel agency, to a broader spatial frame. His flight from the contemporary is also inevitably a flight from self.

The film moves from the individual to the group and from the workplace to a leisure context in the next sequence, which begins with a long shot from a boat towards the island of the film's title. Two buildings stand out: the semaphore station where the group will lodge and, in splendid isolation on the island's highest point, the lighthouse. The opening sometimes shows the group as a cohesive whole – as they disembark from the boat, sit down to a meal or sing together – but it also begins to open up cracks that we suspect will widen. Stéphane, the lighthouse keeper, had been contracted to arrive at midday. He finally turns up at dusk. The adolescents of the group are unimpressed by the run-down accommodation and unhappy to be there. Stéphane says there is lots of expensive equipment in the lighthouse. Asked if he is afraid to be there alone, he pulls a gun and points it around the table before revealing that it is not loaded. He starts to wash up and puts on a loud radio broadcast, bringing the outside world into their space. François angrily tells him to turn it off. When Pierre apologises for the outburst, François replies that Stéphane is paid to be there and should do what he is told. Stéphane responds by saying that the client is always right. In typical Cantet fashion, the film has started to bring a series of tensions to the surface and to explore the blind spots of individuals and the group.

Unsurprisingly, but not necessarily in predictable ways, the film opens up the cracks that have appeared. Firstly, although the group have all agreed to leave the world of convention behind during their stay, they seem unequally committed to their utopian goal. François sounds the most radical, but it is ironically he who is most annoyed by Stéphane's unpunctuality and draws on the employer–employee relationship when it suits him. If the group is split, he is also divided against himself, like a typical Cantet character, by the norms he would like to challenge but still upholds. Other members of the group are less conflicted because their commitment is more superficial. The adolescents are the most predictably conformist. Their rebellion against their parents' plans expresses itself in a desire to escape to Ajaccio and join in the festivities in the town. Later, they go there with Stéphane in the little boat and come back talking of big screens with images from Paris and New York and a massive clock with the millennial countdown. They have successfully locked back into the globalised space and synchronised time that François himself was tied into at the start. Bruno has even synchronised his own watch to the countdown. The adults rebel less obviously against their own plan. It soon becomes clear, however, that their commitment is superficial and they intend to celebrate the millennium's arrival in a broadly conventional manner. Food and drink are ordered through Stéphane. One of them has come with *foie gras*, a typical New Year's Eve dish, in her bag.

Faced with the progressive desertion of the group, François first tries to hold them to what has been agreed, by disconnecting from radios and mobile phones and ignoring the event. This attitude inevitably provokes conflict: the group brings out François's rigidity while he highlights its tepid conformism. One character talks of François's *jusqu'au boutisme* (intransigence). Another asks whether he should carry out his own self-criticism, as people had been made to do during the Chinese Cultural Revolution. Stéphane chips in by reminding him that he is not there to police the others. François feels he is being painted as a fascist or a tyrant. Pierre tells him that his behaviour is that of a masochist. Inevitably, François withdraws from the group and is seen more and more on the edge of events. Catherine, his wife, is the only character who really seeks to go some of the way with him. Provoked by Bruno's talking-clock countdown, she confiscates all the watches, breaking the synchronicity between their group and the broader world. She nonetheless dances with the others during their party on the beach. She is not with them, however, when they sit to watch the firework display in Ajaccio, only semi-detached from convention and the space-time of the globally connected.

As in other Cantet films, much of the drama is played out nonverbally through characters' relationships to space, but here it is used more symbolically than, for example, in the broadly quotidian *Tous à la manif*. Apart from some ruins, the island has only two or three humanised areas: the jetty, which both looks towards the mainland and emphasises their separation from it; the semaphore station with its shared spaces (the dining area and the terrace) and more private ones (the bedrooms); the lighthouse, on the highest point of the island, a space of splendid isolation. The dining area, the terrace and the beach are where the group assembles and its unity is tangible. François's growing alienation is signalled by his withdrawal to the group's edges and escapes to the beach and lighthouse. On the former, he is captured in a high-angle, extreme long shot that brings out his isolation and fragility and the sense that he is becoming lost in the landscape. His escapes to the latter signal his desire for solitude but also suggest an aspiration towards something transcendental. The way in which the lighthouse stands proudly alone and projects its light outwards into an indefinite distance seems to align with his romantic but ultimately doomed search for some indefinable utopia. The fact that his wife follows him on his two escapes to the lighthouse makes manifest her desire to maintain their relationship and to keep him in touch with others. In the film's climactic sequence, as the new millennium arrives, François moves out from the lighthouse towards the rocks. Catherine again follows him as he climbs down towards the beach but vertigo forces her to stop and he vanishes into the darkness.[10] The moment is doubly symbolic. Like other Cantet characters, but more literally, Catherine has an experience of dizziness as the world she knows seems to fall away from her. François's disappearance into the nocturnal landscape suggests a final loss of contact with the human society with which he has refused to compromise.

There is a moment earlier in the film when François asks his assembled friends how they dreamt of the year 2000 when they were young. Laughingly, they talk of an imagined future that might involve having a personal helicopter, being waited on by robots or travelling to the moon. Although apparently trivial and light-hearted, this moment seems to point towards something significant. When the adults were growing up in the 1960s, it was still possible to imagine a utopia associated with the pushing back of technological and spatial boundaries. Now, that kind of future-orientated utopia is no longer available. As we saw at the start of the film, communications technology and mass transportation have combined to connect and shrink the planet, and produce not utopia but uniformity and closed horizons. In the context of this foreclosure of the future, the only alternative is flight. Because the initial escape to the island proves

10 The hero's disappearance is a knowing evocation of Antonioni's modernist classic, *L'Avventura* (1960), a film whose heroine unaccountably disappears when on a small island with friends.

abortive – they bring their existing behaviours and habits of connectivity with them – they must either compromise, as most do, or somehow seek to radicalise their position, as François does, even though there is nowhere to escape to and flight implies a self-destructive separation from human society.

In this context, the group's apparently frivolous evocation of moments like the Chinese Cultural Revolution takes on a deeper significance. In its attempt to create, however temporarily and on however small a scale, a different order, the group of friends repeats, in an almost parodic way, some of the experiences that so marked the century that is coming to an end. To begin with, the group needs to be led by a vanguard figure, in the same way as twentieth-century revolutions required a vanguard party. Then, the initial break with old ways is not found to be complete enough. People bring old habits with them and their attitudes need to be policed either by others or themselves. In the former case, the figure that carries out this surveillance risks taking on an authoritarian role, which is why the words 'police' and 'fascist' come up in association with François. In the latter, the risk is the internalised tyranny of the Cultural Revolution, when people were forced to critique their own behaviour in front of their comrades. More broadly, what the group comes up against is the difficulty of building a non-tyrannical 'we' out of a collection of 'I's. In their drive to move beyond isolated individualism, twentieth-century revolutionary movements tended to imagine collective identities with all the apparent unity and indeed uniformity of the individual self. As we now know only too well, attempts to find a 'we' modelled on the supposed coherence of the 'I' only ended in disaster (Badiou, 2005: 138–9). The question with which those who still hold to some collectivist model must deal is how one can weld together a group of people without seeking to crush them into uniformity. In some ways, *Les Sanguinaires*, with its exploration of the tension between the individual and the group, seems to be asking a similar question, yet, like Cantet's other films, it refrains from easy answers.

The two short films we looked at both had Oedipal relationships at their core. In the strictly biological sense, such a thing is lacking here, yet inter-generational relations are clearly important, notably in the interaction between François, the forty-year-old, and Stéphane, played by the twenty-year-old Jalil Lespert. To the degree that François takes the lead in the group, and lays down rules for others to follow, he could be seen as a father figure. If so, what we see is the loss of his paternal power as the group refuses to follow his lead. In this respect, he is like the fathers of the short films, castrating and castrated, controlling yet fragile. This dual nature is condensed in his interaction with Stéphane. If the latter is initially cast as the subordinate – the employee – then roles soon blur. First Stéphane brandishes the phallic gun. Then he carries François back to his chair to prevent him washing up. Later, when François is on the beach with the other men helping the children saw off a branch to make a beach house, Stéphane appears with a chain-saw, drawing the children to him like a magnet. François's resultant anger clearly reflects how the saw cuts through their romantic desire for a simple life away from the modern world. It also suggests an unspoken jealousy.

In some ways, Stéphane has what François craves. The lighthouse is his solitary domain, yet he can also come into the group when he wishes. Catherine probes him about his private life. He replies that he has no girlfriend but can get one whenever he likes, especially during the tourist season when all the foreign women come to Corsica. He seems to have it all. He can withdraw from the world and reconnect to it when he wants. He controls the boat, after all, and is also seen with instruments of modern power (the chainsaw, the gun). Where François is a fragile romantic, someone who finds his utopian dreams derailed by the resistance of the real, Stéphane is a model of pragmatic, masculine self-sufficiency. What his role therefore brings to the fore is just how much the film's story is one of gender.

Cantet's first three films are clearly very male-centred. The Oedipal or quasi-Oedipal dramas at or near their hearts stage questions of social interaction and transition in largely masculine terms. The mother in *Jeux de plage* is at best an amused bystander but is more often completely marginalised by the drama played out between her husband and son. Her son's girlfriend of a day is more prominent but still not a character in her own right. *Tous à la manif* is, if possible, even more male-centred. Certainly there are some lively, self-confident women students in it, not least the three who embarrass the young barman with their unabashed talk of sex. However, the main drama is played out between father, son and group, with the latter's internal gender dynamics barely touched upon. *Les Sanguinaires* follows a similar pattern. Catherine, François's wife, is a very positive character and shows loyalty to her husband even when his behaviour becomes difficult. However, it is essentially his drama, not hers, and the main elements of it play out between him, Stéphane and the group. In the end, Cantet's dramatisation of the difficult relationship between the individual and the collective is centred on men who struggle to fit in. The way in which Stéphane seems to be an almost parodic version of a dominant masculinity – his self-assured autonomy, instrumental attitude to others, (phallic) lighthouse retreat and power tools – suggests that Cantet is very aware of the gendered nature of his narrative. What Stéphane's presence does is draw out the more subtly masculine dimension of François's quest. By disrupting the latter's plans, he makes the wish for control visible. By flaunting his masculine self-sufficiency, he brings out the gendered dimension of the other man's flight from the group.

Conclusion

There is a remarkable assuredness and maturity to Cantet's early works. They show the emergence of his preferred ways of working with actors, producing a script, engaging with a given context and organising a story. If it would be a mistake to expect to find all the elements of the later works in them, it would also be hard not to recognise the germ of later stories. *Tous à la manif*'s story of a cafe-owner father passing on his trade to his son against the background of student protest feels like a rehearsal for *Ressources humaines*. The latter is different, of course. Its hero, unlike the young barman in the earlier film, has moved away from his roots. Yet the core of the two films, the way they stage the intersection of a class-inflected Oedipal drama with a broader social conflict, is essentially similar. What is striking too is how the most powerful scene of the later film is already rehearsed in its predecessor. There is a moment in *Tous à la manif* when, in the claustrophobic space of the kitchen, the cafe-owner father pointedly asks his son if he is ashamed of him. As they talk, the hubbub from the striking students in the bar can be heard. The scene directly anticipates the moment in the later film when, in front of an audience of striking workers, the hero reproaches his father with having passed on his shame at being working class to him. The *mise en scène* is not identical but the operation of a class-related shame and the sense it bears of being judged by others is present in both films. In a similar way, and on more than one count, *Les Sanguinaires* looks forward to *L'Emploi du temps*. Firstly, it shows how a character's attempt to break with convention is frustrated by both those around him and the social habits that he inevitably carries within himself. Secondly, taking the tension between the individual and the group to its limit, the film explores what happens when the desire for autonomy refuses all compromise. Thirdly, in its very symbolic use of *mise en scène*, the film anticipates the expressive way landscape will be used in the later film. In a more indirect way, there is something of *Jeux de plage* in *Vers le sud*. Although an Oedipal drama set in a French holiday resort might seem to have nothing in common with the later film's exploration of neo-colonial dynamics, apart from the holiday setting, both films figure highly uneasy stories about age-related shame, the voyeuristic look and the consumerist command to enjoy.

Beyond these specific convergences, the early works anticipate the later films more generally in the way they lay out and rehearse what one might call a Cantetian dramaturgy. Oedipal dramas and the problems young people face negotiating their entry into the adult world, the tensions between the individual and the group, the articulation of the inter-personal with a broader social or socio-political context: all these essential features of the later works are already in place. This does not mean that we can somehow read the later films off from the earlier ones. Cantet's cinema is so open to the exploration of new contexts and to the input of new collaborators that it has a process of renewal built into itself.

References

Anon. (n.d.), 'Laurent Cantet: "Substituer à un événement en mondovision, un événement très intime"', *TV5monde*, http://asset2.cinema.tv5monde.com/articles/laurent-cantet-substituer-a-un-evenement-en-mondovision-un-evenement-tres-intime-_1 (accessed 8 April 2014).

Badiou, A. (2005), *Le Siècle*, Paris, Seuil.

Biais, J.-M. and Faure, M., (1994), 'Jeunes: 12 clefs pour s'en sortir', *L'Express*, 27 October, www.lexpress.fr/informations/jeunes-12-clefs-pour-s-en-sortir_600177.html (accessed 8 April 2014).

Bourdieu, P. (1984), trans. R. Nice, *Distinction: A Social Critique of the Judgement of Taste*, London, Routledge and Kegan Paul.

Burdeau, E. and T. Antoine (2008), 'Entretien avec Laurent Cantet', *Cahiers du cinéma*, 637 (September), 10–18.

Chauville, C. (1997), '*Jeux de plage*: Un film de Laurent Cantet', *Quatre courts métrages*, www.le-court.com/lecons_cine/fichiers_analyse/fichier_analyse_185_4cm.pdf, 3–7 (accessed 8 April 2014).

Lefort, G. (1995), 'Tous à Clermont-Ferrand: "Tous à la manif"', *Libération*, 7 February.

Nicklaus, O. (1997), '*Les Sanguinaires*', *Les in Rocks*, 1 January, www.lesinrocks.com/cinema/films-a-l-affiche/les-sanguinaires/ (accessed 15 September 2014).

Pelletier, C. (2009), 'Emancipation, equality and education: Rancière's critique of Bourdieu and the question of performativity', *Discourse: Studies in the Cultural Politics of Education*, 30:2, 137–50.

Rancière, J. (1995), *La Mésentente: Politique et philosophie*, Paris, Galilée.

3

The work diptych

In a founding gesture that seemed to set a pattern, the first French film, the Lumière brothers' famous *Workers Leaving the Lumière Factory in Lyon* (1895), captured exit from the workplace rather than the toil within it. Associated with free time and with distraction from labour, cinema has generally avoided more than fleeting engagement with work (Comolli, 2004: 338–46). Breaking with this more general pattern, some recent French film has shown sustained interest in the workplace (Cadé, 2000). The period since about 1995 has seen a resurgence of cinematic interest in socio-political fault-lines, and the workplace has been one of the key locations explored because of its capacity to bring oppressions to the surface and disrupt any sense of a pacified social order. Documentary has repeatedly recorded the struggles against factory closures that have been such a feature of recent times as the old Fordist bastions have been broken up and production has been outsourced or moved overseas. It has also sought to explore the new transnational processes of labour as one of the main ways to make sense of globalisation. Less over-arching in its scope, fiction has tended to focus on individual workers or small groups as it tracked the dismantling of the old industrial working class and recorded the brutality of the new economic order (O'Shaughnessy, 2007: 55–128).

Cantet's recurrent interest in work and the workplace is therefore less exceptional than it might have been at other historical moments. Work is nevertheless something to which he has been repeatedly drawn and which he has approached in his own, very specific way. His interest in work and the individual's relationship to it was clear from the moment he made *Tous à la manif.* It found more developed expression in his first two major fictions, *Ressources humaines* and *L'Emploi du temps*, the films that are the major focus of this chapter. It would thereafter be present in films like *Vers le sud*, with its focus on the tourist industry and the sex trade, and *Entre les murs*, with its examination of the work of a teacher. Indeed, one of the things that drew Cantet to the latter film was the way it allowed him to home in on a profession where workers' self-reflexion on their professional activity is a routine part of what they do.

Like other contemporary directors, Cantet sees the workplace as a place where oppression and alienation can be forced to the surface. As he noted in an interview when *Ressources humaines* was released, 'J'avais envie de filmer l'usine, et d'utiliser le monde de l'entreprise comme une sorte de loupe sur les rapports humains, qui s'expriment là de façon plus violente qu'ailleurs. L'entreprise peut être un lieu de non-droit, on se permet de parler à des gens comme nulle part ailleurs' (Mangeot and Tijou, 2000).[1] Elsewhere, the director described how visits to tens of factories and discussions with bosses and workers while *Ressources humaines* was being researched had helped convince him that class struggle could not be consigned to the past, despite liberalism's attempts to persuade us of its obsolescence (Larcher, 2000: 50).

What constituted the specificity of Cantet's approach to work was the way he integrated it into his own filmic universe with its intense Oedipal dramas, its strong sense of the tension between the individual and the group, and its melodramatic drive.[2] *Ressources humaines* and *L'Emploi du temps* are both about fathers and sons. The former follows Frank (Jalil Lespert), an upwardly mobile management

---

1 'I wanted to film the factory and to use the world of the company as a way to get close to human relationships that express themselves more violently there than in other places. The company can be a place outside the law where people think it's acceptable to speak to others in a way that they wouldn't do anywhere else.'

2 Cantet does not come to the workplace as a detached observer. He willingly acknowledges that he has no first-hand knowledge of environments like the factory but he is very aware of how heavily what one might call the ideology of work weighs upon his own background and attitudes. Like the father in *Ressources humaines*, his own father believes that leisure time needs to be put to productive use. This same attitude, he recognises, penetrates his own outlook (Mangeot and Tijou, 2000). As with other issues, the questioning that takes place in his films is also directed at himself.

student, as he comes to do a work placement in the factory where Jean-Claude (Jean-Claude Vallod), his father, has always worked, effectively becoming his superior. The latter tracks another high-flyer, this time a mature man, as he seeks to hide his unemployment from those around him, including his own father. *Ressources humaines* dramatises the impossible situation of a young man with a working-class background who has been taught to look down on his own roots. A typical Cantetian drama, it is about someone struggling to find his place in the world. Turning this dilemma on its head, *L'Emploi du temps* is the story of someone who seeks to escape from an all too established place in which they feel trapped. Thus complementing each other at the narrative level, the films also come together to track social evolution: *Ressources humaines* recounts the end of the old, socially inclusive Fordist regime while *L'Emploi du temps* explores the hidden constraints of the new world of flexible, mobile labour. Taken together, the two films form a compelling diptych about contemporary work.

Cantet's films, as we have noted, always tend to locate their strongly drawn melodramatic cores within a well-documented context, with the former driving the fault-lines of the latter to the surface. True to this pattern, *Ressources humaines* locates its father–son story within the context of the implementation of the thirty-five-hour week legislation, a piece of social policy that was absolutely current when the film was being made. Despite this documentary drive, Cantet was not narrowly interested in a specific reform. As he noted, 'je n'avais pas le sentiment de faire un film précisément sur le sujet des trente-cinq heures, ce n'était là qu'un cadre et je n'ai donc pas eu peur de tomber dans le "film à thèse"' (BIFI, 2001: 5).[3] The proposed reduction in the working week interested him because it allowed him to explore an evolving workplace and tensions within it. As he noted, the film could just as easily have been about some other aspect of contemporary labour. He initially thought of building it around what are called 'quality circles', a managerial tool that brings together all those involved in the manufacture of a product to discuss how their output can be made more efficient (Bonnaud, 2000). With its

---

3 'I didn't feel I was making a film precisely about the thirty-five hours. It was only a framework, so I wasn't worried that I might succumb to making a "message" film.'

examination of the power of peer pressure, such a topic would clearly have appealed to a director consistently drawn to the tension between individuals and groups. The project's first name, *Cercles de qualité*, was a title with almost as many potential resonances and ironies as *Ressources humaines.*

As is well known, *L'Emploi du temps* was also partly based on real events, in its case the infamous Romand affair. Jean-Claude Romand was a bright young man who failed his medical studies but hid this from those around him. Building on this initial lie, he developed a fictional life for himself as a high-flying researcher at the World Health Organization in Geneva. Much of his time was simply filled with wandering around. Some of it was used to research his fictional life to give it density and make it more convincing. His fake job helped him embezzle money from relatives and his mistress: by inventing Swiss investments, he persuaded them to part with their cash. He also procured money by selling fake anti-cancer drugs. Amazingly, he was able to sustain his fiction for eighteen years until, threatened with discovery, he murdered his wife, children and parents but failed to kill his mistress. He also apparently tried to kill himself, although the attempt lacked conviction. He is now in prison carrying out a life sentence. His story is the subject of a highly documented but partly novelistic book, *L'Adversaire* (2000) by Emmanuel Carrère, a writer who followed Romand's trial very closely and entered into a long correspondence with the killer. The book spawned a film adaptation of the same name, released in 2002 and directed by Nicole Garcia, starring Daniel Auteuil. When Cantet and his co-writer turned to the Romand story, they were therefore on well-trodden ground. However, Cantet's film was far less true to the Romand case than either of its predecessors. His initial intention was to make a film about someone hiding a job loss. Once he had decided to go in that direction, it was perhaps inevitable that he would be drawn to Romand's story. Elements of the latter clearly come into his film: the high-profile Swiss job, the fake investments, the counterfeit goods, the aimless wandering, the carefully documented fictional life. But thereafter, the resemblance ceases. The murders and suicide attempt remain only as unrealised possibilities. Despite his affinity with melodrama, Cantet was not interested in the more macabre or exceptional elements of the Romand affair. Instead, he moved the story towards the ordinary and used it to explore the relationship between an individual and the world of work. Ultimately, it was this de-dramatisation that allowed the film to become perhaps the key French film about contemporary labour.

Workplace melodrama: forcing class struggle to the surface

The most important line in *Ressources humaines* is undoubtedly the last one, 'elle est où, ta place?'. The film is ultimately about the impossibility of a young man from a working-class background finding a satisfactory place for himself in a world where workers are not only dominated but where even their position of subordinated incorporation is being unpicked. In some ways, the story feels like a classic coming-of-age drama in which the hero or heroine has to shed his or her illusions before taking his or her place in the world. The problem here, the reason that there can be no ultimate closure, is that, for reasons beyond his control, the hero has no ultimately tenable position. The film's sense of blockage can be caught in terms of the impossible movement from one utopian vision of the world to another. One part of its drama is encapsulated in the necessary loss of the utopian world of childhood, in which the child is protected and adored and the parents *seem* admirable and powerful. The second part is the hero's failure to find a suitable substitute world for the one he must leave as he grows up. In the ideal world that he seems to want to inhabit, he could move into a higher social class through education, secure in the knowledge that his working-class father still had a valued place in the world. This second utopia of a meritocratic yet inclusive social order is a personal one – Frank seems to believe sincerely in it – but it is also clearly something akin to a governing ideology, a validation of the existing order. In that respect, it is a conservative utopia, an idealised version of what is, rather than a radical alternative to it.

The film begins, as we noted earlier, by establishing that Frank cannot simply slot back into his old life, not least because his bedroom now has bunk beds to accommodate his sister's children when they stay over. Its closing strike scene shows Jean-Claude sitting with his grandchildren on his knee and Frank at some distance from the re-established family group. Yet, there are moments in between when the parent–child relationship still seems operative. Early on in the film, reaffirming his paternal role, Jean-Claude tells Frank how to behave in the workplace. Frank's mother inspects him before he leaves his house and pronounces him handsome in his new suit, her approving maternal gaze standing in sharp contrast to other looks that he will have to confront. Later, in another assertion of paternal prerogative, Jean-Claude scolds him when he lies in bed after a night on the tiles. On getting up, Frank will assist his father at the work-bench where he makes wooden furniture. Although we are ultimately reminded of the impossibility of its restoration, the traditional parent–child relationship nonetheless hangs over the film, particularly in scenes set within the house, the location where parental authority still seems to hold sway.

Yet, as we know, neither the individual nor the family unit is ever self-contained in a Cantet film. They always open onto and are penetrated by what lies outside them. If the class differences that split Frank against himself come most to the fore, as we shall see, within the factory, they also make themselves felt within the family setting, and notably in the mute deference that is paid to the upwardly mobile young man. When he arrives at his home-town railway station, first his sister and then his mother carries one of his bags for him. Later, when he brings work home, his parents sit whispering so as not to disturb him. Even the mother's admiring gaze on his new suit is tinged with class difference: while the father wears typical manual worker's clothes, the son's elegant attire signals his higher status. The mother is effectively admiring him for leaving his class of origin behind. The parents' deference points to how they have internalised and accepted their subaltern status within the social order.

Other characters cast a less admiring gaze on Frank's success. When his old friends invite him for a drink, it seems nothing has changed between them. However, as soon as he starts to explain that his task at work is to study the implementation of the thirty-five-hour working week, a divide opens up. Patronisingly, he tells them that they will not be interested in what he is doing. Instantly, they pick up on the way he is placing himself apart from them. The gap comes more forcibly to the surface when one friend says he cannot understand how anyone can live in Paris. Frank essentially tells him that he is a peasant. A bout of pushing ensues. Frank's social mobility, and the way it expresses itself in his detachment from the local space to which the less socially mobile are tied, now comes between him and his contemporaries. In a later scene in a bar, we see him sitting alone, separated by some pillars from a group of young workers playing table football. Through its 'text of muteness' (the bag-carrying, the distance between characters) or through moments of melodramatic confrontation (the spat in the bar), the film drives hidden lines of class into visibility.

Class, as Cantet himself noted, makes itself most strongly felt within the workplace, where hierarchies and power asymmetries are present in most concentrated form. In line with the more general movement from the implicit to the openly stated, these workplace divisions only progressively come to full visibility. Frank initially arrives at the factory with his father and his workmates. He talks with them in the foyer as they have a coffee and follows them into the locker room, a transitional space, where Jean-Claude puts on the blue overalls that were traditionally such a marker of working-class status. All seems relaxed. Things change when Frank goes to follow his father into the workshop itself. In a gesture that both emphasises hierarchy and makes visible an unseen barrier, the foreman stops him. He cannot enter without permission. When he is allowed in shortly afterwards, the camera picks him up as he comes through a door on the back of which a poster warns visitors to beware of unfamiliar machinery. This is a literal reference to the dangers posed by drills and presses but alludes more metaphorically to the factory's role as an unknown 'mechanism' that will challenge our presuppositions. A newcomer to the workshop, Frank is effectively our proxy as he begins his tour. Yet the eye-level camera places a distance between him and us by showing him in long shot as he begins his exploration. The distance allows us not simply to see what he sees but also to see him as an outsider. It encourages us to pick up on the glances that those already in the space cast his way. The contrast between his mobile, voyeuristic gaze and the workers' stolen looks tells us all we need to know about his difference from them and the way they are tied to their machines even as he circulates.

The sequence culminates with the moment, described earlier, when one of the foremen humiliates his father in front of him. Jean-Claude has called him over to see his machine and tell him how productive a 'well-trained guy' can be. But his moment of potential pride is completely punctured by the dressing down he receives for slowing production down. The only resistance in the scene comes from

Alain (Didier Emile-Woldemard), the young black worker on the next machine, who literally barks at the foreman, a gesture that is at once a commentary on the latter's action as management guard-dog and a non-verbalised expression of opposition to it. Frank says nothing but his downturned eyes speak of his shame at his father's own shaming and passivity. This scene is in many ways the core of the film. It contains, in as yet latent form, the untenability of both Frank's position and that of his father.

Frank's eyes are cast down again soon afterwards. He is taken on a second tour of the shop-floor, this time with the manager and the head of personnel. This tour begins very differently with an extreme high-angle long shot of the threesome as they move through the space. The shot invites us to distance ourselves from the characters and observe their interactions. What we see is a world that starts to split in front of our eyes. Relationships *seem* cordial. The boss takes an interest in individual workers and shakes their hands. Yet, the way the camera holds his departing back after one such encounter just long enough for us to glimpse a worker's defiantly raised middle finger points to unspoken tensions. Another silent gesture of resistance predictably occurs when he reaches Alain: the latter holds up his oily gloves as his way of refusing the proffered handshake. The boss's trajectory then takes him to Jean-Claude for an exchange that will mirror yet also negate the earlier scene with the foreman. The boss congratulates Jean-Claude for having raised such a promising son. Again, we see Frank bow his head as the impossibility of his position and that of his father is driven a little closer to the surface. The father can be proud of his son but only for his progress in a universe within which he himself is patronised or humiliated. Frank can make his father proud, but only if he is willing to see him treated as an inferior.

In true melodramatic fashion, the final iteration of the scene by the machine during the strike will bring these latent contradictions into emphatic visibility. In front of the striking workers, shouting in Jean-Claude's face, Frank will reproach his father with having passed on his shame at his working-class condition. He will also declare that he is ashamed of his own shame. His reaction is to rebel and force his father to follow suit. Seeking to provoke the latter, he knocks over the tray with the components he has been making and kicks them across the floor. As Jean-Claude struggles to pick them up, he is literally forced to see that he lives on his knees. This is also the sense of the earlier scene when workers and management come up against the factory doors that Alain has soldered shut just before the strike begins. Furious at being locked out, the boss gets out his car jack and smashes the glass in the lower part of the door. He and the other managers stoop to go in, followed by those workers who are not downing tools. The way the latter must virtually crawl to obey the order to return to work is a mute but eloquent manifestation of their position as a dominated group. Jean-Claude is, of course, one of those happy to lower himself to go through. This is a far cry from the start of the film and the impression it gives of a broadly consensual social order.

When he witnesses his father's initial humiliation by the foreman, Frank is content to continue in his managerial role, not least because his boss takes a clear interest in him and the world of power opens up invitingly before him. However, he too is soon forced to confront barriers not simply as they apply to others but also as they affect him. There is a powerful early scene when the works committee brings management together with trade union representatives, with each group on its own side of the table. Frank sits observing the scene but his spatial positioning, beside the boss, and besuited like him, clearly positions him with management. The meeting quickly becomes confrontational as Madame Arnoux, the old CGT representative, enters into a quarrel with the boss, who becomes aggressive in turn. Shortly afterwards, when Frank runs into Madame Arnoux, he looks bemused when she tells him he is a social climber and has clearly chosen sides. As in other Cantet films, characters are forced to confront how others see them. From his own utopian position, Frank operates in a world without class struggle. From that of Madame Arnoux, he appears very differently. A good part of the film is structured by the competition between these two constructions of the film's universe.

Frank's utopian understanding is best expressed through the questionnaire he carries out amongst the workers over what they expect from the implementation of the thirty-five-hour week. As a young moderniser, he sees this as a way of moving negotiations beyond the old confrontation between unions and management to something more inclusive and consensual. He continues to declare his faith in what he is doing even when the boss congratulates him for having divided the unions and the head of personnel rewrites his open-ended questions as multiple choice ones with pre-set answers. The completion of the questionnaire represents the high point of his time in the workplace, not least when, impressed by his competence, the boss takes him aside and suggests there may be a place for him within the larger company that owns the factory. As one father is humiliated, another more powerful and apparently benevolent surrogate seems ready to take his place.

However, in a film where the unspoken is as important as the spoken, there are silent clues that suggest things are less rosy than they seem, even for the upwardly mobile Frank. Just as he is discussing the questionnaire with the head of personnel, the boss asks him to leave the room. Initially the door is left open and it appears that Frank will be allowed to witness what is happening. However, not only does the head of personnel then shut the door, he also lowers the blinds. This secrecy paradoxically drives the company's lack of transparency into visibility. Something similar will happen when a group of managers arrive one day from head office and are met in the car park by the boss. As Frank follows them into the building, the boss lets the door go in his face, as if he were not there. Next, when he tries to join their meeting, he is firmly told that he is not allowed in. The closed doors and hierarchical access to information give the lie to his fantasy of openness and consultation. Just as importantly, they remind him of his own lack of real power within the organisation.

Because the truth is not available on the surface, it is only by chance that Frank discovers the management's true plans. Needing a computer to work on, he borrows the head of personnel's desktop and stumbles upon a letter informing the regional Government of the company's intention to shed a dozen workers, including Jean-Claude. Frank is at a loss what to do. He tells Alain, the young worker from the machine next to his father's. He confronts the boss and calls him a coward for his underhand ways. He tells Madame Arnoux, the CGT representative, who reminds him that few people take her word as an old class warrior seriously anymore. He will need proof. It is at this stage that he and Alain stage a nocturnal break-in to the factory. Frank prints out copies of the tell-tale letter and tapes it to the glass entrance door, which Alain welds shut. Those arriving at work will be forced to see the truth.

In some ways, the break-in represents an improbable generic shift from social realism to something more like a thriller. Yet, within the film's underlying melodramatic economy, it makes perfect sense. Initially, in a world where class struggle is denied and those who voice it (Madame Arnoux) are not listened to, only mute signs (the covert gesture, the closed doors) can point to its underlying presence or concealment. As the film unfolds, and notably through its moments of melodramatic confrontation (Frank seeing his father humiliated or calling the boss a coward), it is driven to the surface. This process culminates logically in the pinning of the letter to the front door, a definitive forcing into view of what had been unseen. Although it still remains for Frank to confront his father about his class shame, the more general struggle can now take place overtly in the form of the closing strike.

Personal politics, unequal voices

When Frank reveals management's plans to Madame Arnoux and effectively aligns himself with the unions in the struggle with management, she pointedly tells him that he is only reacting because he is affected personally. She is right of course. Frank's reaction is doubly personal: not only is his father involved, but he himself has been kept out of the loop. His pride is wounded. The way he reproaches his boss with cowardice also suggests a reaction that is working at the level of the emotional and the individual. The contrast with Madame Arnoux is therefore telling. As an older trade unionist, she speaks the traditional language of collective mobilisation. At the first meeting, her talk is of defending workers' gains, of the parent company's profitability and its unscrupulous overseas investments. Her language is that of the systemic, of class and collective struggle. Part of a different generation, Frank sees things in more personal terms. In a film that, as we shall see, is about a shift in social regimes, the contrast between the two characters points towards a new relationship to politics based less on the old durable collective belonging of class and more on immediate personal refusal. This would seem to be the signification of the scene where the workers come together for a strike meeting in a school gymnasium. As Madame Arnoux speaks, Alain turns and beckons Frank forward to join the workers' group. The latter instead turns tail and breaks down in tears. This would appear to be the moment when he realises that, having burnt his bridges with management, he cannot simply rejoin a class to which he no longer belongs. Like other Cantet heroes, he must work out his own place in the world.

This does not mean that the film somehow consigns collective struggle to the past. If there is one person whose position is validated by events, it is Madame Arnoux. She initially seems stuck in the past. As she herself notes, people think she is a little mad. Her words, the language of class struggle, risk becoming a personal idiom rather than a collective truth. What the film achieves as it unfolds is to stitch the language of struggle and the real back together. As it ends, hers is the most authoritative voice to be heard. It once again bites on a world where struggle has been forced back to the surface. The film does not simply – simplistically – oppose a politics rooted in individual revolt to one based on collective allegiance. Rather, it opens an interrogative gap between the two. This is the lesson of the final scene when the striking workers sit down for lunch. While Jean-Claude has moved back within the group to which his own interests are intrinsically linked, Frank himself sits to one side, aligned with the struggle but also an individual who must work out his own place in relation to it. This, in a way, is where the film leaves us. If it often places us close to Frank, it also distances us from him, forcing us to see him through the eyes of others (his parents, his old friends, Madame Arnoux), not allowing us to align easily with any one position. In the end, like Frank, we must work out our place in relationship to what we see.

This invitation to ponder our position is in stark contrast to the pre-formatted questionnaire that Frank puts to the workers. Although explicitly about the thirty-five-hour legislation, the questionnaire raises broader questions about the democratic process itself. It is driven, as we noted, by the utopian fiction that all voices count equally and can express themselves freely. Yet the reality, as we saw, is very different. As when we choose between the few available parties at elections, the range of possible answers is already decided. The questionnaire, as the boss freely admits to Frank, is designed not to allow real debate but to disarm it. A potentially active public is broken down into a series of numerically countable responses. Voices are counted but clearly do not count. As elsewhere within the film's melodramatic visual economy, the truth is to be found not in what is said but in the mute voice of the visible. The workers are summoned to fill out the questionnaires in the canteen. As they sit and write, Frank, the boss, the latter's personal assistant and one of the foremen circulate, looking over shoulders, offering advice. Anticipating *Entre les murs*, the scene has clear visual echoes of a classroom where an examination is being taken. Jean-Claude later gives the game away when he asks his son if he has had time to correct his *copie*, or examination script. He also confesses to having been unsure of the correct answer to one of the questions. Rather than equal partners in a free exchange, the workers are positioned as minors in a situation defined by others. Within this context, the only tenable position is that taken by Alain, who simply says, 'je n'y crois pas', or 'I don't believe in it.' When all the available choices are fake, the only way to retain one's voice is to point to one's silencing.

When we looked at *Tous à la manif*, we suggested that it hesitated in the space between a Bourdieusian and a Rancierian understanding of what it showed. While a Bourdieusian interpretation would direct our attention towards the acquired attitudes and practices that made people complicit in their own domination, a Rancierian analysis might examine the situation in which only some voices counted. *Ressources humaines* seems similarly poised between the two irreconcilable alternatives. Frank's parents, for example, seem prisoners of their class *habitus*. They bear it in their habits of deference and acceptance of subordination. Jean-Claude, in particular, carries its marks not only in his clothes (his classic blue overalls) but in his submissive, round-shouldered posture. Yet Frank also appears to bear something of his class *habitus* within himself. His suit is too new and well pressed and he wears it too awkwardly for it to seem something he was destined to wear from birth. In a similar way, his attitude to management still has too much of the classroom and the prepared speech to spring spontaneously from an internalised superiority. This, in part, was why Cantet placed Lespert, the film's only (budding) professional actor in the role. Unlike all the other performers who are effectively playing their own social role, Lespert appears to be learning to perform his new status. Yet his exceptional case paradoxically serves to confirm the more general rule that characters bear the mark of their social origins, even when they are leaving them behind.

The film might appear resolutely Bourdieusian if it left things there. However, like other Cantet films, it opens a gap between characters and their role and asserts their capacity as speaking subjects in a way that brings it closer to a Rancierian perspective. While it could be argued that, by eventually going on strike, Jean-Claude merely submits to his son rather than his boss and so remains in his interiorised subordination, other characters establish a clear reflexive distance between themselves and their social position. This is obviously the case with Alain. While he cannot express himself in the management-approved questionnaire, he is more than happy to discuss his relationship to work when he finds Frank sitting alone in the café where the power relationships are very different. The head of personnel feels the need to offer the workers prefabricated answers to questions because he feels they have nothing original to say. What the film suggests, however, is that what really limits their self-expression is the constrained situation in which they are invited to write their thoughts. In other words, moving closer to Rancière, the film explores the barriers and constraints that mean that only certain voices are heard and counted (Rancière, 1995: 43–53). Within the film's text of muteness, the anonymous worker's raised middle finger and Alain's use of his gloved hands to refuse the boss's handshake serve as eloquent reminders that there are voices that circumstances render inaudible.

In this context, it is perhaps telling that the film begins and ends with moments of reflection that remind us that, rather than simply being social objects, the characters are thinking subjects. As Frank approaches his home town at the start of the film, sitting looking out of the train window, he may as yet be unaware of his coming encounter with social barriers and the look of others. Yet, rather than defining him by his circumstances, the film begins with his individual consciousness. He may be forced to rethink his view of himself and the world but he is nonetheless a reflexive being. In the same way, it is significant that the film ends as Alain asks him where he will now go and he in turn asks Alain where his place is. We probably suspect that, while Frank will move on, Alain will continue as a manual worker, not least because of the twin infants he must provide for. Yet we are also invited to see the distance between Alain and his social role, the very distance that is a pre-condition for reflection and possible revolt.

The end of Fordist man

Fordism, as Paul Thompson (2003) notes, is a notoriously difficult term to define. Broadly speaking it tends to be used in three different but overlapping ways. In its narrowest use, it refers to a mode of industrial production of standardised goods on assembly lines operated by semi-skilled workers, as famously practised by Henry Ford in his motor car factories. More broadly, it evokes a macro-economic regime, also advocated by Ford, whereby relatively well-paid production allowed workers to become consumers of the mass-produced goods they made. In its widest sense, with undoubted national variations, it describes the post-Second World War consensus that saw the integration of workers into capitalist societies through guarantees of stable employment and welfare benefits that mitigated the worst effects of markets. Whether one's definition is broad or narrower, it is clear that essential elements of the old Fordist compromise have gone into crisis without some stable 'post-Fordist' settlement being put in its place (Thompson, 2003: 361–6). While neither *Ressources humaines* nor *L'Emploi du temps* ever mentions Fordism explicitly, it is clear that they together track the multi-faceted shift from one social regime to another.

In *Ressources humaines*, during Frank's first discussion with the head of personnel, the former describes his family's relationship to the factory: his father has worked there for more than thirty years; his sister is employed there; he used to receive Christmas presents, as a child, from the firm and would spend summer holidays at the work council's holiday camp. Cutting him short, the head of personnel says that things are now much less rosy and that the company has recently let twenty-two people go. This conversation sets the context for what follows and helps us make sense of the film's use of the thirty-five-hour legislation. A workplace that used to be about inclusiveness, long-term stability and social benefits has now become less stable and inclusive. In other words, the workplace's evolution encapsulates a broader shift from what we might call a Fordist social regime to something very different. Within this context, the film's exploration of the application of the thirty-five-hour week seems to be a way of asking what form the exit from Fordism will take. Frank's initial utopian view suggests what a positive exit might look like for the workers: more free time, more inclusive sharing of work, participation in decision-making in exchange for flexibility. The reality is very different, as we know. Management indeed wants more flexible working, but also plans to replace some workers with machines, older employees like Jean-Claude being predictably vulnerable.

Always wearing the same cap to work and the same blue overalls in the factory, Jean-Claude is an archetypal representative of the old Fordist regime. The predictable world he operates in is embodied by his machine with its endlessly replicated components and its revolving metal plate always coming back with the same task. His predictable response to the variable week that the thirty-five-hour legislation will bring in is to say, 'c'est pas régulier', meaning both 'it's not regular' and 'I don't trust it.' Frank tells him he will have more leisure. Clearly unready to slot into the new, flexible regime, he wants to know if the extra time will follow a predictable pattern. Although he is in many ways the prisoner of his role, someone tied to its routines and his machine and subjected to the foreman's surveillance and the more diffuse monitoring of his productivity, he has also made himself comfortable at work. Richard Sennett, a leading analyst of the workplace, suggests that along with all its constraints (its Weberian iron cage), the rigid, bureaucratic modernity of Fordism also provided a home (Sennett, 2006: 30–2). Jean-Claude is clearly at home in the Fordist workplace. He arrives early to chat with his friends and jokes with them over lunch in the canteen. Sennett suggests that a core part of Fordism's implicit bargain with labour was delayed gratification: workers would put up with the dull, assembly-line routine because they knew that they would be rewarded later through social protection and access to consumption (Sennett, 2006: 30–2). Jean-Claude is true to this pattern. Part of the reason he always arrives early is to earn the end-of-year bonus for punctuality. Alain has always admired his ability to endure toil. On a larger scale, we also know that he and his wife have made long-term sacrifices so that their son will be educated to a higher level and accede to a higher class. His whole life is organised on the principle that self-restraint will ultimately be rewarded. It is this implicit bargain that is broken as the film unfolds. His drama is not simply personal. It is that of a whole social group.

L'Emploi du temps and the new person

If Jean-Claude embodies the vanishing regularities of Fordism, Vincent, the hero of *L'Emploi du temps*, belongs firmly to the new order. Jean-Claude is tied to his home town, and the old Fordist factory with its drills, presses and other heavy machinery. Vincent is a creature of the mobile new. His main tools are his car and mobile phone, devices that free him from the constraints of space. Tellingly, the first time we see him, it is in the car park of a service station, a space for passing through, not for staying still or putting down roots. Later, we find him in other car parks, motorway rest areas and chain hotels, always on the move and ready to take to major or minor roads. Jean-Claude resides in a town full of family memories. Vincent is most at home in what anthropologist Marc Augé calls non-places, anonymous spaces detached from specific local histories and designed for a frictionless passing through (Augé, 1995; Archer, 2008). This is not to say that he has no family ties: during the course of the film, we repeatedly see him drawn back to the characterless middle-class estate where he lives, near where his children attend school and his wife Muriel (Karin Viard), a school-teacher, works. However, the whole film is also structured by his movements away from home and into spaces of apparent freedom and detachment. Whereas Muriel is always there for the children, he is more like an occasional visitor. It is as if a key part of his mobility was the ability to put on but then take off family ties. Where Frank, in *Ressources humaines*, lives a utopian fantasy of social inclusion, Vincent lives one of individual freedom. Both are borne by individuals but both are also fundamentally conformist.

The tensions within Vincent's life are eloquently expressed in the opening sequence although we do not yet fully understand what is going on. It begins with a shot from behind of a figure asleep in a car whose windscreen is steamed up. This is a typical Cantet opening in that it focuses on the individual consciousness before it interacts with the world. It also points to the specificity of the film, however, in the way the fogged windscreen suggests a character who risks becoming detached from his surroundings. Detachment is not so easy to achieve: his mobile phone rings. It is his wife. He tells her he is busy and has meetings lined up for the day. He asks if their daughter is up yet. He then descends from the car and is shown in the car park as a group of children dismount from a school coach. Briefly, he walks just behind two boys, as if they formed a unit. Thanks to the distance procured by his mobile phone, and to the anonymity and fleeting contact of non-places, he seems able to have it all. He can be free, yet in touch with his family. He can be alone, but behave as if he were a parent.

This utopian freedom and miraculous abolition of contradictions is extended in a sequence that shortly follows. Driving alone on a country road, Vincent finds himself next to a small train. Playfully, he races it, as if man, train and landscape had entered into a miraculous harmony whereby he could be alone behind his windscreen, yet also connected to other people and to the world. The moment cannot last. Coming round a corner, he is confronted with a red light that brings him to a halt, his moment of freedom and fusion ended by a reminder of external constraints and social rules.

Later the same day, we pick him up on a motorway service station bridge, as he phones Muriel. He is still tied down, he reports. The team's work project is proving difficult and they are having a crisis meeting over dinner. More positively, his project of moving to a new job in Switzerland may be progressing. As the conversation ends, Vincent returns to his car and reclines the seat, as if settling down for the night. We may not be sure yet but we surely suspect that he has lost his job and is spinning a tale to his wife in order to preserve the freedom that he so obviously enjoys. We may also anticipate tensions to come over the need for money and the pressure of prying eyes.

Vincent's invented career change will take on a momentum of its own once Muriel has spilled the beans to his father (Jean-Pierre Mangeot) and family friends. Their joint expectations mean that what was put forward as a possibility must increasingly be fleshed out. Vincent will go to Switzerland to prospect his 'workplace', the United Nations (UN) development agency in Geneva, from where he will, he says, be helping African development projects. The same invented job will serve as a pretext for getting money from his father towards the purchase of an apartment. It will also allow him to recruit old friends from business school to a bogus investment scheme. He has, he suggests, a colleague who works with ex-Soviet countries and can get astonishingly high rates of return for undeclared investments. Meanwhile, however, as he sits in the lobby of the chain hotel where he meets his friends, he is observed by an older man, Jean-Michel (Serge Livrozet), who quizzes him about the scheme, smells a rat, and offers him something less grandiose but more secure in exchange: participation in the smuggling of counterfeit goods over the Swiss border. Vincent gets involved in the latter scheme, initially reluctantly, but with growing enthusiasm, night-time border crossing on snow-covered roads seemingly bringing back some of the excitement of his earlier freedom at the wheel.

Jean-Claude in *Ressources humaines* works in the same place for thirty years. Between his illicit and invented activities, the flexible Vincent has a multiplicity of projects: the redundancies that, as a management consultant, he seems to be steering as the film opens; the Swiss job; the fake investment scheme; the smuggling. Each project involves him with different networks and contacts: Jeffrey, a well-intentioned colleague from his consultancy job, who wants to help him back into work; his old college friends and their contacts; his father and his contacts; Jean-Michel and those he deals with. He is, then, a man of networks and projects. These are the conditions of his mobility, the ability to shift between projects and draw on different networks being essential to the power of the mobile individual.

Two classics of social analysis, Zygmunt Bauman's *Liquid Modernity* (2000) and Luc Boltanski and Eve Chiapello's *Le Nouvel Esprit du capitalisme* (1999), can help us locate and interpret the broader changes implied by the shift from Fordism to something different. Bauman suggests that Fordism operates essentially as the self-consciousness of what he calls solid modernity. Capitalism, as Marx famously noted, tends to dissolve all that is solid in its restless search for new sources of profit. For a time, however, it renounced some of its mobility. Needing to pin down workers and monitor their behaviour, and committed to machines, it invested heavily in place and accepted solidity (Bauman, 2000: 6–10). As Bauman puts it, 'At that stage in their joint history, capital, management and labour were all, for better or worse, doomed to stay in one another's company for a long time to come … tied down by the combination of huge factory, heavy machinery and massive labour forces' (Bauman, 2000: 57). Now, in the age of the liquid modern, breaking up its old Fordist factories and outsourcing production, capitalism has loosened its ties to specific places. Its trappings have shifted as the heavy concrete and metal of the solid age give way to the flows of the new era. Bauman comments, 'In its heavy stage, capital was as much fixed to the ground as were the labourers it engaged. Nowadays capital travels light – with cabin luggage only, which includes no more than a briefcase, a cellular telephone and a portable computer' (Bauman, 2000: 58). A man of machines and factory routines, Jean-Claude clearly belongs in solid modernity in the same way as Vincent belongs in the liquid. The latter's tools in

L'Emploi du temps – the car, briefcase and mobile phone – are clearly close to those Bauman describes. Besides, his job (the real one), was as a management consultant, precisely one of those people who help companies shed labour and close factories to make themselves more profitable. Exactly such actions were the subject of one of his phone conversations on the first day.

Like Bauman, Boltanski and Chiapello seek to identify the salient features of the new capitalist order. In their model, capital always feeds off critiques addressed to it to steer its own evolution and side-step obstacles in its path. To this effect, contemporary capital has successfully incorporated the kind of attack on its bureaucratic rigidity that came to a head around 1968. As a result, the rigid hierarchies of an earlier capitalism have given way to what Boltanski and Chiapello describe as a 'connectionist' order, a capitalism dominated by flexibility and looser, networked modes of organisation. Projects play a key role in this new order because, given its fluidity, it requires the kind of temporary stabilisation of flows that projects provide in order to ensure both profit-taking and some way to measure individual strengths and capacities. In such a world, the most admired are those who have the best networks and can commit to projects, but can also move on to new ones when the time comes (Boltanski and Chiapello, 1999: 154–238; see also Marks, 2011). It is clear that Vincent belongs to this new 'connectionist' world. His old friends with their more local networks are clearly seduced by his apparently powerful connections and ability to develop profitable new projects. Even outside his fantasy, his ability to assemble money depends precisely on tapping into different networks and making his contacts work for him.

If the main political work done by *Ressources humaines* resides in the way it brings hidden class struggle to the surface, that done by *L'Emploi du temps* relates to its capacity to develop a critique that bites on this new world of mobile capital. Both Bauman, and Boltanski and Chiapello, note that the kind of reproach addressed to an older capitalist model struggles to engage with the new. Bauman stresses how older models of critique sought to defend human autonomy, freedom of choice, and the right to be different from the 'iron grip of routine' and the 'steely casing of a society afflicted with totalitarian, homogenizing and uniformizing appetites' (Bauman, 2000: 16). With the loosening of modernity's 'iron cage', the destructuring of the rigidities of Fordist production and consumption, and the emergence of a society where individuals are obliged to be autonomous workers or self-defining consumers, the old types of critique no longer have the same purchase. Boltanski and Chiapello take up a similar position. Precisely because capitalism reinvented itself along flexible lines by absorbing the critique of its rigidities and hierarchies, it has blunted old lines of attack. Put simply, critique needs to reinvent itself. This is a task *L'Emploi du temps* carries out in brilliant manner.

L'Emploi du temps and the reinvention of critique

L'Emploi du temps underscores how Cantet's film-making can be true to itself yet open to new contexts. Because it involves a framework rather than a specific content (see Chapter 1), it can incorporate what is around it. Thus, *L'Emploi du temps* shares key features with earlier Cantet films yet uses them astonishingly well to analyse the contemporary world of work and the subjectivities associated with it. Like *Ressources humaines*, it is about the encounter between an individual's utopian vision, the frictions of the real and the looks of others: here, however, that encounter is used not to investigate class struggle but to explore the limits to the freedom of mobile man. It uses the tensions between its hero and other groups to explore the ways in which the very networks and connections that empower the new individual also limit him or her. In typically Cantetian fashion, it probes space and spatial boundaries to bring hidden barriers and constraints to light. Yet, unlike *Ressources humaines*, where the main borders were between work and home or within the factory itself, here the boundaries are shown to be more fluid and dispersed but also much harder to escape, as befits the world of liquid capitalism.

The contradictions in Vincent's position are present, although we may not yet recognise them, from the start. His two essential tools, the car and mobile phone, seem to guarantee his ability to be mobile but also connected to others. Yet, as the film progresses, we become aware that, in its effortless ability to shrink distances, the mobile phone actually undoes the more heroic mobility of the car. This comes through in the opening scene when the half-awake Vincent speaks to Muriel, on the phone. If the car seems to wrap a protective bubble round him, the phone can reach inside it and force him to engage with others. The phone appears to be empowering: it allows him to develop the fiction that he is working hard when he is gloriously idle. Yet it also renders him accountable: to be free, he has to show that his time is gainfully used. To be allowed not to conform, he has to develop a conformist persona and split himself in a way that risks a loss of self. Although he invents new ways to liberate himself, he is in constant danger of being reeled back in and becoming a prisoner of the masks he puts on.

This comes through, for example, when he uses the money borrowed from his father to buy a Range Rover. Very different from his previous Renault Espace, which encapsulates his family-man persona, the new vehicle expresses his desire for freedom. Just after he has taken possession of it, the film shows him in extreme long shot as he puts it through its paces, in what looks like a disused quarry. The camera distance is already a comment on his actions: rather than the heroic freedom that he seems to seek, it suggests someone lost in the landscape, like the hero of *Les Sanguinaires*. However, the fantasy is further punctured when he returns to the road. The phone rings. It is Julien (Nicolas Kalsch), his son. Vincent tells him about the new vehicle. Julien asks what it cost and notes that his friend's father paid more for his: Vincent's must be second-hand. Bringing the look of others within the car, Julien's comments show the limits of Vincent's dreams of escape. Unlike his Espace, the Range Rover has a hands-free phone meaning that, combining different mobilities, he can drive and talk at the same time, apparently freer than ever from the ties of space. However, as Ewa Mazierska and Laura Rascaroli perceptively remark, what the hands-free set actually achieves is to make his car more like a mobile office so that what he was trying to flee can more easily follow him (Mazierska and Rascaroli, 2006: 121–2). We see this when he receives a phone call while driving from Fred (Nicolas Beauvais), one of the old classmates, whom he has persuaded to invest in his East European investment scam. On behalf of another investor, but also worried himself, the classmate wants Vincent to account for their money. Vincent has to placate him, the phone once again reeling him in. This capacity to reattach Vincent to the social is nowhere more dramatically in evidence than in the film's penultimate sequence. Vincent's deceptions have all been laid bare because Muriel has phoned Jeffrey, the old colleague, and discovered the concealed job loss. A haggard, angry Vincent has reappeared at home. We fear he may harm his family or kill himself, especially if we are aware of how the film draws inspiration from the celebrated Romand affair. Vincent escapes from the house. We pick him up on a lonely road at night as his father's voice comes over the phone telling him that no issue involving money is irreparable. He parks near a road, his headlights picking out the grass in front of him. As he walks away from the car and into the night – another moment when he seems at risk of losing contact with the world – Muriel's voice comes over the phone telling him how she needs him. The next shot picks him up in a job interview, rejoining normality or abandoning his quest for freedom, depending on how we interpret the end of the film. One last time, the phone has reeled him in.

It is not only through the telephone that Vincent is constantly exposed to the judgement of others. Glass, an omnipresent material in the film, works to similar effect. Tellingly, the walls of his house have large windows on the downstairs rooms. As he approaches it, it seems that, just as he can see in, he is subject to scrutiny. A partial frontier, the glass reminds us that each space has its own separate rules and expectations. Yet, allowing gazes in and out, it also underscores how spaces can be judged by outsiders and how judgements from within can be brought to bear on those looking in. These complex dynamics come into play on several crucial occasions. One occurs in the motel sequence during which Vincent has persuaded an old friend to invest in his scheme. As the latter drives away, Vincent makes as if to follow before driving to a quiet part of the car park to settle down for the night. An ellipsis moves us to a shot from within the car looking out at a torch pointing in. While the windscreen seems to hold the world at bay, it also allows it to look back, in the form of a security man who, having seen Vincent on his closed-circuit television (CCTV), has come to investigate. Initially polite, the man quickly becomes impatient, tells Vincent that one must pay to sleep at the hotel and unceremoniously sends him packing. The chain hotel's car park may be one of those non-places that are made for frictionless passage, but only for those who pass muster when subjected to scrutiny.

Glass, the security man and CCTV again come into play in the compelling sequence where, dressed in a smart suit and carrying a briefcase, Vincent attaches himself to a similarly attired group and bluffs his way into the UN development agency building in Geneva. The building is a palace of glass. Not only do its offices have large windows, they also have glass corridor walls, so that, as Vincent tours the building, those in the rooms can look back at him. In one lovely moment, he looks into a meeting about African development. A man looks out and invites him in, his appearance and interested attitude suggesting he belongs. Yet, soon after, as Vincent talks on his mobile phone to Muriel, the security guard comes and asks him politely what he is doing there. The building, he tells Vincent, is not a public one. The glass suggests perfect transparency, but is also a subtle obstacle and a meeting point between evaluating looks in and out. Less apparently welcoming, the CCTV is a reminder that ostensibly open spaces have their guardians and their rules. Vincent can cross the border between France and Switzerland with no problem, unless he is smuggling, of course, in which case night-time drives on mountain roads are required. But the CCTV cameras, and the inspection of credentials that glass permits, suggest a dissemination and multiplication of points of control and identity checks. Similar dynamics are found in the scene discussed earlier when Vincent confronts Jeffrey outside his old office and is observed through the window by all who work there. Glass is a plane of encounter within a conflicted visual field.

If glass operates (melodramatically) to draw our attention to unseen barriers and voiceless collisions, it also points to the omnipresence of modern methods of control. Following Foucault's famous lead, Bauman suggests that Jeremy Bentham's panopticon, with its unseen central observer, epitomised the type of spatially delimited control mechanism of solid modernity. The typical spaces in which such control was organised and in which the watching gaze was psychologically internalised were the school, asylum, prison or factory, all solid places of enclosure with strong walls (Bauman, 2000: 6–10). We see this earlier form of surveillance in *Ressources humaines*, where those in the workshop are subject to the patrolling foremen's scrutiny. Updating this vision, *L'Emploi du temps* suggests that, in the era of networked mobility, surveillance has become similarly agile and no longer depends on a solid but fixed infrastructure or specialist overseers. All those with whom Vincent interacts, including his family, are potential watchers. Jean-Michel, his later smuggling partner, for example, sits watching him when he is selling his investment scheme in the hotel lobby, and later grills him and tells him that he seemed more convincing when he was talking to his friends. At another moment, when Vincent sits in the middle of nowhere counting the money he has obtained from his friends, he is observed by a passing couple out for a walk. The scrutinising gaze seems to have become ubiquitous.

The home, the traditional place of privacy, is also somewhere where Vincent has to account for himself and seem convincing. In Hollywood films, the family is typically a haven of tenderness in a harsh world; even a film like Jason Reitman's *Up in the Air* (2009) which is very critical of a ruthless, downsizing capitalism, holds the family out as a source of comfort. Far less sentimental, *L'Emploi du temps* shows that the family serves to evaluate behaviours and enforce conformism. Sharply aware of this, Vincent counters the questioning looks of his family once his deceit has been revealed by saying that nothing has changed for them. Despite everything, he has continued to be the good provider that the world and the bourgeois family require the father to be. Tellingly too, it is his own father who procures him the closing job interview that signals the end of his escape attempt. If other Cantet films also show how the family, because it is never self-enclosed, always plays its part in bringing social pressures to bear, *L'Emploi du temps* focuses in a particularly acute way on how it may be implicated in the diffuse forms of contemporary governance. Underscoring this, Vincent himself works as an agent of control within the family, checking on his daughter's punctuality in the opening scene, chiding his younger son for selling his toys below 'market' rates at the school fete, reminding his older son that his mobile phone has been given to him so that his mother can keep in contact and not for chatting with friends.

Debt as governance

The apparently trivial incident with the son's phone points to the importance of debt in governing behaviours in the film. As the parents see it, they have given the son the device and he *owes* it to them to respond to their calls. Not simply a gift, the phone is used to justify surveillance and control behaviours. This may seem banal, the sort of thing that typically happens in families. In the context of the film, however, it points to how debt may combine with networked surveillance to tie down not simply the characters' current behaviours but also their future intentions.

In a recent and important book, Maurizio Lazzarato prolongs Michel Foucault's analysis of neo-liberal governance as developed in his famous Collège de France 'bio-politics' lectures (Lazzarato, 2011; Foucault, 2008). Lazzarato agrees with Foucault that the specificity of neo-liberalism with respect to earlier liberalisms is in the way it generalises the norms of market competition to all areas of human activity from the macro-economic level of State agencies to the micro-economic level of the individual. The latter is recast as an enterprise of the self, responsible for his or her good or bad investment decisions (Lazzarato, 2008: 120). Lazzarato feels, however, that Foucault over-emphasises the freedom of the neo-liberal individual and underplays the disciplines to which he or she is subjected, particularly through the mechanism of debt. As the State protection and secure employment of the era of the Fordist compromise are withdrawn and as collective solidarities are undone, risks are increasingly transferred to the individual. In the end, entrepreneurs of the self are generally limited to managing their employability and debts, the drop in their salary and income, and the shrinking of social services (Lazzarato, 2011: 74). Within this nexus of constraints, debt plays a central role because its moral and temporal reach allows it to govern apparently free behaviours. The individual has not simply to work to pay off debt: he or she has to work upon the self to produce a reliable subject that will convince others of its ability to repay whatever is owed. This implies what Lazzarato describes as a future-directed memory: because the individual remembers contracting a debt, he or she *will* behave in a disciplined way that ensures it will be repaid (Lazzarato, 2011: 33–41). As a result, any previous or future rebellions that might disrupt the predictability of behaviours are ruled out.

Debt is already emerging as a force in *Ressources humaines*. It comes through in the lovely little scene when Frank invites his parents to a meal celebrating the boss's suggestion that there will be a job for him in the company. Jean-Claude tries to pay and predictably pulls out banknotes. Frank rushes over, says it is his treat and proffers a credit card. His father is horrified: Frank already owes the bank money. Frank laughs off Jean-Claude's objections. He is not indebted, he says, not entirely convincingly: rather, the bank has invested in him because they are confident he will earn good money and pay them back. Contributing to the film's broader sense of social transition, this apparently minor moment looks towards the importance that debt will assume in *L'Emploi du temps*. Part of the emerging new world, Frank has access to credit because he promises to be a reliable repayer. While Jean-Claude accepts restraint in the present because of the promise of later reward, Frank has already mortgaged his future.

Vincent is a more developed indebted man and his case shows much more fully how debt acts as a limit to freedom. Although we have no idea of his debt status when the film starts, as soon as we learn he has lost his job, we wonder how he will make ends meet, particularly as has decided to carry on being a reliable provider for his family. He becomes explicitly indebted when he borrows money from his father for the deposit on the fictional apartment in Geneva – a debt to procure a loan! His debt burden worsens when he persuades his friends to invest in his invented Eastern European scheme. What both debts bring with them is an unwelcome exposure to prying eyes: his friends and father need assurances that his schemes make sense and he will reimburse their investment. In other words, he has to generate a convincing, predictable self in order to reassure them. This initially comes through in the scene with the father. The latter is reluctant to lend such a large sum, not least because Vincent already has a mortgage. Vincent can only get annoyed. The more resourceful Muriel steps in and reassures the father that they have done their calculations. Given Vincent's accommodation allowance, she argues, they will be able to repay the debt over two years, thus making a saving as compared to staying in a hotel. Faced with the father's evaluating scrutiny, Muriel has generated a prudent, predictable persona for the couple. Later, the father suggests, only half-jokingly, that he would like to visit Vincent in Geneva to inspect his investment. The same requirement to be open to evaluation is encountered when Vincent is forced to account to Fred when driving.

The power of debt is underscored in the final scene when Vincent seeks to re-enter the job market. As he is scrutinised by the man opposite him, he is asked why he has taken such a long break from work. Erasing his escape attempt, he replies that he has been looking around for a job that would satisfy him fully. His interviewer accepts the reply. His company has decided to invest heavily in a financial 'adventure' that Vincent may be asked to lead. It will expect him to *invest* himself fully in return. No longer merely selling his labour, Vincent is reconfigured as a self-investment responding to an investment. Not only has he to produce a suitably ambitious self that will repay the company, he also has to erase his earlier resistance to hide his unpredictability. The temporal reach of debt is able to extend the power of decentred, networked surveillance into the past and future. Tellingly, as Vincent feels the net closing in on him, the camera slowly but inexorably tracks forward, making him more and more available for inspection, pinning him tightly in the frame. The rather mournful cello music that we hear periodically throughout the film fades in slowly again. Covering the dialogue, it suggests, as elsewhere in the film, that Vincent is absenting himself from an alienating and oppressive situation.[4]

It is no coincidence that the presentation that Vincent overhears at the UN is about how reliable African countries are, in terms of governance, transparent regulation and the primacy of law, at providing an 'investment-friendly environment'. Predictable behaviours and openness to scrutiny are required of countries as well as individuals in a world where investment needs to be repaid. No mere exception, Vincent's case is used to investigate and dramatise some of the key ways in which behaviours are governed in a world ruled by 'free' enterprise. It is of course the character's utopian pursuit of freedom that forces the limits to freedom into view. The tension between the pursuit and the limits are implicitly present from the start, not least in the red light that halts Vincent's playful race with the train. It is only as the film proceeds that they are driven into full view as characters confront each other or give voice to their deeper feelings and fears.

The pathologies of the new individual

The same theorists who explore the workings of neo-liberal governance often draw attention to the pathologies of the neo-liberal subject, the former clearly playing a large part in determining the latter.

4 The original music on the film's soundtrack was written by English composer Jocelyn Pook. Among Pook's credits are Stanley Kubrick's *Eyes Wide Shut* (1999) and other film scores.

Boltanski and Chiapello draw attention to how, no longer able to fall back on their position in a stable hierarchy, their mobile, connected person is torn between the need to adapt to new projects and respond to others' expectations on the one hand, and the need to create a durable, authentic projection of self on the other (Boltanski and Chiapello, 1999: 552–63). Pierre Dardot and Christian Laval likewise note the instability of the kind of persona that the new workplaces require. In the world of networks and projects, the subject can no longer count on the stable framework, linear temporality or durable social relationships that would allow him or her to develop a coherent sense of self over time. Dardot and Laval also suggest that what distinguishes neo-liberal subjectivity from earlier variants is the imperative to go beyond oneself: not to sacrifice oneself for some greater good, nor to cultivate oneself by resisting external pressures, but to realise oneself by setting new goals, performing more efficiently, consuming better and even being a better sporting competitor. The inevitable downside of this contemporary cult of performance and the individualisation of responsibilities that goes with it is depression, fear of failure and potential narcissistic collapse (Dardot and Laval, 2010: 442–52). Less concerned with pathologies, Lazzarato nonetheless notes how, with its insistence on the evaluation of behaviours, the neo-liberal mobilisation of the governmental power of debt inevitably drives people to hypocrisy (Lazzarato, 2011: 103). They must appear to be reliable and predictable even when they are not.

An increasingly haunted character, Vincent exemplifies many of these pathologies. Firstly, he is constantly playing a part to satisfy different people and groups but also wants to project a reliable, stable persona. His way to deal with these competing pressures is to be an accomplished actor, with it being no accident that Cantet cast noted stage performer Olivier Recoing in the role. It is no accident either that, when Vincent wants to persuade people that he works at the UN, he studies leaflets from the organisation, scouts out the building and watches those within it. He is like an actor, documenting himself for a role. It is no accident, finally, that he changes costume and props as he performs for different groups: sometimes the sharp-suited high flyer, sometimes the father in a casual anorak, driving first a Renault Espace and then a Range Rover, able to slot into a lorry drivers' cafe or a high-pressure job interview, he seems more a chameleon than a stable individual. Yet, like other actors, he needs people to believe in him and finds constant acting a strain. He embodies the contradictions and performance anxiety of the new subject.

Secondly, Vincent bears witness to the neo-liberal subject's instability, not only in the shifting roles he plays but also in the spatial trajectory that he covers during the narrative's unfolding. In many ways, *L'Emploi du temps* looks and feels like a road movie: it is about travel, the desire to escape and the quest for authenticity, as in classic exemplars of the genre. It has all the iconography of the road from the car to the lorry, motel and service station (Laderman, 2002: 1–42; O'Shaughnessy, 2013). Yet, Vincent's travels never add up to anything as coherent as a journey with a goal and a linear trajectory. Rather, he has a series of wanderings and new departures, each of which ends with a return home. The house and family are his only stable point of reference. They are also what ultimately puts an end to his bid for freedom.

Thirdly, Vincent seems driven to go beyond himself in both his real and invented lives but is simultaneously haunted by the fear of failure. He implodes, for example, when Jean-Michel tells him that his Eastern European investment scheme sounds unconvincing. He confesses his tiredness to Muriel, his fear of disappointing people and his sense of not really knowing their expectations. This anxiety is the downside of his aspiration to the heights, as expressed notably by his trips to the *gîte* in the snow-covered alpine landscape. However, as Dardot and Laval note, the quest to transcend oneself is a systemic norm rather than a real act of rebellion. It is symptomatic that, the first time Vincent goes to the *gîte*, he studies the UN documentation that will help him pass as a high-flyer. Rather than simply breaking away, he is bearing conformist baggage with himself, just like the characters in *Les Sanguinaires*.

Vincent, finally, is a fake in a world where fakery is a general tendency or, rather, where the boundaries between the authentic and the fake have become inextricably blurred. We know his life is a constant performance driven by a need to convince but we also know that this is a more general tendency of the world of work. His ability to pass as employed draws our attention to the kind of self-presentation that employment more routinely requires. Within this context, it seems logical that he ends up smuggling fake goods, the 'authenticity' of each brand being just as manufactured as that of the individual. A paroxysm of fakery is reached when Jean-Michel mischievously invites himself to Vincent's house for dinner. He passes himself off as someone who works with Vincent but in a different branch – not overseas development, but the tracking down of counterfeit-brand goods. Julien, Vincent's elder son, comments that counterfeit goods are just as good as the authentic ones. If he is right, then the real fakery lies in the claim to uniqueness of the brands. Jean-Michel responds that the counterfeits are in fact shoddy but immediately muddies the waters again by explaining how the fakes are often made in Italian factories where legitimate goods are also produced. Muriel, who has taken it all in, has a moment of *vertige*, or dizziness, reminiscent of the moment in *Les Sanguinaires* when the wife is left on the cliff edge as her husband disappears into the night, but with less obviously dramatic consequences. It is as if the solidity of the world in which she lives has suddenly been lost and nothing and nobody can be taken at face value.

A similar argument might be made about Vincent's recruitment of his friends into a fake investment scheme. If this merely seems a criminal act, we might want to ponder how it points to the importance of confidence and conviction in the financial world. The economy once seemed a solid, reliable thing of gold-backed currencies, heavy factories and durable goods. With the shift of power to finance and markets, it has itself become something 'liquid' (to borrow Bauman's term), as much a question of trust and confidence as Vincent's scheme. The latter works as long as people believe in it and put money in. Once they start to doubt, it becomes unsustainable. While it would be imprudent to suggest that the film somehow anticipates the bursting of the global financial bubble in 2008, it does tap effectively into the dynamics that allowed the bubble to build.

Vincent's fakery adds a new twist to Cantet's repeated recourse to moments of shame to foreground the tension between the individual and the social group. Rather than moving inexorably to scenes of shame, as *Ressources humaines* does, *L'Emploi du temps* is about shame refused or deferred. In a world where an individual's worth is tightly tied to their work, Vincent's unemployment is something he refuses to confront. It is not that he is unwilling to see himself as others see him, as Frank in *Ressources humaines* to some extent is. It is rather that he is too dependent on the approving looks of others to admit he has lost his prestigious job. In a world where individuals are subject to constant evaluation, this is an understandable attitude. This does not mean that the film entirely avoids those moments of exquisite embarrassment that so characterised the earlier works. Rather, the embarrassment often remains latent, as when Vincent is caught asleep in the motel car park but nonetheless keeps up a front. Reminding us how Cantet's films make the spectator's position uneasy, we feel the embarrassment that Vincent refuses to own. We empathise with his job loss and refusal of the un-freedom of work but also see that his position is untenable and eccentric. We look out of the car at the night-watchman with him, but we also look at him through the other's eyes. We too are split and remain unsure where to put ourselves.

Conclusion

Cantet's first two full-length films, *Ressources humaines* and *L'Emploi du temps*, underscore the efficacity of his approach to film-making, his ability to produce works that are simultaneously faithful to a certain way of structuring a narrative and resolutely open to the exploration of a milieu or issue with which he was not familiar in advance. Both films also remind us that, although Cantet may engage resolutely with contemporary issues, he does not make what one might call 'issue' films. As we saw, *Ressources humaines* is far from simply a film about the application of the thirty-five-hour legislation. Nor is *L'Emploi du temps* a simple reworking of the Romand affair. Neither is narrowly about work: instead both use it to probe broader social tensions and transitions. Together they constitute a diptych that tracks the unpicking of the Fordist compromise, the entry into a more mobile and unpredictable world and the shift in subjectivities that comes with these changes. *L'Emploi du temps* shows particular prescience in its capacity to renew critique and to chart the un-freedoms and pathologies of the neo-liberal world.

Both films also underscore the effectiveness of Cantet's way of working at the interface of the melodrama and, if not the documentary, then the highly documented. Cantet's film-making is a sometimes disconcerting blend of the emotional and the coldly detached. The films use melodramatic situations to bring us in, but then find ways to make us stand back so that our response is never simply emotional. We certainly feel for Vincent and recognise the family dynamics that he encounters, yet we also stand back from his situation and judge it from the outside. In any case, Cantet's films always problematise any simple division of inside and outside. Not only are families open to external dynamics, individuals internalise social contradictions. The tools of melodrama, with their attention to unspoken tensions, then come into their own and force what is hidden or silenced to the surface.

The films are undoubtedly social: they explore specific milieux. They are also critical in the way they push us and their characters into self-questioning. Yet, are they political in a more direct sense? They are not if we associate political cinema with works that seek to move their characters or audience into alignment with some greater cause or collective mobilisation. *Ressources humaines* reaffirms the existence of class struggle and the need for resistance but also shows how hard it is for its hero simply to slot back into collective action when he is no longer an organic part of the collectivity concerned. If there is a model of political action in the film, it would seem to be one based on provisional alliances with causes based on a sense of immediate outrage. This, by Cantet's own confession, is the type of political involvement towards which he leans.[5] Yet, at the same time, there is a sense that his film, rather than putting forward one or another model of political involvement, is taking note of a shift in the nature of commitment. Whereas the individual might once have been able to slot straightforwardly into the group, it is now essential to question one's position by asking that essential Cantetian question, 'elle est où, ta place?'. Of course, to put that question to us or the characters, the films have their own political work to do. In our case, they make us question our relationship to what we are seeing, challenging our certainties and creating uncomfortable spectatorial positions for us to occupy. Like us, the characters have their certainties challenged. More importantly, however, the films refuse to tie them definitively to their social roles. They are defined as much by their capacity to think, react and rebel as by their social place.

References

Archer, N. (2008), 'The road as the (non-)place of masculinity: *L'Emploi du temps*', *Studies in French Cinema*, 8:2, 137–48.

5 See *Le Monde* (*Aden*), 12 January 2000.

Augé, M. (1995), *Non-Places: Introduction to an Anthropology of Supermodernity*, trans. J. Howe, London and New York, Verso.

Bauman, Z. (2000), *Liquid Modernity*, Cambridge, Polity.

BIFI (2001), '*Ressources humaines*, un film de Laurent Cantet' (dossier pédagogique), Paris, Bibliothèque du Film.

Boltanski, L. and Chiapello, E. (1999), *Le Nouvel Esprit du capitalisme*, Paris, Gallimard.

Bonnaud, F. (2000), 'Laurent Cantet: Usine et dépendance', *Les inRocks*, 19 January, www.lesinrocks.com/2000/01/19/cinema/actualite-cinema/laurent-cantet-usine-dependance-11228947/ (accessed 9 April 2014).

Cadé, M. (2000), 'A la recherche du bonheur: Les ouvriers dans le cinéma français des années 1990', *Les Cahiers de la cinémathèque*, 71, 59–72.

Comolli, J.-L. (2004), *Voir et pouvoir. L'innocence perdue: Cinéma, télévision, fiction, documentaire*, Lagrasse, Editions Verdier.

Dardot, P. and Laval, C. (2010), *La Nouvelle Raison du monde: Essai sur la société néo-libérale*, Paris, La Découverte.

Foucault, M. (2008), *The Birth of Biopolitics: Lectures at the Collège de France, 1978–1979*, trans. G. Burchell, London, Palgrave Macmillan.

Laderman, D. (2002), *Driving Visions: Exploring the Road Movie*, Austin, University of Texas Press.

Larcher, J. (2000), 'Le Partage des mondes: Rencontre avec Laurent Cantet', *Cahiers du cinéma*, 542, 48–50.

Lazzarato, M. (2011), *La Fabrique de l'homme endetté: Essai sur la condition néo-libérale*, Paris, Editions Amsterdam.

Mangeot, P. and Tijou, B. (2000), 'Un transfuge: Entretien avec Laurent Cantet', *Vacarme*, 11 (Spring), www.vacarme.org/article742.html (accessed 9 April 2014).

Marks, J. (2011), '"Ça tient qu'à toi": Cartographies of post-Fordist labour in Laurent Cantet's *L'Emploi du temps*', *Modern and Contemporary France*, 19:4, 477–93.

Mazierska, E. and Rascaroli, L. (2006), *Crossing New Europe: Postmodern Travel and the European Road Movie*, London and New York, Wallflower.

O'Shaughnessy, M. (2007), *The New Face of Political Cinema*, Oxford, Berghahn.

O'Shaughnessy, M. (2013), 'Nowhere to run, somewhere to hide: Laurent Cantet's *L'Emploi du temps*', in M. Gott and T. Schilt, eds, *Open Roads, Closed Borders: The Contemporary French-Language Road Movie*, Bristol, Intellect, 155–70.

Rancière, J. (1995), *La Mésentente: Politique et philosophie*, Paris, Galilée.

Sennett, R. (2006), *The Culture of the New Capitalism*, New Haven and London, Yale University Press.

Thompson, P. (2003), 'Disconnected capitalism: Or why employers can't keep their side of the bargain', *Work, Employment and Society*, 17:2, 359–78.

1 The father, the son and the rest: socialising the primal scene (*Ressources humaines*, 2000)

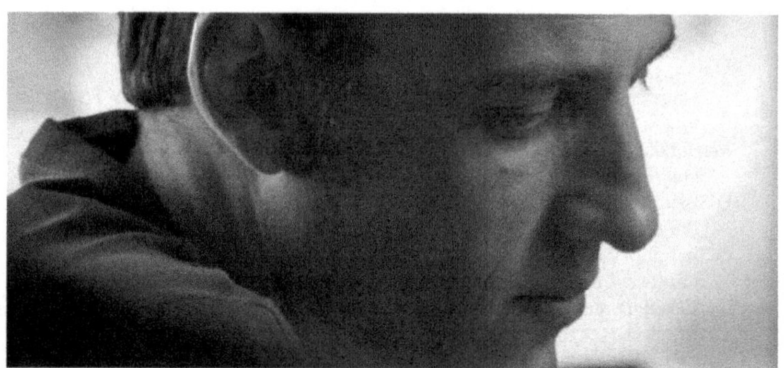

2 The consciousness before it meets the world (*Entre les murs*, 2008)

3 The hero (far right) is part, yet not part, of the group (*Jeux de plage*, 1995)

4 Breaking free or losing oneself (*Les Sanguinaires*, 1997)

5 The text of muteness or the silent voice of the voiceless (*Ressources humaines*, 2000)

6 Mutual surveillance: the glass as plane of encounter and separation (*L'Emploi du temps*, 2001)

7 The 'innocence' of the tourist gaze: taking possession of the beach (*Vers le sud*, 2006)

8 Inequality in the spaces of leisure: the mute eloquence of the image (*Vers le sud*, 2006)

9 Cinemascope: the distance between people (*Entre les murs*, 2008)

10 The unstructured, egalitarian space of the school-yard (*Entre les murs*, 2008)

11 The public shaming of Buttinger: turning the car into a site of struggle (*Foxfire*, 2012)

12 From vamp to ingénue: Violet's use of the masquerade (*Foxfire*, 2012)

13 The non-mirroring of gendered identities (*Foxfire*, 2012)

4

Going global, heading south

The global context is present in Cantet's films as early as *Les Sanguinaires*, with its opening montage of international millennial celebrations. It is an unseen part of the background in *Ressources humaines*, the film's provincial factory being owned by a conglomerate that is busy investing in the third world. It is more prominent in *L'Emploi du temps*, with its Swiss set scenes, invented UN job, and accounts of investments in Africa or the old Eastern Bloc. But, all those films are still predominantly French in terms of their locations, language and performers. As noted earlier, *Vers le sud* is different and represents several new departures. Although largely shot in San Domingo, it is set in Haiti, a country with deep historical connections to France that the film, on the surface at least, chooses not to activate. It has an international cast, its Haitian non-professionals performing opposite British actress Charlotte Rampling, American Karen Young, and French Canadian Louise Portal. It is trilingual, with English, its main language, mingling with French and Haitian Creole. It is an adaptation of a novel: Haitian writer Dany Laferrière's incendiary *La Chair du maître* (*The Master's Flesh*). Unlike all the earlier films, it is set in the past (the 1970s Haiti of the 'Baby Doc' Duvalier dictatorship). Finally, it is largely centred on female protagonists. These shifts, apart from the last ones, might simply seem to suggest a 'natural' transition in Cantet's work to a more international mode of filmmaking as he became better known. Yet this explanation through internationalisation is not enough on its own and leaves important questions untouched. Was Cantet really abandoning present concerns or does his story have contemporary relevance? What was at stake when, a white Frenchman, he filmed an adaptation of a black

Haitian's writing? What was at stake too, when, a male film-maker, he turned his attention to a topic as thorny as women's sex tourism? Could he avoid subsuming or subordinating other voices and experiences as he brought them within his work? What sort of place, finally, would his film, with its deeply uneasy topic, open up for the spectator? We will come to all these questions in turn. Before we do, it is best to give a brief sense of the film.

Vers le sud recounts the interaction of a group of French and English-speaking North American women with a cluster of Haitian males. The former include Brenda (Young), Ellen (Rampling) and Sue (Portal), all in their forties or fifties. Brenda and Ellen are slim and elegant. Sue is plump. The three have different social backgrounds: Brenda, from Savannah, Georgia, seems to have no need to work; Ellen lectures in French literature at the highly selective Wellesley College; Sue works in a warehouse in Montreal. Despite these differences, all three come together as privileged outsiders in comparison to the young Haitians. Informal workers in the romance tourism industry, the latter service the women's emotional and sexual needs in exchange for money, meals and presents. Essentially, they are escorts. Legba (Ménothy César), the hero, must be about eighteen. Neptune (Wilfried Paul), Sue's Haitian lover, looks older. He works as a fisherman when not with her. Eddy (Jackenson Pierre Olmo Diaz), a young hanger-on, may be about twelve or thirteen. Other Haitian characters are less individualised. An older Haitian male, Albert (Lys Ambroise), the dignified manager of the beachside resort where the women stay, does however play a major role.

Much of the film takes place at the resort and revolves around the rivalry between Ellen and Brenda over Legba's time and attention, as well as the broader interactions among the women, Albert and the young escorts. However, the film also ventures into Port-au-Prince, Haiti's capital. It does so at the start, when Brenda arrives at the airport, and at the end, when Ellen departs. It also follows Brenda and Legba there, either when they both visit the market or when the latter is there on his own. If the resort seems a safe haven, the city is a place of danger. Firstly, the Tonton Macoute, the dictatorship's much feared paramilitary force, lurk there. Their presence brings menace to the initially peaceful scene within which Legba plays football and chats with young acquaintances. Secondly, there are other risks. A young woman (Anotte Saint Ford) to whom Legba has been close but who has been forced to become the mistress of a colonel, has her chauffeur-driven limousine pick up the young man, an act that makes him a target for the soldier's ire. Later, when returning from the market with Brenda, Legba finds himself pursued by the gun-waving chauffeur. As the film draws to an end, we see what may be the same limousine draw up at the beach and dump the naked bodies of Legba and the young woman at the water's edge. We are not sure if they have been killed separately or caught together and shot. What we do know is that forsaking the safety of the resort has proved fatal to Legba. His death leaves both Ellen and Brenda distraught: the former, who has been coming to Haiti for many years, no longer knows what she is doing there and leaves for the North American home that offers her nothing; the latter, who is on her second trip, leaves Haiti too, not to return home but to visit other islands and, presumably, find other young lovers.

From novel to film

Laferrière was born in Port-au-Prince in 1953 and began his career as a journalist in the Haiti of the Duvalier dictatorship. Following the murder of a fellow journalist, he went into exile and has since moved between Miami, New York and Montreal. He is what one might call an American writer rather than simply an exilic one, as long as one takes American to refer to the Americas and not to the United States. He came to literary fame with the publication of his first novel, *Comment faire l'amour avec un nègre sans se fatiguer* (*How to Make Love to a Negro without Getting Tired*; 1985), a work whose self-consciously inflammatory title points to the decidedly edgy subject matter of the writings and his willingness to engage with inter-racial dynamics while mobilising and subverting stereotypes. *La Chair du maître* works on similar ground. An episodic, multi-character novel, it narrates a series of often sexual encounters between blacks and whites and Haitians and foreigners. These are never simply erotic, although they are almost always that: rather, the flow of desire is used to highlight and subvert uneven power dynamics. In a country where a gulf separates rich and poor, sex can break down barriers and brings those who would not normally interact into intimate collision. If this bridging capacity might seem potentially utopian, one should underscore how, in Laferrière's work, sex and domination are too tightly entwined for the former ever to exist beyond the grasp of the latter. However, the novel does suggest that, in a country where the poor have so little, sex may be empowering, desire a tool for revenge, and the poor person's body a credit card (Laferrière, 2000: 16).

Cantet came to Laferrière by chance. His parents, who are members of a non-governmental organisation, often went to Haiti for humanitarian work. Having gone to visit them, he found himself somewhere that other westerners were almost all engaged in aid work. He felt profoundly out of place, almost as if he were one of his own characters who simply did not fit in. At the airport on his way home, wanting to get closer to Haitian reality, he looked for a novel by a Haitian novelist, found *La Chair du maître* and read it on the plane. Its capacity to straddle the deeply intimate and the overarchingly social spoke immediately to his own concerns (Morice, 2005). He would read other Laferrière works but his film would rely essentially on *La Chair du maître* and especially on some of the stories contained in its loose narrative. This turn to adaptation raises a series of questions, some general, others more specific.

The last ten years have seen a tremendous renewal of the field of adaptation studies with important works by Robert Stam and Alessandra Raengo (Stam and Raengo, 2004, 2005; Stam, 2005), Linda Hutcheon (2006) and others. Such works have moved on from regressive analyses of adaptation in terms of (an impossible) fidelity to literary texts and the supposed incapacity of film, in its concreteness, to translate the rich connotations of the written word. Analysts now rightly start from the recognition of the material differences of the two media. Stam's introduction to his co-edited 2004 volume is very useful in this respect. He suggests that adaptation can be better understood as a shifting and complex range of transformations, rather than a single process. These include: selection (what is chosen from the original text), amplification (what is given more weight than it originally had), concretisation (the way cinema necessarily puts specific faces and decors to what literature leaves more open to the imagination), actualisation (the bringing up to date of a text), critique (the establishment of distance from values contained in a text), popularisation (the way film may take a text to a wider audience), reaccentuation (an alteration of the emphasis of a text) and transculturalisation (the relocation of a text in a different cultural context) (Stam 2004: 14–46). While we would not want to apply these different transformations mechanically to Cantet's use of Laferrière, some are of clear relevance to our analysis. To begin with, Cantet's use of Laferrière's book is very selective but some of what he uses is considerably amplified. There is also a distinct reaccentuation at work, for the tone and emphasis of the film are clearly different from those of the novel. The latter is overtly transgressive and vividly erotic while the former is more implicitly questioning and restrained. Locating itself in the late 1970s like the novel, the film does not explicitly actualise its content. However, it is less rooted in a specific Haitian context and moment than its literary inspiration, and more interested in probing neo-colonial relationships at a general level and in a way with clear contemporary relevance. It does not critique the novel but borrows a critical dimension from it and turns it sharply on its wealthy incomers. To this effect, the novel's rounded exploration of social dynamics between Haitians, returning exiles and outsiders is pared down to a focus on the interaction of poor Haitians and tourists, a potentially problematic shift.

The title sequence of Cantet's film acknowledges a debt to three stories from Laferrière's novel without specifying which. Two of the book's chapters, 'Vers le sud' (2000: 226–44) and 'La maîtresse du colonel' (2000: 182–225) clearly provide the backbone of the film, with the former also giving it its title. However, both are substantially transformed, not least because they are woven together as two sides of the film's story while they remain separate episodes in the book. Elements of the film are also taken from elsewhere in the novel but cannot be pinned down to a single story. The narrator's prefatory chapter is the source of two important moments. There is an anecdote in it about a mother who raises her daughter according to a strict moral framework until, laden with debt, she must make the girl walk the streets. This is obviously the source of the film's opening scene. Another anecdote entitled 'La peur' ('Fear') describes the omnipresence of danger in Port-au-Prince when the narrator was growing up (2000: 15–16). He evokes two particular moments when he instinctively feels there is danger behind him: in one, he turns to see a car being driven at him; in the other, he spins round to see a man with a revolver following him. Pulled into one episode, merged with the story of the colonel's mistress, these two moments anticipate what will happen to Legba when he visits the market with Brenda. Another chapter of the novel, 'L'après-midi d'un faune', describes, among other things, a conversation between a character called Fanfan and another young man, in which the former explains to the latter why he, Fanfan, is successful with women, while his friend is not (2000: 31–33). This conversation provides the core of interchange between Legba and his friends just after the film's football game. Two other chapters, 'Les garçons magiques' and 'Le bar de la plage', contribute to the general context of the film's story without feeding directly into any episode. The first describes how a hotel owner cultivates the presence of young Haitian men to attract women from the north. The second evokes a barman called Albert who seems not to realise that he is working in something akin to a brothel. This Albert seems very much like the one in the film.

Although first-person narration can be found at various stages in Laferrière's book, the chapter entitled 'Vers le sud' nonetheless stands out formally. Rather than foregrounding a single narrator, it consists of the polyphonic interweaving of four voices belonging to characters named Sue, Brenda, Ellen and Albert, who recount their interactions and particularly the events leading to the death of a young Haitian called Legba. The voices are used differently in the film. Elements of what they recount are dispersed and amplified to give the film its interpersonal core and most of its resort-based action: for example, Ellen's confession in the book that she attacks Sue for her weight gives rise to a sequence on the beach where we see such a targeting occurring; similarly, the discovery of Legba's body at the water's edge becomes a sequence in its own right. At the same time, important parts of each character's confession from the novel are preserved as voice-over monologues but separated from each other and detached from the murder. Typically they follow a sequence within which the character has come under particular strain or left something important unsaid. This dynamic interplay of the unspoken and the confessional is typical of the melodramatic economy of a Cantet film but is very different from the sustained, explicit drive of Laferrière's novel.

Cantet's film often uses Laferrière's monologues verbatim, yet elements of them are omitted and, more importantly, what is kept is recontextualised. The most significant omissions relate to Brenda and Albert's stories. The novel underscores that Brenda is a Methodist and her husband a Baptist who has touched her only eight times in their married life. This religious dimension disappears in the film where Brenda's sexual frustration is less tied to a specific context. The 'seduction' of Legba is handled differently too. In the novel, Brenda's husband encourages her to have sex with the boy and watches events unfold. His absence from the film makes the episode less obviously perverse and blurs its unequal power dynamics. The novel's intercourse is painted very graphically: Brenda describes the length and fragility of Legba's penis, his hot sperm spurting into her and the force of her own orgasm. A lot of these explicit details disappear from the film. What remains is still graphic enough but is tempered by how the scene is handled. As Stam notes, film is a multi-track medium that mobilises image, sound, language and music (Stam, 2004: 18–24). Our response to Brenda's story is inflected by her increasingly distressed features, unkempt hair and tears. It is also shaped by a sad Haitian folk song (frequently heard in the film) that comes in as she falls silent. While Laferrière's borrowed words still carry a powerful account of the intercourse, the film's overlaying of music, image and voice soften the emotional tone and interracial dynamics of the episode.

There are other changes in the uses of the four characters' accounts. One of the most obvious concerns Albert. In the novel, he confesses that he has come across the sleeping Legba on the beach, started to caress him and made love to him. There is nothing of this homoerotic nature in the film. Cantet is clearly more interested in the untenability of Albert's position than in the discovery of a repressed sexuality. He is also more tightly focused on the unequal relationship between the young Haitian men and the northern women than on the polymorphous play of desire. The novel leaves the reasons for Legba's death open: there are suggestions that it relates to his drug dealing but Sue suspects Brenda or Ellen, while Ellen suspects a jealous Albert. There is little of this uncertainty in the film: although we do not know the details, we know that Legba has been killed because of his involvement with the colonel's mistress. Were the women potential murderers, we would hold their experience at greater distance. However, because they look on Legba's body with only an indirect sense of guilt, they are much closer to our own unease when we witness the suffering of the globally disadvantaged. This probing of a more everyday responsibility is typical of Cantet.

The story of the colonel's mistress is also handled very differently in novel and film. As we would expect, it has a provocative, erotic charge in Laferrière's chapter. The mistress of the chapter's title is tremendously sexy and entirely off limits. This perverse chemistry is largely absent from Cantet's film. In both film and book, the young woman has had no choice but to accept the colonel's attention. As a poor woman, it is not in her power to refuse. However, the novel's character is more than she seems. She effectively uses the hero as a decoy while she prepares the murder of the colonel in revenge for his killing of her brother. The character in Cantet's film has none of this capacity to resist. More than anything, she is a female double of Legba. Both are essentially prisoners of their situation. She is also a partial double of the young girl we see in the opening scene in the airport, the one whose mother tried to give her away, knowing that she would draw the attention of predatory men. It might seem strange that Cantet, a director whose characters never simply accept their situation, would neglect a story of resistance in his source. Its removal does, however, make sense if we remember that the film chooses to concentrate its action on the interplay between tourists and Haitians.

The stories of the northern women and the colonel's mistress are two unconnected chapters in Laferrière's multi-chapter, multi-character work. They are brought together to create the heart of Cantet's film. With Legba becoming a central character of both, they are made to constitute the two complementary parts of his story. The part of his life that the women see is associated with the beach. It is where he is safe but where he has to perform a role for them. The part of his life that they do not see but where the other story develops occurs in the town. Legba is more able to be himself there but is in increasing danger. The women's vision is doubly faulty. There are important things that they cannot see but those that they do see and seem to take at face value are the product of a performance in their honour. Ultimately, the film is more interested in exploring the limitations of their vision than seeking to develop an impossible insider's view of Haitian reality.

Laferrière's book is written in French even when it is recording dialogue between Haitians. While it incorporates a multitude of voices, not least by having multiple narrators, it is essentially a monoglot text. Cantet's film, on the other hand, is trilingual. The Haitians sometimes use Creole among themselves but use French to talk to the white women. The women switch between French and English although Sue speaks some Creole. This trilingualism brings a dimension to the film that the novel lacks. It highlights differences of power and status, access to English, for example, being limited to the more privileged characters. It also draws attention to non-communication and the kind of social barriers to which Cantet's films are always drawn. Yet, it would be a mistake to explain these linguistic differences simply as choices made by the author or the director. Laferrière's work is written in French, the traditional literary language of Haiti, because it is initially targeted at a francophone audience. It is also widely translated into English because of Laferrière's status as an international writer. Cantet's film circulates differently. Being essentially an arthouse film, it is made for an international circuit within which the subtitled film is routine fare. It can be trilingual because those who watch it will generally accept subtitles without complaint, unlike more popular cinema audiences. With its ability to combine sound and image, voice and subtitle, cinema is simply more able to convey a polyglot reality. However, with its many contrasting voices, Laferrière's novel may in fact be much more multi-vocal than the film even if its voices are conveyed in French. Any discussion of the difference between film and novel needs to be aware of this kind of nuance. Similarly, we should hesitate before suggesting that film, as a medium drawn to the visual and concrete, is somehow better able than the novel to grasp the material realities of places or the interplay of bodies as Françoise Lionnet, for example, suggests (2008: 233–4). Like his earlier works, Cantet's film does indeed have constant recourse to the silent eloquence of its image and its capacity to bring the unspoken into view. Yet, Laferrière's text also creates astonishingly vivid images of people and their embodied interactions. While we should necessarily be aware of the specificities of individual media, we would do well not to essentialise differences between them. As if to demonstrate this, Cantet relies on Laferrière's words to convey Brenda's first sexual encounter with Legba, perhaps the most striking *image* of the film.

Laferrière's text strays only once or twice from the era of Baby Doc. It does so in its closing story, 'La chair du maître', the one that gives the novel its title and anchors all that has come before. In it, an old woman explains that a picture on her wall of a large black man and a young white women is in fact of her ancestors, he an ex-slave, she the slave-master's daughter who seduced him. The couple's story has occurred at the time of Haiti's revolution, an event that both sought to extend the French Revolution's emancipatory drive and that led to Haitian independence in 1804 as the first black-led, post-colonial nation in the world. Before the revolution, Haiti, then named Sainte-Domingue, was France's richest colony. After the revolution, supported by an American trade embargo, France imposed such a level of reparations on its ex-colony that Haiti was in debt to the 'mother' country until 1947. It was far too important an example to be allowed to prosper (Hallward, 2004). Laferrière's engagement with this history is typically subversive. Cantet cannot bring it into his adaptation. He does however take up another historical reference from the book, this time when, in his voice-over monologue, Albert evokes the American occupation of Haiti from 1915 to 1934. Beyond this brief reference, the film works less by grounding itself in history than by revealing just enough history to point to its silencing. A history of oppression and resistance is something to which the characters either cannot or will not connect.

There are well-known adaptations and rewritings of classic texts that seek to bring out the colonial or neo-colonial oppression ignored or marginalised by the original work. We might cite, for example, the different novelistic and filmic reworkings of novels like *Jane Eyre* or *Robinson Crusoe*. There is also a film like *Mansfield Park* (dir. Patricia Rozema, 1999), which develops the British upper classes' connection to colonialism in a way that Jane Austen's classic novel failed to do. These reworkings remind us that adaptation can be a form of critique and that, in some cases, the success of an adaptation may be measured by its capacity to generate distance from its source rather than to stick close to it (Stam, 2004: 28–30). Yet, when the adaptation is of a novel already written from an anti-colonial or anti-racist perspective, the question shifts from whether the film can develop a critique to whether it can preserve an existing one. Thus, for example, Anthony Minghella's 1996 adaptation of Michael Ondaatje's 1992 *The English Patient* has been reproached for diluting the novel's anti-colonialism and reducing the importance of its Indian character (Deer, 2005). Similarly, there were serious questions asked about Steven Spielberg's film of Alice Walker's 1982 classic, *The Color Purple*. While it was acceptable for a black woman to write a book very critical of black men, could the same thing be said when the story was filmed by a white, male, Hollywood mainstreamer like Spielberg (Stam, 2005: 41)?

One could argue that Cantet was also badly placed to adapt a black writer's incendiary novel. After all, his film softens the novel's tone, pares down its portrayal of Haitian society and privileges the viewpoints of the white women over those of the black men. Such an argument would be unfair. The film eliminates most of the novel's loosely linked collection of episodes in order to provide itself with the kind of story arc that most films feel they need: in other words, some of the explanation for the drastic pruning of characters relates to the change of medium rather than the adaptation by a white film-maker of a black novelist's work. While it might seem harder to explain, the decision to organise the film around the perspective of the white characters can best be seen as a redirection, not a dissolution, of critique. We know that the project began with the director's unease at his position as a visitor to a damaged, impoverished country. The film borrows Laferrière's perspective to explore and extend that unease, using the Haitian's vision of prosperous outsiders to question both their position and, by implication, that of the film-maker. While understandable, this way of proceeding raises its own issues. Firstly, because the North American women are made to carry the burden of the film's critique of the white outsider's view, the film's engagement with the gendered dimension of their desire and ageing may be outweighed by other factors. Secondly, because the tourists' position is so intrinsically limited, the film may deny itself access to the broader Haitian history that would explain contemporary realities. These are questions to which we will need to return.

The film's opening and the tourist gaze

The first shot of *Vers le sud* has some of the hallmarks of a classic Cantet opening. It begins by showing the hand of a man as it writes a name on a little blackboard of the sort that people typically hold up when greeting someone at an airport. As the hand writes, a woman's hand, also black, but more slender, closes over it. The camera pulls back to show first the torsos, then the faces of the characters. Both are smartly dressed and look of similar age, somewhere in their fifties. The woman asks the man if she can talk to him. He replies that he has little time. This destabilising movement from self-absorbed activity to the need to engage and negotiate with another person is one we are familiar with. Widening the circle further, the woman's voice then brings in a broader context. Her husband was a public health inspector. Their life was good. Then, one day, he was taken away never to be seen again. She has been left without resources to bring up their beautiful teenage daughter and knows that she cannot protect the girl from men drawn to her. She wants the man, whom we later discover to be Albert, to take her child from her. He refuses. She leaves him with an enigmatic warning that suggests that deceit and self-deception may be important in the film: the good masks are mixed with the bad, she says, but all wear a mask. As the pair talk, we see passengers waiting to collect their luggage from the airport carousel behind a pane of glass. A blonde woman waves at Albert. On the other side of the pair, behind a different pane of glass, we see the woman's daughter waiting.

Inspired, as we saw, by a short section of Laferrière's book, this little scene contributes little to the film's main plot. It does, however, tell us much. To begin with, it contains something akin to a family group: two mature adults and a teenage girl. Yet, it also tells us that normal family life is impossible. The impoverished mother cannot protect her child. Albert, a possible substitute father, either chooses to do nothing or is effectively impotent. Social structures and their reproduction through the family are effectively in crisis. In some ways, the scene is an indirect evocation of the broader situation in Baby Doc's Haiti. As Laferrière notes in the early pages of his book, Haiti was a land of absent fathers in which Baby Doc, the obscene patriarch, could seem the father of all. Papa Doc, his father, had been an authoritarian traditionalist. In contrast, the son allowed in foreign music, pornography, violent films and drugs as a new permissive authoritarianism took over (Laferrière, 2000: 11–16). This is the context for Laferrière's novel. It can also be felt in Cantet's film.

The use of glass in the opening scene has clear echoes of other Cantet works, notably *L'Emploi du temps*, although its presence is less prevalent in this case. Again, it suggests the presence of social barriers that people choose not to see. Albert is caught uneasily between two panes of glass, separated, on the one hand, from the woman's vulnerable daughter who cuts an isolated figure, and, on the other, from the international travellers entering the country. Divisions implied here will harden as the film progresses and inequalities become more apparent. We also see, again in a typical Cantetian way, how a character's self-image and plans are challenged by others. Albert is effectively pinned by the expectant looks from the black woman, her daughter and Brenda. The fact that he only responds to the latter points to the power relationships in play.

The next sequence shows Brenda being driven to the hotel. Her viewpoint is immediately privileged. Shots of Port-au-Prince from inside the vehicle are mingled with shots of her looking out. As opposed to the understated opening sequence at the airport which gave us an insight into the harshness and economic conditions of people's lives, these shots construct the Haitian capital as an exciting spectacle of movement and human colour that is quite simply there for the tourist. The latter is protected in her bubble, moved through the scenery but safely insulated from it by the car windows. Her way of seeing is not simply that of the tourist. It is also akin to that of the cinema-goer or television watcher for whom the world is likewise a spectacle held at a distance. We are being aligned with Brenda not simply so that we empathise with her position but so that we will begin to question our own. The sequence ends as the car arrives at the beach resort.

As Brenda dismounts from the vehicle, we take in the setting and particularly the palm trees whose leaves sway in the breeze. The palm is not just a tree amongst many. It plays a key part in the stereotypical iconography of the Caribbean when, in tourist or travel literature and images, it is constructed as a tropical paradise. As Mimi Sheller notes in *Consuming the Caribbean*, the tree was once associated with economic utility, politics and power. It had particular symbolic significance in a Haitian context as it became the 'tree of freedom' planted around the island in the same way as the French planted liberty trees at the time of their revolution. For this reason, it is found in the centre of the Haitian flag. This history has subsequently been occluded. More than anything, the palm now connotes leisure, relaxation and carefree living (Sheller, 2003: 65). When Brenda walks among the trees, she is entering a space seemingly without history or conflict. As the sequence ends, she goes under an arch with the hotel's name, crossing a threshold from the broader world into a tourist area. After a few seconds, Albert appears behind her, carrying her bags. Like the bar in *Tous à la manif*, the hotel is an apparently unconstrained space where the leisure of some in fact depends on the labour of others.

The next sequence picks up Brenda as she leaves her individual chalet and walks over the wooden bridge that takes her to the bar-restaurant and the beach. Albert greets her at the threshold of the former and introduces her to a young Haitian waitress. The latter follows Brenda onto the beach to cater for her needs. A young black man in a swimming costume places a lounger on the sand for her. She looks off-screen, heads down the beach and stops. The film cuts to a view from behind her as we are invited to see what she sees: alone, against a background of palm trees, lies a young black man on his side with his back to us. A long tracking shots holds Brenda in close-up, the ocean behind her, as she walks towards the young man, her eyes fixed firmly on him. She reaches him and looks down on his motionless, beautifully toned body. She calls his name, Legba, and, as he sits up, sits opposite him. They talk about why she is there until a voice breaks in calling him away.

The sequence partly continues the dynamic of its predecessor and partly changes it. As on the drive, the world is literally there for Brenda, an idyllic fantasy of sand, sea and palm tree over which her tourist gaze can wonder. In the same way as a chair appears for her when she needs it, Legba, the young man that her hungry gaze has been seeking, is miraculously there, waiting for her voice to bring him to life. Beautiful and unthreatening, he is at her feet. Where the sequence differs from the drive is that Brenda is no longer separated from the world but moves through it, touching the sand and water, sharing the space with Legba, all barriers seemingly removed. However, the space is only frictionless and reassuring in this way because the broader world is held at bay. Those parts of it, including Legba, which are let in are there to service the tourists' needs, formal and informal workers in the service economy. Thresholds, as we know, are important in Cantet films. The threshold Brenda crossed when she entered the resort was the one between Haitian reality and the enclave of the resort, a space outside of the broader society.[1] Sheller's comments on Caribbean tourism in general apply particularly well here. She notes how 'the "untouched" Caribbean of

---

1 In Haitian Voodoo, Papa Legba is an important spirit, a figure who stands between the human and spirit worlds and controls the crossroads between them. It is no accident therefore that Cantet's Legba finds himself at the crossroads between tourists and the much harsher experience of indigenous Haitians.

tourist fantasy must be held in place behind walls, gates, and service smiles in order to afford the tourist the experience of getting close to it' (2003: 30). Brenda seems to be on a deeply personal quest to recapture her earlier idyll with Legba. Yet, as is often the case with Cantet, her personal utopia is clearly a deeply conformist one, a collectively shared fantasy of tourism and of consumption more generally. The world, as we are told in a thousand ways, is there for us because we are worth it.

The network of inter-textual cross-connections of any cultural production is potentially infinite. Every novel or film is involved in the recycling, rearticulation or reworking of dense networks of cultural references and meanings. What is interesting, in the end, is to consider which inter-textual references are important for which works. Laferrière's novel is full of references to North American high and popular culture and to French literature, not least because it contains a number of characters who are cultural producers of one sort or another. It also functions through a constant and subversive reuse of racial and sexual stereotypes and taboos. Cantet's film is both similar and different. It has none of the rich web of explicit cultural references, culture not being on its characters' minds. It does, however, draw on some of the same stereotypes and taboos while adding others of its own, notably concerning the sexuality of older women. Moreover, as a film, it connects more easily to other visual representations. Not a noticeable presence in the novel, advertising, with its endlessly recycled images of sandy beaches, sea and palm trees is clearly a privileged inter-text of the film. In her classic *Black Looks: Race and Representation,* bell hooks notes the pervasive commodification of otherness in the contemporary period. As the world becomes offered up for consumption, otherness (world music, exotic holidays, foreign food) promises new delights, a way of 'spicing up' the jaded consumer's experience and making it more intense and satisfying (hooks, 1992: 17–21). Brenda's apparently personal encounter with Legba makes sense within this broader picture of exoticised consumption.

There is a paradox about the way in which Brenda takes possession of the beach. She seems to be walking into a virgin space to encounter a young black man as if it were a romantic meeting with no history behind it. Yet, in the same way as the myth of unspoilt nature is just that, a myth – Haitian nature having been shaped and reshaped by people, not least at the time of the slave plantations and colonial estates – Brenda's walk outside history is full of historical echoes. Others before her have taken possession of the land and gazed upon it as if it were there for their pleasure or ownership. What has changed is that, in the era of neo-colonialism and of tourism, the overt violence and domination of earlier eras has gone underground. Cantet's film will bring the violence back into view.

The individual, the group and the broader society

The voice that calls Legba away from Brenda belongs to Ellen, the rather cynical university professor who reigns over the beach. It exercises a double constraint. It both reminds Legba that he is expected to be there when wanted and breaks into the utopian moment when it appeared that Brenda's world had become frictionless. As elsewhere in Cantet, the encounter with the group forces the individual to confront the looks and desires of others. What Brenda has to come to terms with as she engages with those at the resort is that Legba is not simply there for her. This is precisely what Ellen tells her when the pair later watch him dancing on the bar terrace with a young blonde woman. Brenda is clearly not happy. Ellen tells her that Legba belongs to everyone and can decide with whom he wishes to be.

We noted the presence, in *Ressources humaines*, of a kind of social primal scene, repeated with variations, wherein the hero's worker-father was humiliated in front of witnesses as he stood by his machine. Brenda's idyll on the beach with Legba, a socio-sexual primal scene, undergoes similar repetition and variation. The first iteration is the one that we do not see but hear described in Cantet's softened reuse of Laferrière's text. It is effectively the moment of lost plenitude, the unspeakably intense first orgasm that Brenda will spend the film seeking to recapture. It seems within reach when she finds Legba but is snatched away when he is summoned by Ellen. She joins him on the beach where Ellen is holding court, only to see him kissing the latter. The next iteration occurs when Ellen leads the group along the shore on horses for a picnic. Because Legba is once again at the disposal of the other woman, Brenda dances with young Eddy, who may be about twelve, first at a distance but then close together, with the young man's hands on her haunches. While the other picnickers applaud in their amusement, Legba intervenes and pulls the boy away. Embarrassed at her behaviour in front of the group, Brenda confesses that she does not know what she was thinking. We realise, however, that she has been grasping at anything (even young Eddy) that will bring her closer to the lost moment. Her shame, that key Cantetian sentiment, can be seen as resulting not simply from her present action but also as a deferred acknowledgement of the wrongness of her earlier seduction of Legba brought on by the eyes of others. The next iteration is more positive. It comes after Legba has returned from his run-in with the Tonton Macoute. Brenda insists that Albert feed him in the restaurant although it is against the rules for the young escorts to eat there. When he has eaten, he and Brenda leave the others and walk onto the nocturnal beach where they make love. This is the high point of Brenda's return, the moment when her romantic fantasy seems to have been realised. It is also the last time she will make love to Legba. The next, tragic iteration of the scene occurs when the young man's naked body is dumped with that of the young black woman on the sand. This moment effectively destroys Brenda's fantasy. If her idyllic construction of her relationship with Legba has required the exclusion of the exterior world and its oppressions, this is when the excluded breaks in and hidden violences are forced to the surface as they inevitably are in Cantet's films. The presence of Legba's dead body was already anticipated in that opening scene where he lay motionless on the beach.

More complex in its narrative organisation than earlier Cantet films, *Vers le sud* is characterised, as we noted, by a series of partial mirrorings between characters and events, with Eddy being a younger version of Legba, Ellen a cynical double of Brenda and so on. One of the consequences of this is that Brenda's scenes with Legba are to some extent paralleled by scenes between him and Ellen. Unsurprisingly, therefore, Ellen's most positive moments are when she is alone with the young man. One such scene occurs early on in her beachside cabin. Mirroring the earlier moment with Brenda, it begins with Legba seeming to be asleep. The young man sits up, tells Ellen she is like a doe ('une biche') and pretends to bite her, calling himself a tiger. She objects and instead has him lie on the bed face down, naked and pretending to be asleep while she photographs his body. As when he makes love to Brenda on the beach later in the film, he is playing a role in a neo-colonial fantasy of which he is not the author.

Underlining the two women's complementarity, there is an exchange of roles at the end of the film. Up until then, Ellen had always opposed her cynicism to Brenda's romanticism. At the same time, she seemed to accept that she could not monopolise Legba's time. However, when the women realise that Legba's life is in danger, things change. High-handedly expelling the workers from the restaurant kitchen, Ellen pulls Legba in behind her and tells him that he must leave with her for the United States so that they can always be together. We realise that her desire for Legba is no less possessive than Brenda's. As Sue will tell her, everyone knows that she too loves Legba. When he is killed, she is more defeated than Brenda. The latter, now the cynical one, decides to move on to other islands while Ellen resigns herself to her lonely life in Boston. The women bring out each other's blind spots and force hidden feelings to the surface. If Ellen's cynicism makes Brenda recognise how others see her behaviour, Ellen's rivalry drives Brenda's attachment into the open.

When Ellen addresses Legba in the kitchen, we realise that, in typical Cantetian manner, the space is not properly enclosed. What seemed a private encounter is witnessed by others through a hatch. As Ellen follows Legba back into the dining area, this social observation becomes more obvious. Heads turn towards her and follow her departing back. Just as the group had watched Brenda and Eddy dance in an inappropriate way, public scrutiny is now turned upon Ellen as she reveals previously hidden feelings. Unlike Brenda at the picnic, but like her later in the film, when she searches publicly for Legba, Ellen is effectively shameless. She refuses whatever judgement the group may bring to bear upon her. Were it not for the neo-colonial context, the mature woman's defiance of the weight of social expectation might seem an admirable affirmation of autonomy. The context makes it far more ambiguous and challenges us to ponder, Ellen's empowerment coming, as it does, at the cost of Legba's vulnerability.

Race, gender, age and class: blurring the divisions

The ostensible subject of Cantet's film is sex tourism, a subject that we probably feel we understand well enough to judge until our certainties are unsettled by the swapping of the expected gender roles.

As Jacqueline Sanchez Taylor writes, 'the stereotypical image of the "sex tourist" is that of the Western man who travels to Thailand or the Philippines to engage in brief, highly commodified exchanges of sex for cash or kind with prostitute women or children' (2006: 83). She comments, 'dominant understandings of the term "sexual exploit-ation", preclude the possibility that a woman can sexually exploit a man' (2006: 43). When men are those selling their services, she notes, there is still a tendency to see them as 'agents who either eco-nomically, emotionally or sexually exploit tourist women rather than being exploited by them' (2006: 46). At the same time, she adds, ana-lysis of the sex trade in terms of exploitation tends to be framed from a radical feminist perspective that explains it predominantly in terms of patriarchal power and marginalises the racial and global relations that underpin the phenomenon (2006: 45). Unlike its male counter-part, therefore, female sex tourism challenges preconceptions and must be approached with careful thought. Although the film cannot develop the same explicit argument, a similar desire to prevent us slotting what we see into existing stereotypes of gendered behaviour or North–South relationships clearly lies behind its choice of subject. This is implicitly announced by Cantet at the start of his film.

The opening, as we noted, gives us a strong sense of the perverse situation with which poor Haitians must live. It is presented using a stock cast: the powerless mother, the innocent daughter and predatory men. We have an immediate moral grasp of the situation. However, this comfortable clarity is quickly taken from us. When Brenda appears on the scene and finds the far from fragile Legba, we have to think harder about what we are seeing. The Manichaean world of the prelude gives way to something less easy to gauge. An older woman, travelling alone in search of love and sexual satisfaction, is not an obvious predator. Legba, who seems able to choose partners, is not an obvious victim. In some ways, Brenda and Legba seem as similar as they are different. Economically, they are poles apart. Yet each must bear disadvantages of class and nationality or age and gender that may pull them together in a way, it being a Cantet film, that is not without its utopian dimension.

Our main insight into the women's situation is provided by the conversations that they share and the to-camera monologues that each is granted. What emerges from both is the degree to which they feel frustrated and constrained when they are at home in North

America. Sue gets on well with the men with whom she works. However, when she has spent the night with one of them, she has found that he ignores her the next day, probably fearing what his colleagues will think. Ellen, who lives in Boston, notes that there is nothing there for women over forty. The only men interested in her are 'born losers' or those whose wives are cheating on them. A strong, intelligent woman, she is scornful of her women students who 'spread their thighs' to get a husband and cry when men leave them. The more fragile Brenda feels hemmed in by the patronising way her husband, family and friends look upon her at home. In contrast, all three women are empowered in Haiti. Sue comments that she feels free and alive, like a 'butterfly'. Elsewhere, this might make her the object of ridicule, she notes, aware of her plumpness, but not in Haiti where people's difference is accepted. Brenda, we know, has found sexual satisfaction but, more than that, is seen in active pursuit of what she desires even if she cloaks it in romantic guise. Ellen is more cynical and forthright: she has always told herself that, when she was older, she would pay men to love her. She is at ease with this and feels others should be too.

This unaccustomed sense of empowerment and recognition comes through in the scenes at the resort in Haiti. Ellen quite simply holds court on the beach. Brenda forcefully overrides Albert and the resort's rules when she insists on inviting Legba to eat at her table. Sue can frolic on the beach with her black lover, without a care in the world. The unacknowledged corollary of this, however, is the relative disempowerment of the black men. The pattern is set from the early scene when Brenda finds Legba lying on the sand, a body available to her searching gaze. Legba wears only a tight swimming costume and a gold chain, the latter, we assume, just one of the presents that the white women give him instead of direct payment. Later, we see him in a new shirt that Brenda has bought for him. We also see the different women provide food and drink for the young Haitian men. Quite simply, as the women take on the role of providers traditionally associated with men, the latter are pushed into a more classically feminine role of being looked after and bought clothes and jewellery.

The film also seems to privilege the women's voices over those of the men – Albert, the older male, being the only one of the latter to be granted a monologue, and conversations being more generally dominated by the women. However, the film's melodramatic visual economy works to undermine the women's self-justification by bringing the underlying truth of social relations into view. Thus, for example, when Legba joins Ellen's entourage at the start of the film, we see a shot within which Ellen and two other mature white women sit on loungers. A young black waitress stands behind Ellen with a drinks tray while a young black man sits behind another of the women massaging her shoulders. A third Haitian sits on the ground between the women. What seems a scene of interracial harmony and relaxed pleasure is, on closer examination, one where clear lines of power and status are visible. In the end, the women's vocal privilege only serves to underscore their failure to see. The same failure is clearly conveyed by the film's narrative structure and the way it sutures together what were two separate stories in Laferrière's novel. Legba is part of both stories, the one on the beach and the one in the town, but the women only really see the former. The two stories cross on only one or two occasions. On the first of these, Brenda and Legba have gone to the market. Outside the resort area, Brenda might feel that she is experiencing the real Haiti. However, when she buys local products and takes pictures of people, even as Legba dutifully accompanies her, she is still behaving and being treated as a tourist.[2] It is only when the pistol-waving chauffeur appears during the same excursion that she becomes aware, not of Legba's life in the round, but of the limitations of her knowledge. Later, when the two bodies are dumped on the beach, it is as if the staged *mise-en-scène* of the tourist resort were being rent asunder. Despite the differences between the two films, this resembles the moment in *Ressources humaines* when the stolen letter about the impending sackings is stuck up in the factory entrance. It is as if an act of violence were needed to force something previously denied to the surface. Even then, the women do not entirely get it. Ellen suggests to a policeman that they too may be in danger. The latter tells Albert in Creole that tourists never die. Albert and the policeman are both fully aware of the line that divides

---

2 Sanchez Taylor underscores how local people's informal economic activity is important to the more formal tourist economy. The former offers tourists something more 'authentic' outside the staged reality of the resort. However, as she notes, what they are in fact experiencing is a stage behind the stage. She adds that the power relations of the front stage (the resort) are also woven into the fabric of the back stage of the informal economy (2006: 55). *Vers le sud* makes a very similar argument at the implicit level.

the experience of the two groups. Not only do tourists never die. They never really see.

This is also clear when Albert tries to prevent Legba eating in the restaurant. Brenda interprets his actions as racism and expresses her shock to Sue. The scene is followed by Albert's turn for one of the film's voice-over monologues. In contrast to those of the women, however, Albert's is neither delivered to camera nor from the comfortable privacy of a chalet, the same level of interiority clearly not being available to all. Instead, we hear his thoughts as he reluctantly prepares the meal Brenda has demanded for Legba. We learn that he comes from a family that resisted the American occupation of the island in 1915. His father never shook a white man's hand, while his grandfather saw white people, above all the American invaders, as animals, not humans. Had his grandfather known that he was now waiting on Americans, he would have been ashamed. The new invaders, comments Albert, do not carry guns, but dollars that corrode everything they touch. The different presentation of Albert's inner thoughts is highly revealing: the way his anger at the 'invaders' is expressed even as he serves them points to the impossibility of his position and the unbearable tension he is exposed to. If we think about what he says, we can deduce why he does not want Legba in the restaurant. As long as the prostitution of the young Haitians stays on the beach, he can exist in denial of the situation. By forcing him to accept Legba in the restaurant, the women make him confront his role in a more generalised corruption. The fact that they attribute his attitude to individual racism again underscores their failure to see the underlying social structures that condition all inter-personal interactions in the neo-colonial context.

Albert cannot speak openly but is allowed to express his thoughts. Legba is quite simply silenced. At the resort, he has to perform a role for the women. When faced with the brutality of the Tonton Macoute he has to bite his tongue. When Ellen expresses surprise that Haitians accept the yawning gap between the luxury in the presidential palace and the poverty of the population, he asks, 'Qui t'a dit qu'on accepte?'.[3] Given the impossibility of speaking frankly in either the resort or the town, he can only point out that silence does not mean agreement. Effectively, his movements and gestures speak for

---

3 'Who says we accept?'

him as when, without making a comment, he pulls young Eddy away from Brenda or, more generally, in the way he moves restlessly back and forth between town and resort, at ease in neither. Like Albert, he is in an impossible situation but cannot vocalise it. Initially, his ability to shift between spaces and from one woman to another suggests agency. Increasingly, it resembles flight. Town becomes too dangerous, yet, when he escapes to the resort, Ellen gives him orders. There is effectively nowhere he can be himself. Unlike Brenda and Ellen, he cannot move on in ways of his choosing.

As part of her discussion of the consumption of otherness, bell hooks explores the dynamics of the racialised sexual encounter. On the one hand, she notes how it seems to offer something exciting and threatening to members of dominant groups. Because young black men are associated with the tension between pleasure and danger, death and desire, they seem to possess a vibrant intensity that can rescue their more privileged partners from the numbness of mainstream American life. On the other hand, the latters' transgressive embrace of otherness seems to move them away from their dominant position in the status quo. Encounters within which seduction and longing play a key role are able to blur, if not erase, structural inequalities (hooks, 1992: 21–7). As hooks comments, 'the desire to make contact with those bodies deemed Other, with no apparent will to dominate, assuages the guilt of the past, even takes the form of a defiant gesture where one denies accountability and historical connection' (1992: 25). However, as she also notes, this encounter with difference cannot be equated with a durable renunciation of mainstream privilege (1992: 23). Although she is discussing a North American rather than a Haitian context, her analysis converges with the diagnosis implicitly offered by Cantet's film. The women's individual liberalism, blindness to structural inequality and desire to feed off the fragile vitality of the young men all fit what she describes.

At the start of *Vers le sud*, there seems to be some symmetry in the relationship between the Haitians and the white women, the former gaining material benefits from the women, the latter taking romantic and sexual satisfaction from the men, both groups seeing themselves positively reflected in the eyes of the other. By the end, the asymmetries of power and wealth have overwhelmed any symmetry there may have been. In between, we have been invited to take careful stock of the situation rather than assume that we know it in advance as we might have done if the tourists had been men.

Tourism, consumption and contemporary subjectivities

When we looked at *Ressources humaines* and *L'Emploi du temps*, we suggested that, taken together, the two films showed a shift in subjectivities from the regularities and fixed identities of the Fordist era to the mobile, networked person of the contemporary period. *Vers le sud* continues and develops this exploration of a transitional moment. In conversation with Claudine Haroche, leading French social theorist Robert Castel distinguishes between two types of contemporary individuals, the individual 'by default' and the 'excessive' individual. Both are products of the move away from the more rigidly defined roles, social and moral disciplines, and institutionalised welfare protections of an earlier period, but the former is resource-poor while the latter is resource-rich. The former is called upon to be an individual and stand alone but lacks the necessary means. The latter develops an inflated sense of his or her autonomy and cultivates his or her own subjectivity, often in denial of connections to others (Castel and Haroche, 2001: 107–46). Although Cantet's film is set in 1970s Haiti, its social world mirrors Castel's diagnoses of the current moment. Legba largely resembles the individual 'despite himself'. Although Ellen describes him as 'his own man', he is too dependent on others to stand on his own two feet. In contrast, the three women seem entirely capable of self-definition. Whereas once they might have been defined by family roles and conventional morality and the oppressive limits these placed on women's behaviour, they can now seek unlimited self-realisation. In this respect, Brenda's first orgasm marks a symbolic transition, anticipated in *Jeux de plage*, from repression to the pursuit of pleasure. As the film closes, she tells Sue that, although she may not really have loved Legba, she loved the way he looked at her. All the contradictions of her position are contained in that line with its solipsistic narcissism yet its recognition of a need for others. Ultimately, the excessive individualism of modern times cannot escape bodily limits or the needs and judgements of others.

In *La Vieillesse* (*Old Age*), her classic discussion of women's ageing, Simone de Beauvoir discusses how age is both an inner, subjective experience and a consequence of the objectifying encounter with the look of others, a moment not dissimilar in its structure to the Sartrean account of shame. While the individual can still feel unchanged on the inside, it is the way others look upon her that forces the unwelcome realisation that she is no longer considered in the same way as she was (Beauvoir, 1977: 315–29; Casado-Gual, 2012). There is a scene where Ellen swims with Legba that fits this Beauvoirian account of ageing particularly well. It finds the pair in apparently idyllic isolation as they laze in the tropical water. Ellen ducks playfully beneath the surface. When she comes up, her usually elegant, flowing hair is matted and stuck to the sides of her head. Legba comments disapprovingly that she now looks like an old lady. She comments ironically on the 'kindness' of the remark. We know nonetheless that she has been confronted with the way she appears in the eyes of others.[4] Despite the apparently unconstrained and paradisiacal setting, she faces two limits. She can control neither the way that Legba sees her nor the marks of ageing. She is played by Charlotte Rampling, one of the actresses whose public image most embodies the impossible demand placed on older women to defy the effects of time if they wish to remain socially sanctioned sexual beings. Yet, rather than brushing away the ageing process, Rampling's character is used to show its ineluctability. While Cantet's film explores the violence that lies behind the surface of tourism and consumption, it also explores the limits of their promise of empowerment.

The 1970s, the period when Cantet's film is putatively set, was the heyday of second wave feminism with its sustained intellectual debate, far-reaching critique of patriarchal society, vibrant collective mobilisations, and important social and political gains. Cantet's film bypasses this history. Although his characters seem moved by authentic feminist urges (autonomy, recognition, sexual enfranchisement), their actions and attitudes belong far more to what is usually called post-feminism, although the term itself is far from uncontested (Gill, 2007: 147–8). Were one to seek to summarise the meaning of

---

4 By noting Ellen's ageing appearance, Legba also holds up an unflattering mirror to himself as a young man involved with an older woman, rather than a simply glamorous one. This process of mutual mirroring underscores the way that both the young men and the older women need the approving looks of others to shore up their sense of self.

post-feminism in a few lines – an impossible task of course – one might say that it referred to an incorporation of feminism within the dominant values of the neo-liberal era. As Rosalind Gill notes, 'the autonomous, calculating, self-regulating subject of neoliberalism bears a strong resemblance to the active, freely choosing, self-reinventing subject of post-feminism' (2007: 164). Taken this way, post-feminism is what remains of feminism when it is shorn of its radicalism, collective mobilisation and capacity to challenge the status quo, leaving only a shrunken discourse of (already achieved) individual empowerment in its wake (McRobbie, 2009). Cast in terms of personal self-realisation, it offers no meaningful way to bridge to other struggles. Representatives of a post-feminist rather than a feminist mind-set, Cantet's women are unable to make common cause either with each other or oppressed Haitians. Instead, they are used to show the illusions and exploitative nature of apparently empowered consumption.

Conclusion

Vers le sud is a powerfully intelligent but not unproblematic film. Like all Cantet's cinema, it strikes a judicious balance between questioning and critique. If it points unerringly to oppressions of gender, age and socio-economic condition, it also makes it impossible for us to come to any easy conclusions. It challenges any preconceptions that we may seek to bring to bear and makes us question our own privileged position as western/northern consumers in relation to what we see. Importantly, too, it includes the director himself in the circle of critique. In the same way that Cantet's films always revolve around the exposure of individuals to the critical gaze of others, Cantet borrows the eyes of a post-colonial writer to problematise his own gaze upon a poor country of the global South. Where he differs from his source is that he is less interested in Haiti per se than in neo-colonialism more generally, and less focused on the 1970s than a more diffuse but broadly contemporaneous period. This is the root of the film's strength – it feels absolutely current – and its problems. It delivers a subtle but ultimately devastating critique of tourist and consumer subjectivities, but tells us relatively little about the specific Haitian realities and histories that are so vibrantly narrated in Laferrière's source novel. It somewhat belatedly brings women's experience to the centre of Cantet's film-making, and shows a real sensitivity to gendered oppressions but allows them to appear as relative privilege by playing them off against neo-colonial injustices. There were good reasons why Cantet did this, not least his desire to challenge his spectators by forcing them to weigh up different oppressions and their complex interactions.[5] He would nonetheless feel the need to return more single-mindedly to gendered injustices in the recent *Foxfire*. With its exploration of the collective mobilisation of a group of young women against patriarchal oppression, the later film provides a necessary corrective to the *Vers le sud*'s elision of the radical and collective dimensions of feminist struggle.

References

Beauvoir, S. de (1977), *Old Age*, trans. P. O'Brian, Harmondsworth, Penguin.
Casado-Gual, N. (2012), 'Unveiling "the Other within": The crucible of internal alterity in Laurent Cantet's *Heading South*, in J. Dolan and E. Tincknell, eds, *Aging Femininities: Troubling Representations*, Newcastle upon Tyne, Cambridge Scholars Publishing, 133–44.
Castel, R. and Haroche, C. (2001), *Propriété privée, propriété sociale, propriété de soi: Entretiens sur la construction de l'individu moderne*, Paris, Fayard.
Deer, P. (2005), 'Defusing *The English Patient*', in R. Stam and A. Raengo, eds, *Literature and Film: A Guide to the Theory and Practice of Film Adaptation*, Oxford, Blackwell, 208–33.
Gill, R. (2007), 'Postfeminist media culture: Elements of a sensibility', *European Journal of Cultural Studies*, 10:2, 147–66.
Hallward, P. (2004), 'Option zero in Haiti', *New Left Review*, 27 (May–June), 23–47.
hooks, b. (1992), *Black Looks: Race and Representation*, Boston, MA, South End Press.
Hutcheon, L. (2006), *A Theory of Adaptation*, London and New York, Routledge.
Laferrière, D. (2000 [1997]), *La Chair du maître*, Paris, Le Serpent à Plumes.
Lionnet, F. (2008), 'Postcolonialism, language and the visual: By way of Haiti', *Journal of Postcolonial Writing*, 44:3, 227–39.

5 Núria Casado-Gual writes, 'The spectator of *Heading South* is left with the uncertainty of not knowing which is the most alienating form of "Otherness" in the complex interaction of age, gender, racial and ethnic difference shown in the narrative' (2012: 143).

McRobbie, A. (2009), *The Aftermath of Feminism: Gender, Culture and Social Change*, Los Angeles and London, Sage.

Morice, J. (2005), 'Une île et des elles: Laurent Cantet tourne *Vers le sud* en République Dominicaine', *Télerama*, 25 January 2006.

Sanchez Taylor, J. (2006), 'Female sex tourism: A contradiction in terms', *Feminist Review*, 83, 42–59.

Sheller, M. (2003), *Consuming the Caribbean: From Arawaks to Zombies*, London and New York, Routledge.

Stam, R. (2004), 'Introduction: The theory and practice of film adaptation', in Stam and A. Raengo, eds, *A Companion to Literature and Film*, Malden, MA, Blackwell, 1–52.

Stam, R. (2005), *Literature through Film: Realism, Magic and the Art of Adaptation*, Malden, MA, Blackwell.

Stam, R. and Raengo, A., eds (2004), *A Companion to Literature and Film*, Malden, MA, Blackwell.

Stam, R. and Raengo, A., eds (2005), *Literature and Film: A Guide to the Theory and Practice of Film Adaptation*, Malden, MA, Blackwell.

5

Between Republican walls

Awarded the Palme d'Or at Cannes, *Entre les murs* (*The Class*) was the film that cemented Cantet's reputation as one of France's leading film-makers. It also confirmed the director's convictions about how his films should be made, in terms of both their production and their relationship to contemporary issues. Based on François Bégaudeau's novel of the same name, *Entre les murs* was shot with an entirely amateur cast that included the novelist himself as the main character, teacher François Marin. Set in a school in north Paris, the film raised questions about Republican education at the beginning of the millennium, particularly relating to the treatment of ethnic diversity and the traditional Republican principle of equality.

Unlike some other major countries, notably the United States and the United Kingdom, France has traditionally consigned people's origins and beliefs to the private domain. Confident of the value of its own culture and language, the country has also held to a highly assimilationist understanding of the role of education. The school was where young peasants and immigrants shed their particularity and became simply French. With the perceived difficulty of assimilating the children of post-war, ex-colonial immigration, and the increased critique of the assimilationist model as an alibi for class and ethnic discrimination, Republican integration is today held to be in crisis. Linked to this is a broader, common-sense view that France is a divided country, split not so much along class lines as between the included and excluded. Some of these broader anxieties have converged around the country's *banlieues*, the site of a succession of high-profile confrontations between young men and the police. Often ethnicised in their reporting, these clashes have tended to cement a perception that the country is alienated from its disaffected youth. Famously, in 2005, after much the largest youth revolt, the then Interior Minister, Nicolas Sarkozy, labelled the rioters 'la racaille' (the rabble), an inflammatory and populist appellation (Moran, 2011). Without directly citing these incidents, Cantet's film explores their context and probes the capacity of the school to adjust to new circumstances, asking whether it can still (if it ever could) promote egalitarian values. If the film was lavishly praised for its festival success, this intervention in controversial issues also stirred up debate.

The film tells the story of a class of thirteen- and fourteen-year-olds as they relate to François, their French teacher and form tutor. The class is ethnically diverse with children of white French, North and West African, French Caribbean (Antillean), Chinese, and Turkish heritage. Although their social background is not necessarily obvious, most of them are clearly more working than middle class. The school is in one of those remaining socially mixed areas of Paris, a city whose poorer inhabitants have more generally been pushed out to its edges. The story is a relatively simple one. Its hero is a child-centred rather than a more traditional pedagogue. The film follows him as he tries to build bridges between the culture of the school and that of his pupils. In some cases, he seems to be successful. In others, he fails, more or less spectacularly. Conflict builds between the school and Souleymane (Franck Keita), a boy of Malian extraction, leading to his eventual expulsion. Another black student, Henriette (Henriette Kasaruhanda), steps forward at the end of the year to say that she has learnt nothing. Esmeralda (Esmeralda Ouertani), a student with a mixed French and North African background, announces that she has learnt nothing worth knowing in school but has read Plato's *Republic* on her own account. The teachers and pupils end the year with a good-natured football match in the school-yard, a conclusion that counterbalances but does not erase the exclusion of Souleymane. Although an account of the school year, the film is less interested in the institution's daily routine than in moments of interruption and conflict when authority is challenged and the classroom or the yard temporarily become spaces of democratic interaction.

If the film raises questions about the power dynamics operative within the school, it also puts similar questions about the film-making process itself, giving it a greater reflexivity than any other Cantet work. The film's François is not simply a double of the book's author,

François Bégaudeau, effectively playing himself. As he stands in front of the class, organising and structuring the situation, he is like a director on a set. When the film investigates classroom inequality, it is also implicitly scrutinising its own orchestration of voices and asking to what extent, even in (educational *and* filmic) contexts that seem intrinsically unequal, an egalitarian interchange may take place. To unpick this complex interrogation of social and vocal hierarchies, I will draw on Bourdieu, Rancière and Bakhtin: Bourdieu to probe the social inequalities of education, Bakhtin the dialogic exchange of voices, and Rancière at the intersection of these two domains.

The film's reception

Having received a late invitation to the 2008 Cannes film festival, *Entre les murs* was not among the favourites to receive a prize even after its screening had been followed by a prolonged standing ovation. Much to everyone's surprise, however, the festival jury, presided over by the famous left-leaning Hollywood star Sean Penn, awarded it the prestigious Palme d'Or for best film, making it the first French film to carry off the top prize since Pialat's *Sous le soleil de Satan* in 1987. The award had an immediate effect: not only was the film released on a greater number of copies than originally planned within France, it was also bought for far more foreign markets than any preceding Cantet film. Its director and cast found themselves in demand, so much so that the teenage stars had to be sheltered from an over-inquisitive media. Politicians quickly become involved too, the combination of a French triumph and the film's theme (the school system) being too big a temptation to resist. Christine Albanel, the then Minister of Culture, was one of the first laudatory voices, alongside a famous Socialist predecessor, Jacques Lang, and the Minister of Education, Xavier Darcos. Cantet's production company, Haut et Court, had to be careful to make sure the director did not become photo-opportunity fodder for politicians keen to associate themselves with the film's success. The production company was happy, however, for the film to be shown by the Socialist-run town hall of the twentieth *arrondissement* of Paris where it had been shot. They were also happy when Socialist Mayor of Paris, Bertrand Delanoë, organised a screening for the capital's head-teachers and offered free tickets to thousands of pupils from schools marked out for special support. Further success followed when the film was chosen to open the 2008 New York film festival. Having taken his teenage cast to Cannes, Cantet now led a smaller group to New York, saddened that he could not take them all.[1]

After such a wave of acclaim, a backlash was perhaps inevitable. Having praised the film unreservedly before seeing it, Education Minister Darcos retreated ingloriously to a more nuanced if not outright critical position, identifying the film as the story of a failed pedagogy (Debril, 2008). Writing in leading paper, *Le Monde*, conservative *nouveau philosophe* Alain Finkielkraut was overtly critical. Seeing the film's teacher as a representative of progressive, pupil-centred pedagogy, he leapt to the defence of a more traditional, 'Republican' model of education within which great literary texts, with their capacity to engage with complexity, and teach precision, nuance and courtesy, played a central role (Finkielkraut, 2008). Veteran populist and leftist politician Jean-Pierre Chevènement adopted a similarly conservative stance. Noting that the film was based on a novel that favoured child-centred learning, he advocated a more traditional, back-to-basics approach centred on hard work, merit and discipline (AFP, 2008). Complicating matters, Philippe Meirieu, the public standard-bearer of the child-centred *pédagogues*, also came out strongly against a work that he felt brought the methods he championed into disrepute. In particular, he reproached the film's school-teacher for an approach that was too reliant on emotional proximity, sought an impossible equality between teacher and pupil, and failed to consider the vital mediations needed to bridge between the school curriculum and pupils' own knowledge. While he recognised that the film gave a reasonably sound portrayal of life in a difficult *collège* (secondary school), he accused it of failing to show a single properly constructed episode of learning with demanding content, clear instructions and properly framed activities (Meirieu, 2008). The broad thrust of these criticisms was echoed by some of the teachers invited by the press to comment

---

1 For an overview of the film's release and reception, see Olivier De Bruyn, '*Entre les murs*: Une palme d'or, et après?', http://rue89.nouvelobs.com/2008/06/11/entre-les-murs-une-palme-dor-et-apres; and '*Entre les murs*: Comment résister à la star-académisation?', http://rue89.nouvelobs.com/2008/09/18/entre-les-murs-comment-resister-a-la-star-academisation (accessed 15 September 2014).

on the film. One teacher, Valérie Sultan, for example, suggested that the film simply showed verbal jousting without a coherent educational goal (Lefort and Soulé, 2008). Pointing to one potential reason for some of this broader disquiet, at least two articles (Ledoux, 2008; and Polony, 2008) criticised the film for its misleading 'effet de réel' (reality effect), the way in which its amateur cast, location shooting and filming style made it seem like a documentary while it was in fact something else.

Some of these criticisms were clearly unfair if not outright wrong-headed. But they were also a telling response to the film. *Entre les murs*, as Cantet made clear, was not interested in smoothly functioning teaching but in those moments when routine was interrupted and something more interesting came to the surface. As he also underscored, his film in no way set out to be a documentary (Lefort and Soulé, 2008). Yet, at the same time, and like the book that it was based on, it deliberately probed some key contemporary issues and thus, like his earlier works, provoked reactions that went well beyond the normal limits of film criticism. In 2004, the Government had launched a major public consultation, the Thélot Report, about the future direction of the French school system. The consultation asked for responses to a long series of questions about the values of the Republican school system: what the contents of the curriculum should be; how the school should respond to the diversity of its students; how students can be motivated, and violence and incivility addressed, and so on (Thélot, 2004). The questions are reproduced verbatim and without any explanation in Bégaudeau's book, in a way that suggests that it is mocking them (how can a list of discrete questions begin to engage with something as complex as the school?) but also implicitly responding to them in its own holistic way (Bégaudeau, 2006: 61–2). They were in the film script but did not find their way into the released version, although their presence can still be indirectly felt.[2] But the film is not simply about the school system. As Cantet underlined, the interest of the school, or the workplace (*Ressources humaines* clearly being on his mind), was its ability

---

2 Evidence of the original intention to include the questions spoken by Francois's off-screen voice can be found in the script published with a commentary by Bégaudeau *et al.* (2008: 45).

to function as 'une caisse de résonance' (a sound-box) for broader social issues (Widemann, 2008).

From novel to film: towards polyphony

As the son of two teachers and the father of two children, Cantet had a more than passing interest in the education system. What he lacked was any direct experience of its functioning. As had been the case with *Vers le sud*, he was drawn to novel adaptation as a way to access the kind of insider knowledge that he lacked. In the same way as Laferrière's work opened up Haitian reality for him, Bégaudeau's experience as a teacher could provide a way into the world of the school. Laferrière's writing was above all important for its radical otherness: allowing access to the unfamiliar, it also enabled Cantet to take a distance from his own position and to see his viewpoint as a western outsider through other eyes. The relationship with Bégaudeau was different. Sociologically, as a white member of the cultured middle classes, the novelist was close to Cantet. More importantly, as his close collaborator in the film, he was, as we have noted, something akin to a double. During filming, Cantet and he would meet every morning to discuss what they would seek to achieve that day. Standing in front of the class, leading his pupils' activities, he was effectively the director's on-set proxy (Burdeau and Thirion, 2008: 13).

Cantet had been thinking about a school-based film for some time. When the shooting of *Vers le sud* had to be postponed on account of events in Haiti following the ousting of President Aristide, he had time to write an initial outline centred on a boy's disciplinary hearing (the story of Souleymane in the film). Later, when *Vers le sud* was released, he met Bégaudeau in a radio studio and their encounter relaunched the idea of a school-centred film. Cantet was there to discuss his new work, the writer to talk about his novel. The director was gripped by the extracts that the novelist read out and mentioned his own story outline. The film project grew from that encounter (Burdeau and Thirion, 2008: 15). The understanding between the two creators was undoubtedly helped by the fact that, apart from being a teacher and writer, Bégaudeau was also a film critic in *Les Cahiers du cinéma*, where, among other things, he had defended *Vers le sud*, a film that not everyone had liked. Cantet; Campillo, his usual co-writer; and Bégaudeau set about turning the book into a film with the disciplinary hearing at its heart and with the writer watching over the documentary dimension of the work (Domenach and Valens, 2008: 28).

As with *Vers le sud*, but less dramatically so, the adaptation required a significant reshaping of the original work. Bégaudeau's book takes the form of a chronicle, an unfolding account of a year's work with a class, with its many ups and downs. The film has far more dramatic shape. The root of almost all its scenes and much of its dialogue can be traced back to its source, but the way it builds its tension to a multi-faceted crisis bears witness to a significant reworking. In the novel, the incident where the teacher calls two pupils 'pétasses' ('slags', or 'prostitutes', as they take it to mean), comes relatively early on, as does the moment when one of the same pair, Sandra (the film's Esmeralda) reveals she is reading Plato's *Republic* at home. The novel has not one but three exclusions dispersed throughout its length. As it nears its end, we also learn that the mother of Wei (Wei Huang), a Chinese pupil, is to be expelled from France. The film concentrates and rearranges this action: only one exclusion, that of Souleymane, is retained and is moved near the end of the film, making it a much more climactic event. The 'pétasses' incident is pushed back and tied into the exclusion, becoming one of its triggers.[3] The announcement of the expulsion of the Chinese mother is brought forward: an event around which the teachers unite, it contrasts sharply with the tense and divisive moments to follow. The novel ends with a discussion of what has been learnt during the year and with the staff–student soccer match. These episodes are kept in the same place, but Sandra's revelation about her reading of Plato is included in the year's summing-up, giving it greater narrative impact. To the same activity is also added Henriette's confession that she has learnt nothing and fears she is destined for the *lycée professionnel* rather than the more prestigious academic route. The combined effect of these changes is not simply to give the film a stronger dramatic structure, with mounting tension leading to crisis; it also makes its conclusion more ambiguous: the film does not simply build to the exclusion of

3 In the novel, during the *conseil de classe*, an oral discussion of progress, the teacher describes a pupil called Youssouf as 'limited'. This moment is refocused on Souleymane and becomes another reason for the outburst that leads to his exclusion.

Souleymane, a failure for school and pupil. It ends with the interplay of the exclusion, the quiet failure of Henriette, the independent success of Esmeralda (her reading of Plato) and the harmony of the football match. Neither the school in general nor the teacher in particular can simply be cast as successes or failures. As is typical with Cantet, we are confronted with complexity and challenged to think.

Beyond the interplay of its multiple endings, one of the main ways in which Cantet builds complexity into his film is through his inclusion of different voices. Bakhtin, and his distinction between the dialogic and the polyphonic, is again a useful reference. As we noted in Chapter 1, any instance of speech or writing is inevitably dialogic in Bakhtin's eyes; that is, it must of necessity enter into conversation with utterances that precede or follow it. We can immediately see how this could apply to Bégaudeau's source novel with its capacity to incorporate not simply the speech of its teacher-hero and the other teachers around him, but also a range of voices, from the popular language and slang of the children to the wooden language of the official questionnaire that the novel quotes at length. It is not my intention here to examine the polyphonic credentials of Bégaudeau's novel. What interests me is how Cantet's film manages the interplay of voices and whether it is simply dialogic or achieves a more genuine polyphony.

On the face of it, the classroom is an archetypical space where multiple voices are subordinated to a controlling voice. This can be seen in all those scenes where François draws on examples from pupils to illustrate a more general point or, perhaps more typically, to show how *not* to say something. Thus, for example, when he explains to his pupils how to produce a self-portrait, he discusses how shame might restrict their self-expression. Pupils then produce examples of shame tied, in one case, to body image; in another, to eating in front of a friend's mother; and in a third, to finding oneself, as someone from North African origin, in a social event where everyone else was 'native' French. The details are unimportant at this stage: what matters is how the pupils talk at the level of the personal, embodied and specific, while the teacher manages the transition to the more general and abstract. Some voices are put in the service of others. Similarly, when the teacher wants to look at the imperfect subjunctive, a rarely used tense and mood in French, or the difficult conjugation of the verb *croître* (to increase), he uses pupils' partial or wrong answers to work towards the correct model. Again, the rightness of his voice is confirmed by the inadequacy of others in an unequal orchestration of opinions. At the same time, as Cantet's film repeatedly demonstrates, the classroom is a place where the organising voice can be challenged. Indeed, as we saw, the film is driven more by interruptions to the teacher's plans than by their smooth execution, partly because the teacher himself latches onto pupils' opinions to drive his lessons, partly because the pupils themselves are far from docile learners.

It is not only the teacher's voice that is questioned. Those of the book's author and the director are also implicitly challenged in the film. Although this kind of problematisation was perhaps implicitly present in Bégaudeau's source text, the way Cantet made his film played a crucial role in its development. The film can be seen as an ideal example of the application of the director's method because of the way in which it was cast and rehearsed. Slotted into the school summer holidays, shooting itself only took seven weeks: five weeks working with Bégaudeau and the children and two more to shoot with the other adults. But the film's preparation period was much longer and stretched out over the preceding school year (Domenach and Valens, 2008). On Wednesday afternoons, the time when French children typically have no lessons, Cantet worked with pupils from the Collège François Dolto, trying out ideas from the book in workshops, extracts from which are included on the French DVD of the film. Over the course of the year the original fifty participants were whittled down to the about twenty-five who appear in the film, while members of staff were recruited to play the teachers, and parents to play parents. Rather than being submitted to the rigid discipline of a pre-existing script, each group was given a looser framework within which to work and could thus inflect the direction that scenes took and comment on the situations that they developed (Burdeau and Thirion, 2008: 16–17). Bégaudeau's original authorship was not simply reworked by Cantet and co-writer Campillo. It was opened up to the input of parents, teachers and, above all, children in a way that challenged any fixed authorial role. As elsewhere, when he had turned to amateur performers, Cantet trusted people to be experts on their own lives and to use their experience to inform their roles. Describing his work with the teachers, for example, Cantet said: 'On a passé des heures à improviser mais aussi à discuter des enjeux de chaque scène ... il y avait des choses qu'on avait écrites, et des choses qu'ils ont proposées, des doutes, des questionnements qui sont les leurs' (Burdeau and Thirion, 2008: 17).[4]

This effective democratisation of the film's preparation was prolonged into the shooting itself, which took place in the Collège Jean Jaurès, a stone's throw away from the Collège Dolto from which the pupils came and which was in turn only a few blocks away from the school where Bégaudeau worked. For the classroom scenes, which made up the film's core, Cantet and his cinematographer used a three-camera set-up. A corridor was built for the cameras down one side of the classroom. Because they were high-definition video cameras rather than film cameras, they were able to record whole scenes in a single take. Sitting at his table, Cantet could let the scenes unfold, thinking about his editing, even as he watched what was being shot. Typically, one camera tracked Bégaudeau at the front of the class, another followed his main interlocutor(s) in the scene, while the third picked up other performers as they responded to interactions (Domenach and Valens, 2008: 30). Giving the scenes time to develop, this mode of shooting also permitted a degree of spontaneity in performance: rather than being pre-programmed by the needs of editing, the dialogue could develop more freely and voices were therefore less constrained. At the same time, the staging of scenes as a to-and-fro between teacher and pupil(s) – Cantet compared it to a tennis match – meant that interchange rather than something more monological was favoured (Domenach and Valens, 2008: 30).

Cantet's own voice was everywhere and nowhere in the film. It was present in the way his preferred method was so fully applied. It also made itself strongly heard in how the story was organised. His films typically show characters who struggle to fit in with groups. *Entre les murs* is no exception in this respect. Not only does it show pupils like Souleymane who cannot carve out a place for themselves, it also explores the double isolation of its teacher-hero who, on the one hand, finds himself on a collision course with his class and, on the other, is something of a loner in his relations with colleagues. The first shot of the film, a typical Cantet opening, finds him alone

---

4 'We spent hours improvising but also discussing what was at stake in each scene ... there were things we'd written and things they suggested, doubts and questioning that are theirs.'

in a cafe, a consciousness ready for its encounter with the world. The second shows him join two other male teachers as they approach the school only for him to draw ahead and enter alone. Subsequent staff-room scenes tend to accentuate his tendency to stand back from the group, a detachment that peaks at the time of the 'pétasses' incident when his unconventional methods make him stand out from his colleagues and pit him against his pupils.

The film's use of cinemascope, itself a relatively late decision, lends itself perfectly to the exploration of the relationship between the individual and the group. As we know, whatever the format, more distant shots typically emphasise the group and the context, while closer ones foreground the individual and his or her reactions.[5] What widescreen changes is that, even in those closer shots, the individual can rarely fill the frame and there are always other heads and bodies in view. The result of this is that the image can capture the distance between people and the non-alignment of viewpoints, especially when one face is in focus and other heads and bodies are blurred. There are excellent examples of this throughout the film but none so striking as when Souleymane is brought before the disciplinary hearing. A series of shots where he and the teachers are visible but only one or the other is in focus underlines the distance between them. One wonderful shot catches Souleymane and his mother (Fatoumata Kanté) in profile, both looking towards to the teachers' group off-screen, their bodies aligned but their looks condemned not to meet. Cantet may have come to cinemascope accidentally, but, in its capacity to make the screen a space of interaction and deliberation, to show the gaps and connections between people, and to bridge the intimacy of the close-up with the contextualisation of widescreen, it seemed to fit his world like a glove.

The group–individual tensions that run through the film and that scope brings into such compelling visibility also make shame, that archetypically Cantetian sentiment, central. It is present from the pupils' discussion of their disquiet at revealing private information when asked to do their self-portraits, through the hero's deep

---

5 The excellent Artifical Eye DVD of the film has an interview with Cantet, a 'making of' documentary, commentary of selected scenes by Bégaudeau and the director, and examples of some of the improvisations with the students. It is during the interview that Cantet discusses the late decision to use cinemascope and the thinking behind it.

embarrassment at his loss of self-control when he insults the girls and calls Souleymane 'limited', to the latter's own shame when he has to translate his non-French-speaking mother's defence of him as a 'good boy' to the disciplinary hearing that will exclude him. Alongside shame, the other typical Cantetian motif present is utopia. As Cantet noted, Bégaudeau and his alter ego in the novel, François Marin, seek to espouse a pedagogy that is 'presqu'égalitaire', or almost egalitarian, with *almost* being the key word and the one that drives the film (Lefort and Soulé, 2008). If shame allows Cantet to force the tensions between individual and group into full view, the utopian drive and its frustration open the gap between the world as it could or should be and the world as it is. Because the Cantetian utopia is never purely individual, François's testing of the limits of an egalitarian classroom is also a probing of a key leftist and French Republican value.

The beauty of a narrative construction driven by the *general* tension between the group and the individual or the utopian and the existing is that it can open up any given context without imposing a specific content on it. Driving towards a questioning rather than the identification of answers, it is both recognisable, like a personal signature, and self-effacing. When we watch *Entre les murs*, because of the way it was made and its story constructed, we can hear the voices of the teacher, his colleagues, the pupils and their parents without those individual accents being swamped by a controlling, authorial voice. Indeed, not only are these other voices heard, they are able to answer back because, in its reflexive questioning of the teacher-director-author's control, the film opens up a space of dialogue and probes its limits. It works towards developing the kind of polyphonic text described by Bakhtin but, at the same time, explores the factors that restrict the equality of voices.

The learning of inequality

Up until the 1950s, the French Republican school was very clearly and obviously divided on class lines. The children of peasants and workers, on the one hand, and of the bourgeoisie, on the other, went to different schools. The *lycée* and, even more so, the universities and the prestigious *grandes écoles*, were the preserve of the wealthier, more educated classes. In more recent times, this system of effective educational apartheid gave way to something more apparently inclusive and egalitarian. It was in the context of this seeming democratisation of the education system that Bourdieu and Jean-Claude Passeron wrote their classic book, *Reproduction in Education, Society and Culture* (1977), first published in France in 1970. The book's style was rather opaque and jargon-laden but its core thesis was clear enough: despite its egalitarian pretensions, the educational system was a formidable apparatus of social reproduction that worked to legitimise the existing order by making it appear just. The system had its own history and logics and seemed an objective assessor of merit and talent. But, it was precisely its apparent independence that made its work of social reproduction seem fair and natural. Beneath the surface, it was a powerful tool in the service of class interests. Through its work of symbolic violence, or indirectly exercised class domination, it imposed the legitimacy of the dominant culture and delegitimised the culture of the dominated. The latter thereby tended to be excluded from the system or, better still, excluded themselves, having been taught to devalue what they brought with them to the school and to consider that their rightful place was not within it (Bourdieu and Passeron, 1977: 41–2). Within this context, language and the relationship of different social groups to it had a special place. No-one's primary socialisation teaches them the specialist academic idiom that the school or university requires, but the gap between the language of home and that of the institution is far less for bourgeois students. The latter are socialised into the confident and detached relationship to language that educational institutions value. In contrast, the language of the popular classes is more attached to the concrete, prefers banter, rudeness and ribaldry to fine words, and adjusts less well to the school (Bourdieu and Passeron, 1977: 115–17).

Writing more than twenty years later in *La Misère du monde* (1993), Bourdieu, and a new and broader set of collaborators, would arrive at an updated but not altogether dissimilar judgement about the school system. They began by noting the apparently increased inclusiveness of French education. But they also observed that the much higher staying-on rate of children from the popular classes tended to lead to disillusionment: a sense that, even though they now had access to the *lycée* and even university, they were still excluded from the upper social reaches, as if the rules had somehow been changed and their elimination merely postponed. Although faced with increased competition from below, the middle and upper classes were still favoured by their possession of the symbolic capital that the children of immigrants or the working class lacked. They could also bring their greater financial and cultural resources to bear. They invested increasingly in their children's education and knew which courses to pick or avoid. They also knew which schools were desirable and which to shun. They thus helped build an increasingly segregated educational environment, one of the consequences of which was the creation of 'sink' schools, institutions that tended to concentrate far more than a proportionate share of ethnic minority pupils and social problems. In some ways, this looked suspiciously like the same world as Bourdieu and Passeron had found in 1970, one in which the cultural capital of one group gave it an overwhelming advantage in what was meant to be an egalitarian system. In other ways, it was different. Its discriminations were no less real but more diffuse (the choice of course or school, the amount of parental support) and the filtering out of the disadvantaged more gradual (Bourdieu, 1993: 597–646). What was also noticeable was how what had been told as essentially a story of class was now complicated by questions of ethnicity and the new-found prominence of the 'children of immigration' in the discussion of disadvantage and segregation. This was a different social terrain, one that Cantet's film would set out to explore.

Soon after the film begins, the hero has his first difference of opinion with his pupils. They waste, he suggests, fifteen minutes out of every hour of class owing to the time they take to arrive, line up and settle down. They thus put themselves at a disadvantage in comparison to all those French schools where a lesson means an hour spent learning. Not so, says Khoumba (Rachel Régulier), a black, female student: lessons everywhere last only fifty-five minutes. The point, as François and Khoumba both know, is trivial and designed more to mark Khoumba's refusal to be a docile pupil than be a substantive point of difference. The episode does, however, mark the first attempt to open up the question of comparative disadvantage and how it might be addressed even if its crudely quantitative answer falls obviously short.

In the first more meaningful interaction with the class, François asks them to pick out unfamiliar words from a text. Two of those put forward are *condescendance* and *succulent*. Inadvertently providing a perfect illustration of the former, François asks the pupil if he has 'une petite idée' (a little idea) of what *condescendance* means. Then, he puts *succulent* into a sentence to which he thinks his pupils will relate: 'Bill déguste un succulent cheeseburger' (Bill samples a succulent cheeseburger). If the condescension provides a perfect example, à la Bourdieu, of how the school inculcates a sense of cultural inferiority in non-bourgeois children even as it instructs them, this building of bridges between refined language and a popular idiom might seem a valiant attempt to break down cultural barriers between the school and its pupils. It is not, however, received as such. Instead, Khoumba and Esmeralda take François to task for using 'Bill' in his example rather than a name more typical of the class. What name would they prefer?, François asks. Aissata, they suggest, after some deliberation. François is happy to put 'Aissata' into his sentence. While the incident underlines the pupils' willingness to challenge the school's unspoken exclusions, its outcome suggests a change that is more tokenistic than real.

The gap between teacher and learner is also underlined by the lesson within which François asks the pupils to conjugate some verbs in the imperfect of the indicative. The discussion is side-tracked onto the imperfect subjunctive, a form usually associated with literary French and rarely used in the spoken language. Khoumba comes up with the correct first-person singular for the verb *être*. François rather mockingly tells her that she has vaguely remembered an ending for the conjugation and gives an example of how it would be used in a sentence. Not convinced, the pupils say that the imperfect subjunctive sounds like French from the Middle Ages, something even their old relatives would not use. François says they should learn it before they dismiss it. He also comments that, used in spoken French, the tense is rather snobbish, but that he and some friends were using it just the other day. What does 'snobbish' mean?, asks one child. François explains, with some gestures, that it means mannered and pretentious. Picking up on the gestures, Boubakar, a teenager with a Malian background, asks if he means homosexual. Another child asks how they can tell whether French is in written or spoken style. In the end, says François, it comes down to intuition. Can intuition be learned?, asks the pupil. Over time, answers François.

The episode feels like a textbook working-through of a Bourdieusian analysis of the school and its distance from children from the popular classes. The latter want what they learn to be of immediate use and to connect to their experience. With his more educated background, François wants them to have a less instrumental attitude to learning. For them, to take on the imperfect subjunctive would imply distancing themselves from their own background: the tense is not part of their lives. For François, the cultural gap between the object of study and everyday usage is still there – he is not a *frequent* user of the imperfect subjunctive – but it is smaller. In a classically Bourdieusian way, he can draw upon the kind of intuitive relationship to language that is learned through prolonged social exposure. This socialisation is precisely what gives the higher classes an inbuilt educational advantage. However, the classroom interchange also underscores, again along Bourdieusian lines, how the distance between the different social groups and the object of study is not only linguistic. It also involves the relationship to the self and the body. While adopting a refined style might simply seem mannered to François, it goes against Boubakar's and others' sense of their masculinity. The gap between the social groups clearly does not look the same from either side of the divide.

It is perhaps in the light of this that we can understand François's decision to ask his pupils to develop a self-portrait. The exercise takes us closer to a sense of who the pupils are and what they stand for. In a typically Cantetian way, it takes place at the uneasy interface of the public and private. The self-portrait exercise springs from Francois' decision to read Anne Frank's *Diary of a Young Girl* with his pupils. Although a young Jewish girl in hiding from the Nazis might seem to have nothing in common with young people in modern Paris, what she shares with them, as shown in the extract read in class, is a heightened sense of the self and its public vulnerability. François is able to use the book to build a bridge from the more formal culture of the school to the pupils' sense of themselves. Their self-portraits, although they may seem superficial, underscore the complexity of self-identification and the exposure of the self to the group. A telling example is provided by Carl (Carl Nanor), a boy of French-Caribbean origin. His self-portrait is captured in a single long take to camera. He is caught in medium close-up but the widescreen image means that we see the empty space of the blackboard on either side of him, its bareness underscoring both the institutional context of his public–private disclosure and his isolation when exposed to the looks of others. He defines himself in terms of sporting, televisual and musical tastes; where he lives; his background (his holidays in the Caribbean); his family (including his brother in prison); his subcultural affinities and dislikes (Goths and skateboarders); and his relationship to politics (an animosity towards politicians and racists). What sounds like a straightforward list of preferences is in fact a complex combination of social, spatial, familial, national and subcultural moorings grounded as much in a transnational popular culture as in something more nationally specific. Carl is just one pupil. Other self-portraits and other activities will reveal the complex web of personal identifications, subcultural belongings and national allegiances to be found in the multi-ethnic group. It is this multi-faceted network that François must deal with if he is to make the links that his pupil-centred pedagogy requires with the cultures of his class.

François's counterpart, the figure to whom he is most repeatedly opposed, is Frédéric, or Fred (Frédéric Faujas), the history and geography teacher. Their interaction condenses the broader educational debate between the partisans of traditional Republican education and the modernising *pédagogues*, a debate echoed, as we saw, in the way the film was received. Fred is the voice of traditional Republican rigour. Because he is studying the *Ancien régime* with the pupils, he would like François to do some canonical Enlightenment literature with them. The non-conformist François chooses Anne Frank, as we know. When the pair discusses discipline in a staff meeting, François wants to be able to exercise his discretion and turn a blind eye to mobile phones in the classroom. Fred, like a true Republican, is for the uniform (blindly egalitarian) application of the rules. When the class council meets to discuss pupil progress, François explains how he feels it counter-productive to punish Souleymane and better to home in on things that interest him. Fred is unimpressed. He wants the school to set the same high expectations of all pupils, not buy social peace. The two are poles apart on every issue. As is typical in Cantet, each tends to throw the other's blind spots into view: the inevitably arbitrary dimension of François's flexible, pupil-centred pedagogy; the blindness of Fred's approach to individual needs and socio-cultural differences. The film does not make it easy for us to choose which of the two, if either, we should align with. It certainly positions us close to François. We can see the value of what he is trying to do, but whether he is successful is another question.

The challenge of mixity

There was a moment after the famous World Cup victory of 1998 when it was fashionable to celebrate *La France black-blanc-beur* and what it had achieved. More recently, the booing of the French national anthem at France–Algeria (2001) and France–Tunisia (2008) friendly internationals in Paris seemed to suggest that, rather than showing how France might come together, soccer brought out its divisions and failure to integrate one or more generations of immigrants (Dine, 2003). *Entre les murs* plays off these precedents from the early moment when, responding to François's request to make name cards, one of the pupils puts an Algerian flag on his. Divisions become more obvious when Khoumba and Esmeralda challenge François over his choice of Bill in an example, rather than a name more representative of the class. As part of the same discussion, Esmeralda acknowledges that she is half-French but adds that she is not proud of the fact. Later, during a football match in the school-yard, Souleymane and Carl nearly come to blows. Souleymane, with a Malian background, shouts out that Thierry Henry, the great black French footballer, is a 'pédé' ('fag'). Discussions continue more jokingly in class when pupils are asked to demonstrate how to put an argumentative position. Nasim, a boy of Moroccan extraction, steps forward to sympathise with the Black Africans about the absence of Mali from the final of the African Nations Cup. He notes how their African-ness seems to fluctuate according to the success of their teams. Carl comes forward in turn to complain about African pupils' obsession with the Cup. The others stop him: what country does he support? France, he says. Boubacar challenges him: why then does he normally say he is *Antillais* (from the French Antilles) and not French? Carl responds that the Antilles are departments of France and cites great players who have their roots there, like Thierry Henry. Souleymane throws in the name of Alou Diarra, a French player with a Malian background. He never visits Mali, comments Carl, calling Souleymane 'mon frère'. The latter retorts that he is not Carl's brother, becomes insulting, and ends up being thrown out of the room. The class, and indeed individual pupils, are internally split.

If the school classroom was one of the primary sites of national integration, *Entre les murs* seems to suggest that it no longer works as it once might have done. Although the traditionalists among the school staff might still seek national uniformity, the institution is now prey to fragmentation. The modernisers like François who seek to build bridges between the school's culture and that of the pupils are also faced with the failure of their project. Rather than bringing their students together, they risk throwing their differences into relief. The film seems to lead us to an impasse: either we embrace mixity but accept the resultant fragmentation of the school community or we retreat to traditional Republicanism while acknowledging that its capacity to integrate comes with an inevitable baggage of social and cultural hierarchies and exclusions.

Spaces of inclusion and exclusion

The school's most obvious failure, but not the only one, is Souleymane, the boy who is excluded late in the film and may be sent by his Malian father back to the family's country of origin. His increasing disaffection is signalled early on: his seat at the back of the class, his failure to bring the right equipment, his reluctant participation in the self-portrait exercise, a confrontation with François during which he calls the latter by the informal *tu* form of address and is sent to the head-teacher's office. Things take an upturn when he brings in, not a written self-portrait, but one made up of a series of photographs to which François persuades him to add captions. François prints out the work, puts it on the wall and calls the class over to admire it. Souleymane is both embarrassed at his life being exposed to public view and pleased at the approval. Yet, this upturn is short-lived. Things go sharply downhill after the *conseil de classe* during which, to justify his disciplinary light touch with the boy, François says he is academically limited. Although they have seemed inattentive during the meeting, not least because of a period of whispering and giggling, Esmeralda and Louise, the two student delegates, take note of the comment and pass it on to Souleymane in a later lesson. It is at the stage that François loses his cool and tells them that they have behaved like 'pétasses', or sluts. Responding to this insult, but also to being effectively labelled an educational failure, Souleymane loses his temper, insults François and makes to leave the room. When Carl seeks to restrain him, he struggles and accidentally clips Khoumba's head with his rucksack, causing her eyebrow to bleed profusely. He is excluded and summoned to the *conseil de discipline.*

Before the hearing takes place, some teachers gather to discuss it in the staffroom. François feels that the outcome is inevitable. The previous year, they held at least twelve such hearings and all ended in exclusion. Souleymane is a clear case where the school has failed, the exclusion negating all they have tried to do. Fred intervenes without directly disagreeing. It is not the school that is excluding Souleymane, he says. Through his attitude and behaviour, the pupil has already left them. Whether the Bourdieusian echo here is deliberate or not, we cannot but think of the sociologist's classic analysis here and the way it suggests that, transferring responsibility from the institution to the student, self-exclusion occludes the school's role in the reproduction of inequalities.

The hearing itself is much the most formal and theatrical scene of the film. The sequence opens with a rectangular group of tables in what looks like the school library, like a stage set awaiting human figures. The head-teacher and his assistant, two parent representatives, what may be two students, and three teachers, including François, walk past the camera and into shot, followed finally by Souleymane and his mother. They all take their places around the table, with Souleymane and his mother facing the head, and the teachers and parents opposite each other on the other two sides. In a film that is generally characterised by a considerable amount of fluidity, the set-up stands out through its formality and the way in which people seem to be playing scripted roles. The different voices are heard. Souleymane's mother says what a good son he is and asks for pardon on his behalf. One of the parent representatives expresses his misgivings that François is there both as a party to the dispute and someone who will decide its outcome. Souleymane and his mother have to leave the room when the vote is taken, using ballot papers and an extravagantly large, transparent box. But, what we already knew would happen comes to pass and Souleymane is expelled. The young man himself has no illusions about the process. What can he say?, he asks. They should do what they have to do. The final shot of the scene lingers on François, in focus, his profile aligned with that of Fred, out of focus. The two are together in their institutional role but François is alone with his failure. The next shot is a haunting high-angle long shot of the school-yard as Souleymane and his mother leave the school, two isolated figures in its concrete expanse.

In some ways, the disciplinary hearing is the kernel of the film, condensing many of its tensions, like earlier social 'primal' scenes in Cantet's work. François looks ill-at-ease throughout. He knows that he is partly responsible for the failure that they are dealing with. As a teacher of French, he is supposed to be in command of his language. As a practitioner of child-centred pedagogy, he has tried to bridge the gap between himself and his pupils. Yet, he has failed in both areas. He has lost control of his language not once, but twice, calling Souleymane limited and the girls 'pétasses'. He thought he could use the same banter as the pupils, putting himself on their level, but has instead insulted them and created an ugly incident. In some ways, like Souleymane, he is on trial. This is the point raised by the parent who asks how he can judge an incident involving himself. But it had already come up earlier when François confronted Esmeralda and Louise in the school-yard because they made a complaint about his use of language. He asked them if they expected a teacher to be punished like a pupil. 'Yes', they optimistically responded, but of course he is not. In all of François's dealings with his pupils, no matter how close he felt he was getting to them and no matter how much he thought he was relying on his personal style and charm, the power of the institution was behind him.

As James Williams persuasively argues, all Cantet's films are highly conscious of spatial power dynamics (2013: 147–86). Each Cantetian space has its own internal qualities but is also open to the outside. The yard is within the school but is also a space within which some of its rules and hierarchies are suspended. François usually sees it from above, either from his classroom window or from the stairway. He is both outside it and, as a teacher, superior to those who circulate within it. Although he seeks to make his classroom a relatively egalitarian space, his position standing at the blackboard, with all the desks turned towards him, underscores the institutional authority he can always lean on. When he comes down into the yard to confront the girls, he literally finds himself on a new level, in a disorderly space within which the pupils congregate freely and challenge his viewpoint. When he first appears there, a medium close-up catches him amongst a cluster of faces. As the confrontation develops, the shots become more crowded and more bodies join the dispute. Longer shots emphasise how François has become surrounded by a sea of faces. Carl says that teachers who exclude are 'des enculés' (arseholes). François is outraged at the acceptance of this term by pupils who were so upset by the use of 'pétasses'. The two words are equivalent, say the pupils. Faced with this collective refusal of his power to define the situation, François beats a hasty and flustered retreat.

The truth of the film, if such a thing can be found, lies as much between the different spaces as within them. The staffroom is a place of informal, egalitarian interchange, somewhere where teachers reflect on their practice and role. The classroom is very different. Hierarchy is built into it. Yet it is also a space where, going against the grain, in moments of interruption, *almost* egalitarian interchange and reflection can take place. The yard, a more disorderly space but also an area of free exchange and circulation, is where the pupils can more truly express themselves in a way that brings out the limits of what can be said elsewhere. The disciplinary hearing is the most formal space. It has the trappings of justice and democracy (the ballot box), yet is also the most rigid and pre-scripted arena. Each space casts light on what happens in the other spaces, bringing out their potential and limitations. The school itself is also set within a larger social context that impacts upon it and that it can only partially shut out. At a more anecdotal level, we are aware of this outside through its effect on individuals. The arrest of Weï's mother by the police and Souleymane's potential exile by his father impact on the school community but lie outside its control. But, on a much more general level, the school, as Cantet had noted, is a sound-box for social and cultural differences that come from outside its walls but play out within them (Widemann, 2008). The film's truth lies partly in the interplay of its internal spaces but also involves the relationship with the outside, what lies beyond and *before* the school.

While the exclusion of Souleymane seems to be a verdict on the Republican school, we should remember that the film is more about the interplay of exclusions and inclusion than one single story strand. The very public, quasi-theatrical, exclusion of Souleymane is preceded by the off-screen arrest of Weï's mother, which may lead to the child's deportation, and the low-profile confession by Henriette that she has learnt nothing and fears she is destined for the technical baccalaureate. The latter two cases are different, both from each other and from Souleymane's story. Although the staff's support for Weï's mother is from Bégaudeau's book, it also connects directly to Cantet and other film-makers' activism in support of illegal migrants in general and their children's right to be educated in France in particular (see Chapter 1). Wei, the Chinese boy, is smart and thrives in school: the school seems eminently capable of integrating him as it has earlier waves of migrants. Coming from outside the school, the threat to him allows the teachers, like the film-makers, to come together in a generous, politically progressive gesture of support without their own role seeming in question. In contrast, Henriette's case points to a failure that is at least partly that of the school. Souleymane's exclusion, which may be his own, the school's or the broader society's fault, or a combination of all three, at least partly puts François and the institution on the line. He and the other teachers belong to an institution and a society that fails to integrate some of its members. While Wei's problems seem external to them, those of Souleymane put them doubly on the spot, as professionals and as white, middle-class French people. On the latter score, Cantet (and many of his film-making colleagues) would also seem to be inadvertently complicit. In the same way as *Vers le sud* questioned the privileged position of westerners, including the film-maker, *Entre les murs* asks the liberal middle classes to examine their role.

Socrates, the ignorant school-teacher and the equality of voices

When François asks his pupils to look back over what they have learned, and Esmeralda mentions, to his enormous surprise, that she is reading Plato's *Republic*, he does what he always does and probes her knowledge. Her replies show that she has indeed read and made sense of the book. Although she cannot remember his name, she knows that it figures someone who teaches by constantly questioning. As she puts it: 'Un gars-là ... Socrate. OK, il vient. Il accoste les gens dans la rue et tout. Il leur dit, "Oui, est-ce que tu es sûr de penser ce que tu penses. Est-ce que tu es sûr de faire ce que tu fais?". Et tout ça. Après, les gens ne savent plus où ils en sont et tout. Ils se posent des questions.'[6] The moment drips with irony because it

6 'There's this guy ... Socrates. OK, he comes and stops people in the street and so on. He says, "Are you sure that you think what you think? Are you sure you are doing what you do?". And so on. Afterwards, people no longer know where they are and so on. They ask themselves questions.'

so disconcerts François, a probing, mocking figure with an obvious resemblance to the Socratic teacher as described by Esmeralda.

François is a sustained questioner – not simply, as one would expect, on the content of what students are learning, but, more generally, on comments they make and values that they bring with them. When, for example, Souleymane asks him about rumours he is gay, he quickly turns the question around and asks why he wants to know and what sexual issues of his own lie behind the question. He is equally forceful with a young Goth who has stepped forward to defend his right to be different. How can the pupil defend his difference by dressing in the same way as a whole group? In his way, but not in the same words, he repeatedly asks his pupils if they are sure that they think what they think and are doing what they think they are doing. Picking up on this tendency to question and tease people about their positions, Esmeralda and Khoumba tell him, 'vous charriez trop' (you tease too much).

The critique addressed by Bourdieu and his co-author to this kind of Socratic methodology is relatively predictable. Because it *seems* to invite the person questioned to find the truth in and by themselves rather than having it given to them, it serves all the better the school's ideological purpose of masking its work of symbolic violence (Bourdieu and Passeron, 1977: 13–14). Rancière's critique, as developed in his book about Joseph Jacotot (1770–1840), *Le Maître ignorant* (*The Ignorant Schoolteacher*), is different. While the practice and writings of Jacotot, the exiled revolutionary, point towards what a truly egalitarian pedagogy grounded in the *self*-emancipation of the learner might look like, Socrates is a prototype for the *pédagogue savant*, the knowing pedagogue, Jacotot's polar opposite. The problem with the Socratic teacher is that he questions others in a way that relies on his greater knowledge. While he teaches, he also teaches the pupils that they know less than he does and that they need someone to help them to grow, organise their learning, ask them the right questions in the right order, and so on. The learners are thus locked into a system of endless deferral. Following an education that is meant to make them equal citizens, they are placed in the position of eternal minors. The teacher does not simply work on the ideological level, he or she actively teaches students that their intelligence is inferior. They will always need help (Rancière, 1987: 51–3). The difficulty with Bourdieu's position, as Rancière has pointed out, is that it duplicates the functioning of the very thing it critiques. Setting out to unmask a system of domination, it tells us that we in fact need someone with superior knowledge to help us see things as they are and thus puts us back in the inferior situation of the pupil (Pelletier, 2009). Rancière and Jacotot's way out is very different. It relies on the ignorant school-teacher of the book's title and pre-supposes the equality of intelligences as an axiomatic starting point and not as an endlessly deferred point of arrival. Rather than asking students to submit their intelligences to his (superior) intelligence, Jacotot asks them to submit their wills. Because everyone is able to learn, what is needed is an effort that it is the teacher's role to verify. When Jacotot questions, he questions as an equal, as one person questioning another in order to find something out and not seeking to check whether someone else has acquired knowledge that he, the teacher, already possesses.

It could be argued that *Entre les murs* initially looks Bourdieusian – it shows how the school teaches the pupils the inferiority of what they bring with them – but, on closer inspection turns out to be more Rancierian. In its treatment of voices, the film suggests an underlying belief in their equality. In its different fora, we repeatedly see how parents and students are willing to challenge the authority of the teachers and school. Thus, for example, François is taken to task at parents' evening by a woman who feels he does not understand her son. Another mother tells him that the school is not one of the better ones and its teachers are only average. More significantly, and from the very start, the pupils are shown to be willing to challenge François's authority, not simply, or mainly, at a disciplinary level, but in terms of the way he structures and selects what is to be learned and defines the classroom situation. Coming to a head at the time of the *pétasses* incident, this process means that François tends to lose his mastery and to be placed in the position of learner. This role reversal is underlined when, because he omitted the *pétasses* incident from his report about Souleymane, he is sent to produce a corrected version by the head-teacher, like a pupil told to rewrite an assignment. François is the character supposed to know: not simply because of his superior educational status, but also because he is returning, like other Cantet characters before him, to a situation that he thinks he masters. As he loses control, he is forced to learn anew, to become an ignorant school-teacher, discovering things with his students even as they discover them themselves.

Yet, there is an obvious risk here. Even as he undermines François's assurance and reasserts the equality of on-screen voices, Cantet may place himself above his characters, replacing François as the knowing, Socratic master, the one who makes his characters, and his audience, question their position, even as they discover a situation that he, as writer-director, already understands. It is at this stage that we might want to return to our earlier discussion of Bakhtin and the way in which Cantet's film, through both its on-screen organisation and its participatory mode of preparation, studiously worked to create an interchange of voices in which no one voice allows itself a controlling, over-arching position. Because Cantet does not feel he knows the school from inside and trusts his participants to be experts in their own lives, he puts himself as much in the position of an *ignorant school-teacher* as he can, discovering things with us, asking that we pay attention and reflect rather than arrive at a pre-determined conclusion. Of course, it is inevitable that, through his control of the filming process, he will be drawn towards the position of power and knowledge that he has tried to avoid. But the way in which his film refrains from working towards a truth about the school and seeks to retain a polyphonic interplay of voices shows us what *almost* egalitarian interaction can look like.

Conclusion

The school has found itself at the heart of several very successful French films in relatively recent times, two of the most notable of which are Nicolas Philibert's hit documentary *Etre et avoir* (*To Be and to Have*, 2002) and Abdellatif Kechiche's *L'Esquive* (*Games of Love and Chance*, 2003). Philibert's film was set in a small rural school where children of different ages shared a single classroom. Its countryside location and its caring, protective teacher gave it a strong, nostalgic appeal. It seemed to look back to a more innocent age of the Republican school and indeed of French society. Its classroom was more a haven from the contemporary world than an echo chamber for it, as it is in Cantet's film. Kechiche's fiction is more of the present time and might seem to have much in common with Cantet's. It features rehearsals for a Marivaux play, *Le Jeu de l'amour et du hasard* (*Games of Love and Chance*) by pupils from a multi-ethnic school in a Paris suburb. It is refreshing in the way it breaks with stereotypes of *banlieue* youth that typically revolve around violent clashes with the police. Interspersing Marivaux's eighteenth-century French with the *tchatche* (patter) of the young people, it finds an equal pleasure in the linguistic play of both. At the same time, it draws on parallels with Marivaux's drama, with its story of roles exchanged between masters and servants, to explore the extent to which people are tied to their existing social identities. Although there are certainly important points of convergence between *L'Esquive* and *Entre les murs* on this latter point, Cantet's film is much less interested in the linguistic creativity of young people from a popular background and much more in exploring the power relations that constrain linguistic interchange.

It is therefore tempting to see *Entre les murs* as an indictment of the hidden exclusions and cultural assimilationism that lie behind the apparent universalism of French Republicanism, and there are certainly elements of that in the film. But things are not that straightforward. The film is certainly driven by a desire to engage with a social mixity of which ethnicity is a major component. It does not, however, seek to tie people to their history or their origins, or narrowly equate social justice with the recognition of such factors. Indeed, as we saw in the case of Carl, the identities that the film uncovers are more complex, layered and shifting than any appeal to origins can account for. Besides which, and as we should by now expect from Cantet, it is precisely when we think that we know a person or context that we are likely to have to rethink. Esmeralda does not particularly seem to surprise François when she rejects the French part of herself. However, he is truly taken aback when she reveals that she has engaged with Plato. This has nothing to do with her identity, although it certainly tells us something about *his* prejudices. It is all to do with her capacity to resist definition and be an active intelligence and independent voice as much as a set of objectifiable socio-cultural characteristics. If part of the politics of the film resides in its (Bourdieusian) investigation of social hierarchies and exclusions, another important part is the way it works towards an egalitarian interplay of voices and intelligences. To the extent that a film driven by questioning and polyphonic interchange more than monologic certainty can have a truth, its truth lies in this tension.

The ending underscores this point. After François has dismissed his class at the end of the year, on apparently good terms with them all, we cut to the yard, where teachers and pupils come together for a good-natured football game. The yard has previously been the place of the pupils. Football had seemed a key marker of division, a sign that, when the school opened itself to diversity, it produced fragmentation. Now, it is a place of coming together and football, a ludic, egalitarian sharing that suggests that, some of the time at least, the school does work and can pull people together. This is the result neither of some austere Republican principle, nor of a planned pedagogic alternative, but arises from an unstructured egalitarian interaction that only works intermittently. We know, after all, that the school also excludes and devalues, sometimes more quietly, sometimes more noisily. In case we have forgotten this, the last image of the film is a stationary shot of François's now empty classroom, its disorderly chairs and tables bearing silent witness to events that took place in the space during the year. As the image is held, we can still hear the noise of the playful football game from the yard. In this closing disjuncture of image and sound, the film reminds us of its refusal to arrive at a settled truth about the school.[7]

References

Agence France-Presse (AFP) (2008), '"Entre les murs": Chevènement critique', *Le Figaro*, 24 September, www.lefigaro.fr/flash-actu/2008/09/24/01011-20080924FILWWW00430-entre-les-murs-chevenement-critique.php (accessed 3 January 2015).

Bégaudeau, F. (2006), *Entre les murs*, Paris, Gallimard.

Bégaudeau, F., Cantet, L., Campillo, R. and Haut et Court (2008), *Le Scénario du film 'Entre les murs,'* Paris, Gallimard.

Bourdieu, P., ed. (1993), *La Misère du monde*, Paris, Seuil.

Bourdieu, P. and Passeron, J.-C. (1977), *Reproduction in Education, Society and Culture*, trans. R. Nice, London, Sage.

Burdeau, E. and Thirion, A. (2008), 'Entretien avec Laurent Cantet', *Cahiers du cinéma*, 637 (September), 10–18.

Debril, L. (2008), 'Pour Xavier Darcos, *Entre les murs* est "l'histoire d'un échec pédagogique", *L'Express*, 26 September, www.lexpress.fr/education/pour-xavier-darcos-entre-les-murs-est-l-histoire-d-un-echec-pedagogique_576469.html (accessed 3 January 2015).

7 Cantet originally intended to end the film with a coda showing Souleymane in Mali. The sequence was shot but eliminated during editing because it would have prioritised the young man's story over other strands and given the film a more fixed conclusion (Bégaudeau *et al.*, 2008: 159).

Dine, P. (2003), 'The end of an idyll? Sport and society in France, 1998–2002', *Modern and Contemporary France*, 11:1, 33–43.

Domenach, E. and Valens, G. (2008), 'Entretien avec Laurent Cantet: Une envie d'accidents', *Positif*, 571 (September), 28–31.

Finkielkraut, A. (2008), 'Palme d'or pour une syntaxe défunte', *Le Monde*, 3 June, www.lemonde.fr/idees/article/2008/06/03/palme-d-or-pour-une-syntaxe-defunte-par-alain-finkielkraut_1053101_3232.html (accessed 14 January 2015).

Ledoux, S. (2008), 'Palme des malentendus', *Le Monde*, 25 September 2008, www.lemonde.fr/cgi-bin/ACHATS/acheter.cgi?offre=ARCHIVES&type_item=ART_ARCH_30J&objet_id=1052163&xtmc=entre_les_murs_cantet&xtcr=50 (accessed 14 January 2015).

Lefort, G. and Soulé, V. (2008), '"J'ai fait un film, pas un documentaire": Laurent Cantet et deux professeurs de français confrontent leurs expériences et leur vision de l'école', *Libération*, 22 September.

Moran, M. (2011), 'Opposing Exclusion: The Political Significance of the Riots in French Suburbs (2005–2007)', *Modern and Contemporary France*, 19:3, 297–312.

Meirieu, P. (2008), '*Entre les murs*: Un film en dehors de l'école', *Télérama*, 30 September, www.telerama.fr/idees/entre-les-murs-un-film-en-dehors-de-l-cole,34130.php (accessed 10 April 2014).

Pelletier, C. (2009), 'Emancipation, equality and education: Rancière's critique of Bourdieu and the question of performativity', *Discourse: Studies in the Cultural Politics of Education*, 30:2, 137–50.

Polony, N. (2008), '*Entre les murs* sur les écrans: La Palme du malentendu', *Marianne*, 27 September, 49.

Rancière, J. (1987), *Le Maître ignorant: Cinq leçons sur l'émancipation intellectuelle*, Paris, Fayard.

Thélot, C. (2004), *Pour la réussite de tous les élèves: Rapport de la Commission du débat national sur l'avenir de l'école présidée par Claude Thélot*, Paris, La Documentation Française and CNDP, available at www.education.gouv.fr/archives/2003/debatnational/upload/static/lerapport/pourlareussite.pdf (accessed 3 January 2015).

Widemann, D. (2008), 'Laurent Cantet: "La salle de classe est une caisse de résonance de notre société contemporaine"', *L'Humanité*, 24 September, www.humanite.fr/node/490866 (accessed 3 January 2015).

Williams, J. (2013), *Space and Being in Contemporary French Cinema*, Manchester and New York, Manchester University Press.

Before and after the political

While he was editing *Entre les murs*, Cantet was given Joyce Carol Oates's classic American novel, *Foxfire: Confessions of a Girl Gang* to read. First published in 1993, the novel presented itself as a mature woman's account of her 1950s youth and involvement with a gang of girls spurred into revolt against an oppressive, male-dominated society. Cantet was gripped by the book and unsurprisingly drawn to an adaptation. The novel contains so many of his favourite themes: the collision between the utopian and the real; shame and refusal of it; the tensions among individual, group and society. Finding in the novel's heroines – especially Legs, its lead character – the same spirit and energy that he had admired in Esmeralda in *Entre les murs*, Cantet thought of shifting the action to contemporary France, the novel's rebellious young women finding their 'natural' counterparts in the French suburbs. But the transcription would not work. Despite living in a patriarchal society and belonging to the working class, Oates's adolescents were remarkably free, as much because of neglect as anything else, and able to buy a car, rent a house and leave home. Cantet could not conceive of such a thing in contemporary France. Social services would intervene were there a situation in any way similar (Mangeot, 2012: 7). Reluctantly – he had just spent a year touring the world with *Entre les murs* – he decided to make the film in North America and situate it in the same period as the novel. A script was developed with Campillo, his usual collaborator, and a location found, not in New York State where the novel was set, but in Ontario, Canada, now a frequent filmic stand-in for the United States. Applying his usual method, Cantet spent the winter months of 2010/11 going round places in Toronto where young people could be found, auditioning young women and assembling his cast. Again in typical fashion, he spent about two weeks work-shopping with the chosen actors, setting out situations for them, allowing them to improvise, feeding their ideas and personalities back into the script. Shooting took place in the summer of 2011 in the Ontarian town of Sault Ste. Marie, its downtown, with some judicious reworking, a passable substitute for 1950s USA (Mangeot, 2012: 10; Rigoulet, 2011).

The film raises a series of major questions. Firstly, it takes us to a place and time – the American 1950s – more tightly tied to cinematic nostalgia than perhaps any other era. To what extent can it sidestep the perils of the period piece and speak to our current moment as Cantet's earlier films do? Secondly, it again poses the question of adaptation and what happens when, as with *Vers le sud*, the source novel is by someone whom one might for convenience label radic-ally other (in this case, a North American woman)? Is this a case of a male *auteur* simply overwriting a woman's voice, or is something more interesting taking place? Thirdly and relatedly, it brings women further to the centre of Cantet's film-making, but does it do so only to relativise their oppression, as *Vers le sud* did, or can it be considered a more properly feminist film? Fourthly, and finally, how does it use its story of the emergence, radicalisation and eventual disbandment of a rebel girl gang to explore broader political questions? Is the gang's trajectory in some way emblematic of a broader political history? The latter three of these four questions are clearly linked, the relation-ship between the male-authored film and the female-authored book clearly opening onto the questions of gender and the film's broader politics. Less obviously connected, the treatment of the 1950s is also crucial. Put simply, were Cantet to follow in the footsteps of previous films set in the era and make a nostalgic work or one captivated by the *look* of the period, it would be unclear how his film could engage meaningfully with issues.

The 1950s: sidestepping the stereotype, probing the surface

In his classic study of post-modernism, Fredric Jameson is drawn more than once not to the cinema of the 1950s but to cinematic works that retrospectively seek to recreate that period (Jameson, 1991). He is particularly interested in how the latter group of films bear witness to a desperate attempt to reclaim a lost past and its radical failure. All the films can do is to recycle commodified images from the popular culture of the period and return obsessively to cliched icons such as cars, diners, dresses or haircuts (Jameson, 1991: 279–88). The films, and other cultural works, are particularly drawn to small-town America as the site of a lost innocence. The milieu seemed comforting because of its apparent self-enclosure, a characteristic itself allegorical of a broader American worldview whereby the country felt it was a bastion of security in contrast to other populations and cultures with their 'violent and alien histories' (Jameson, 1991: 281). However, even by the 1950s, the isolation of small-town America was ending. With the spread of television and other media, it was subsumed into a 'continuum of identical products and standardised spaces from coast to coast' (Jameson, 1991: 281). Any real connection to the past had been lost. More seriously, with the completion of capitalist modernisation and the elimination of older social forms that might permit some contrast, a broader sense of history had collapsed. While the nineteenth-century bourgeoisie could read the past for the genealogy of its collective rise, and the left could see it as something whose injustices and unrealised hopes could be assumed by a redemptive historiography, all that we are left with is a present that we struggle to locate in any broader unfolding (Jameson, 1991: 18).

The work that Jameson credits with inaugurating the nostalgic stereotype of the 1950s is George Lucas's *American Graffiti* (1973). Writing in *Cinema Journal*, David Shumway pursues Jameson's analysis of it and other nostalgia films, focusing particularly on how they use popular music to create a reified collective memory even for those too young to have lived through the period. He underlines how *American Graffiti* uses, not the music that might have been playing on any particular radio station in the period when the film is set, but what he calls an 'idealized fifties music' (Shumway, 1999: 41). Given the pervasiveness of music in the film, he notes the difficulty deciding whether it is diegetic or not and comments, 'Music doesn't come from particular places in the film's space; it pervades that space. Its function is not mainly to convey this or that mood or emotion but to constantly keep the viewer located somewhere else, in a time and a place that is gone, lost, but not related historically to the present' (1999: 41–2). He concludes that music is the *primary* means by which 'the fifties' are produced for the viewer, but also notes how virtually all the characters in the film (the delinquent gang, the cheerleader, the nerd etc.) are already familiar from films and television. This leads him to conclude:

> not only the music but the entire film is a representation of a well-known representation of youth in the 1950s. It is the seamlessness of this system that has allowed *American Graffiti* to be used as a prime example of the postmodern image society, in which images are supposed to replace any more substantial understanding of our past and present. (Shumway, 1999: 42)

Earlier films had, of course, used recorded music to evoke a lost past. What constitutes the novelty of *American Graffiti* (and the broader post-modern turn that it embodies) is that the past evoked depends *entirely* on recycled cultural representations and products.

How then does Cantet deal with the 1950s without producing another 'fifties' movie trapped in the recycling of cultural stereotypes? The response to this question is necessarily multi-faceted and involves close attention to stylistic and other choices. We can begin with the use of music. In some ways *Foxfire* seems to practise the musical recycling typical of 'fifties' evocations. There are faster and slower rock numbers ('Wild wild women' by Johnny Carroll and his Hot Rocks, 'Let's get high' by Rosco Gordon etc.). There are show-business numbers or film songs from the period or earlier ('Que sera, sera', Doris Day's signature tune; 'Where is your heart', the song from John Huston's *Moulin Rouge* (1952); Carmen Miranda's late 1930s hit, *Mamãe eu quero*). But, partially connecting to but also cutting against these songs, there are instrumental and vocal pieces from the contemporary Canadian group Timber Timbre, who were commissioned by Cantet to provide background music for the film. Given this complexity, any assessment of the film's use of music needs to consider how individual tracks are used as well as their effect in combination.

We might begin by noting how the period pieces tend to be used in a way that both reactivates their preferred meaning and reorients it. 'Wild Wild Women', for example, is sung by a male group and centres the male voice, the 'I' who drives women wild, leaves them or tames them. Cantet's film uses the song to accompany a scene of the girls without any men – authors, one might say, of their own wildness. The stereotypical teen rebellion of the 1950s is evoked but in such a way as to question the gendering of voice and agency. Something similar might be said about the use of 'Que sera, sera'. The song tells of a mother teaching her daughter to accept her destiny as she moves from girlhood, through heterosexual romance, to motherhood (the daughter prolonging the cycle by singing the song to her own daughter). In the film, however, the song is sung by the girl gang as they move to their communal house outside town. What is retained from the original is the period evocation and the female solidarity. However, the mother–daughter pairing is replaced by the group, while acceptance of woman's 'fate' is overwritten by the collective decision to break with the subordination to patriarchal norms required of women in the conservative 1950s. The song from *Moulin Rouge* is used in a similar way: it is initially played on the radio of a stolen car. Its lyrics and haunting performance by Felicia Sanders suggest the tribulations of heterosexual romance and notably a woman's anxiety about her man's true feelings. But, played over a scene of intense bonding among the girls outside and in defiance of male authority, its emotion is reoriented and expresses the girls' feelings and doubts about their own group. The pattern is clear. Because Cantet's film centres on a challenge to patriarchal power and gendered norms of behaviour, the story cuts against the soundtrack and destabilises meanings it bears. The film attaches itself to the period and borrows the affects of popular songs but undercuts the values associated with them. Rather than the past simply being evoked in an unquestioned way, it is problematised.

When we put Timber Timbre back into the mix, things become yet more complex. The rawness of their music and their use of guitars and sometimes driving rhythms seem to echo fifties rock, but their songs are also recognisably not of that period and thus work against the kind of seamlessness that Shumway linked to *American Graffiti*. Instead, they operate a temporal breach in the surface of the film, implicitly inviting us to see it as something other than a time capsule.

An analysis of the film's visual style might lead us towards similar conclusions. To begin with, it often uses what one might call the nondescript rather than the cliched. This intention is signalled in the title sequence when we see a montage of almost deserted side streets, gravel pits, a window with fading graffiti, a run-down house. We later realise that these locations are connected to the as yet unseen action of the film, mute signs of its coming (rather than frozen) pastness. Yet the *initial* absence of the more obvious icons is an announcement of the film's intention to avoid the immobilising cliches of the period. When some of this familiar iconography does appear, it is a site of struggle or presented in new and de-familiarising ways.

The treatment of the car is exemplary in this respect. The first time it appears is as the story commences. It is night-time. A girl, whom we do not yet know to be Legs (Raven Adamson), the future leader of the girl gang, walks high up on a roof as a car appears in the street below with rock music issuing from its open windows. A high-angle shot positions us behind her as she crouches down, making herself invisible. A cut takes us inside the car and shows us the Viscounts, the male gang that occupy it, as they survey the street. Another high-angle shot moves us back above the car, looking down on it from something like Legs's perspective. It is as if the film were teasing us, proffering the cliches (the young men, the car, the music, Main Street) before making it clear that the period will be viewed from a different angle. The car is again central soon after when the young women carry out their first offensive action in retribution against the maths teacher, Mr Buttinger (Ian Matthews), who has been sexually harassing Rita (Madeleine Bisson), one of their number. They paint 'I'm Buttinger. I teach Math and eat little girl's pussy' on the passenger side of his vehicle. As the unsuspecting teacher drives home, he appears in total control, an authority figure at the wheel of his car, listening to music on the radio, comfortable and relaxed. But, he soon finds himself the object of public ridicule and hostility. Rather than evoking nostalgia for the consumerist surface of the period, the car becomes a site of struggle whereby male power is made visible and shown to be vulnerable. Something similar happens later in the film when the girls first steal a car and later buy one, thereby challenging the class, gender and generational hierarchies that meant that the democratisation of mass mobility promised by post-war prosperity was not in fact equally spread.

Other icons of the period are also subject to struggle. When we finally see a diner, for example, it is a place where the girls are picking up the older men from whom they extort money. In such a conflicted and seedy context, any nostalgic temptation is clearly blocked. The same happens with the suburban house, another icon of fifties stability. There is a sequence when the girls go trick-or-treating, disguised as witches, at Hallowe'en. We find ourselves looking into a comfortable middle-class household as they press their false, crooked noses up against the glass. The mother comes to the door and gives them some treats. They stare mutely at her as she is joined by her children. The mother retreats uneasily inside and returns with money to distribute to the girls, who then depart. The film is a social drama rather than a horror, yet there is something deeply uneasy about this scene and the way it enacts, at the threshold of the house, a collision between, on the one hand, conformist middle-class comfort and female domesticity and, on the other, rebellious young women from a lower social group. Rather than returning us to an unproblematic past, the film draws out some of the subterranean conflicts that had to be repressed for that past to appear reassuring. As elsewhere in Cantet, the doorway is less a simple space of passage than a site of encounter where values meet and looks collide, with the norms of one group being made strange by the eyes of another. Later in the film, Legs and another of the group, the beautiful Violet (Rachel Nyhuus), get invited to the home of the wealthy Kelloggs, whose daughter, Marianne (Tamara Hope), had visited Legs in the detention centre to which she was sent after the theft of the car. The house is full of luxurious objects that inevitably draw the eye. The mother and daughter wear the beautiful frocks so associated with the period. The point, however, is that the Kelloggs' home stands out from the mundane, dowdy or run-down locations of the rest of the film. As a result, we do not simply see it as a commodified surface but as evidence of class privilege. Moreover, we inevitably view it through the eyes of Legs and Violet. As both are from humble backgrounds and the former is hostile to the class privilege and decorous femininity that the house enshrines, we inevitably look beyond the surface to the tensions beneath.

As Cantet noted, he sought to avoid any form of pictorialism when representing the 1950s. One of the reasons that the location was chosen was because it was a passable stand-in for the USA of the period. It could generally be filmed in the round rather than with more static or restricted framings. The desire was to create a sense of lived space in which the cameras could follow the actors rather than the latter being positioned for the former. The performers' freedom was also maintained by the filming of whole scenes in long takes with two hand-held, high-definition digital cameras (as opposed to the three used in *Entre les murs*). This way of shooting avoided the need for shot–reverse-shot constructions and allowed the performances to flow more spontaneously. At the same time, the filming was deliberately restrained, the lack of excessive or ostentatious camera movements giving the film a classical feel. Just as the soundtrack, with its blend of contemporary and 1950s music, tended to detach the film from any particular period, Cantet hoped this tension between rawness and classicism would help produce an atemporal look (Melinard, 2013; Mangeot, 2012: 7).

The film's narrative organisation had a similar effect. The story has an intra-diegetic narrator: Maddy (Katie Coseni). Her voice-over is heard as the story begins and attention is periodically drawn to her role as narrator, as when she obtains a typewriter in one of the gang's first victories, or her voice warns of disasters to come near the end. When recounted retrospectively by the older Maddy, the story seems to be held at a distance. Yet, much more than in the novel, explicit narration takes a back seat and the present of the story as an intense, unpredictable unfolding comes to the fore. This is, of course, a partial consequence of any adaptation to the screen, whereby a novel's emphasis on telling *what has happened* inevitably shifts to a film's showing of *what is happening*. Yet, there is also a clear choice to privilege immediacy over distance. As we will later see, Cantet's film positions its story of rebellion not only as a story of the 1950s but as part of a sequence of revolts. This sense of an ongoing if interrupted history is reinforced by the indeterminacy of the ending when an older Rita and Maddy meet and the former shows the latter a blurred press photograph of Fidel Castro's forces in Cuba in which one of the figures bears an uncanny resemblance to Legs. This conclusion suggests that, although Foxfire (the gang) has gone, its participants dispersed, Legs may carry on the struggle in other ways and in another place.

In contrast to the vein of reified fifties nostalgia described by Jameson, Cantet's film sets the 1950s in renewed motion, challenging the cliches, moving behind the surface, opening the period up to a sense of unfinished struggle. What we now need to look at is how exactly that struggle is framed. We will begin by considering what happens when Cantet, a male auteur, adapts a work by a female author, before opening out onto the film's broader politics.

The politics and practice of adaptation

Compared to the complex temporal to-and-froing and dense succession of episodes of Oates's novel, Cantet's film has a more straightforward and symmetrical structure, with two successive arcs, each with an upturn and downturn. After the affirmative prefatory sequence where Legs appears on the roof and is welcomed at Maddy's window, the first arc begins with things at a low ebb. We see Rita dragged into a shed by the Viscounts and presumably raped. We also see her humiliated in front of her class by Mr Buttinger before being confronted by her girlfriends for her passivity. We then see the girls begin to resist. They form Foxfire, their gang, take an oath of loyalty and secrecy, and tattoo each other with a flame (the gang's symbol). Next, they humiliate Buttinger in the way described earlier. They also beat up Maddy's middle-aged Uncle Wirtz, who had demanded sexual services from her in return for his discarded typewriter. Emboldened, they put on animal masks and demonstrate in front of a pet shop where dogs are kept in small cages. They don more disguises, as witches, on their Hallowe'en outing when they paint graffiti on shop windows in the town. The fact that this latter action is witnessed by the male gang underscores a clear progression from hidden oppressions and acts of revenge to public actions. The trend continues when the Viscounts harass Violet on the school steps. Legs puts a knife to the throat of their leader. The girls steal a man's new car and head into the countryside, only to be pursued by the police and crash. At this stage, the first up-curve of their story is brought to a sharp end. The girls are arrested, tried and convicted, with Legs being sent to the young offenders' centre and the others given suspended sentences.

After a hiatus in the group's fortune comes the second upturn, when the gang rents the house outside town and establishes an independent space, with some working for wages, others doing what they can, all chipping in. They buy a car and triumphantly cruise Main Street as the Viscounts had done at the start of the film. However, this utopian phase cannot last: they simply cannot make ends meet. They turn to extortion and, taking it in turns to dress up seductively, entice mature men, and extort money from them through the threat of public exposure. This sequence of actions ends when Maddy decides that, to prove herself to doubting members of the group, she will take her turn. She is hurt and almost raped by an older man. The girls' action becomes more dangerous: Legs decides that they will do one last sting by cultivating the relationship with the wealthy Kelloggs, kidnapping the father and demanding a ransom that will solve all their financial problems. By this stage, Maddy has left the group, unhappy with the turn to violence, followed by Rita, who has been seeing a boy on the side, in defiance of gang rules. Other frictions have arisen, as when the gang votes against admitting a black girl whom Legs got to know when imprisoned. This second downturn reaches its nadir when, against all the girls' expectations, the kidnapped Mr Kellogg (Rick Roberts) refuses to co-operate and is shot by VV (Lyndsay Rolland-Mills), one of the new, younger and more radical members of the gang. Legs tells them all to run, calls for an ambulance, takes flight herself with VV in tow, and outruns the police. A coda moves us several years on: Maddy, who was always fascinated by the stars, is working at an observatory. She drives into town and bumps into Rita, who has a young child. The two sit and chat in Rita's suburban house. It is then that Rita produces the picture that may be of Legs with Castro's troops.

One thing that Cantet says draws him to novels is the way their complex plotting and narrative organisation resist the over-neat causality of many films (Mangeot, 2012: 6). Yet, what is also clear is how he and co-writer Campillo modified their source to produce something more tightly structured. The film's symmetry is underscored by the way in which each of its arcs culminates in a car chase, the first ending with crash and capture, the second with eventual escape. The first half of each arc is associated with hidden or less visible resistances and the second with increasingly public battles with the broader society and the law that the girls cannot win. This tight structure is achieved by the elimination of some episodes of the novel. The most important of these are as follows:

1. Early in the novel, Legs enters a pole-climbing competition and wins it by beating all the male participants.

2. Legs comes across a 'dwarf' woman on a farm and witnesses her chained to a table, having sex with a whole group of men yet being a willing participant in the situation. Legs sets fire to the grass around the farmhouse and leaves the scene.

3. Legs cross-dresses to apply for a clerical job. The prospective employer, a gay man, makes a pass at her, thinking she is a he. She slashes him with a knife and steals his money.

4. Legs's father's woman, Muriel, comes to live with the gang in the communal house with her sickly baby.

5. The house comes under attack from men from the town. Shots are fired at it. Later, the gang's dog is shot and killed.

Other episodes, most notably Legs's period in the detention centre, are pared down but kept. The changes streamline the narrative and sharpen thematic lines but may also have more specific explanations. For example, the story of the 'dwarf' woman was presumably too shocking for inclusion, although its lesson about some women's complicity in their own oppression would have fitted well thematically. The reasons for the exclusion of the cross-dressing episode are less obvious. Had it been retained, it would have complicated the rising curve of violence from the easily achieved sting operations, through the attempted rape, to the kidnapping and shooting. It would also have brought the theme of male homosexuality into the film without allowing it fuller development. The shedding of the assaults on the house means that direct attacks by men on the group are concentrated in the first half of the film while the second half focuses more on the struggle against economic necessity and the girls' increasingly criminal agency. The overall consequence of the changes is to sharpen the contrast between the two halves of the film, the first showing the difficulty the girls have living within a male-dominated society, the second underscoring the impossibility of moving fully outside it or evading the more diffuse power of money.

Although the film takes all of its episodes from the novel and keeps them in a similar order, there are some major changes in terms of chronology and narrative organisation. Firstly, the film's time-frame is shorter in terms of both the story itself and the distance between Rita, the mature narrator, and Rita, the participant. In the novel, Rita, the narrator, gives her age as fifty. She locates the story of Foxfire as occurring when she was aged between thirteen and seventeen and ending in 1956. This would position the moment of narration in 1990, just a few years before the book itself was published. The chance encounter with the grown-up Rita occurs in 1968 and the newspaper report where the young women think they recognise Legs is from 1961. The film's action is concentrated into the period from 1955 to 1956. The meeting with the older Rita is not dated but, given her infant child, is presumably also the 1960s. Maddy, the narrator, seems to be contemporary with this same period rather than the older figure of the novel. The film's condensation of the action is almost certainly motivated by the difficulty of either using the same actors to cover four teenage years, given how much young people change, or the impossibility of using different performers, given the need for close resemblance. The film's narration by a younger Rita means there is less of a gap between the narrator and her younger self but a greater distance from our present. While the action might seem further from us, it is more vivid for the character, a choice that underscores how, compared to the novel, the film privileges a present unfolding over retrospective telling.[1]

Other major changes are implicit in my earlier discussion of the soundtrack and visual texture. The blending of period and contemporary music to create a sense of atemporality can have no direct equivalent in the novel. Nor does the latter need to confront so directly the risk of getting sucked into reproducing the cliched representations of the 1950s, typical of earlier cinematic representations. A multi-track medium as opposed to the novel's single track (the words on the page), cinema has of necessity to find its way through a complex inter-textual web of images, dialogue and music (Stam, 2004: 18–24). Thus, some of the differences between the film and the novel are clearly to do with their very different material bases. However, one difference that does merit considerable attention is that of authorship. Oates's book is one by a woman about young women fighting gendered oppressions and other inequalities. The male authorship of Cantet's film clearly complicates matters. It would indeed be ironic if the screen adaptation of a feminist novel placed the male voice back in control

When I discussed *Entre les murs*, I suggested it achieved something akin to a Bakhtinian polyphony by questioning the director's authority and opening itself up to a non-hierarchical interplay of voices. Much the same can be said of *Foxfire*. Cantet's voice is strongly present but also self-effacing so that Oates's voice and those of the character-performers are heard and can articulate a critique of patriarchal power that is implicitly directed at the director as well as male spectators. This comes through, for example, in the treatment of shame.

---

1 The film does have moments of anticipation, notably at the start and towards the end, when the closing drama is announced, yet its narrative is far more linear than that of the novel.

The film begins by showing how young women like Rita are shamed into conformity or silence. It then shows how, in a society where men must be seen to be in command, the women are able to reverse the dynamics of shame and to silence the males whom they have humiliated or from whom they have extorted money. As in other Cantet films, shame arises where individuals are forced to confront social pressures as embodied in the looks of others. Yet in *Foxfire*, the specific dynamics of the shame and its capacity to underscore patriarchal power and its frailties are drawn from Oates's book. Two voices cohabit in the same space.

Something similar applies to how the film explores tensions among individual, group and society, on the one hand, and between the utopian and the real, on the other. These are typical Cantetian concerns, yet, because they have no concrete content, are able to open themselves up to another voice. Thus, for example, we see how the girl gang empowers individual members but also pressures them. We see too how the gang comes up against the overt power structures of a patriarchal society (the school, the law, the detention centre) and the more diffuse power of money. In the process, we note how the group's utopian solidarity cannot be sustained in the face of internal tensions or external obstacles. The film works through these typically Cantetian tensions while maintaining a space for the voice of Oates with its concern for gendered oppressions and resistances. However, before we suggest that this preservation of a female voice in a male-authored film is enough to make *Foxfire* a feminist work, we will need to explore its gender politics in greater detail.

Foxfire and feminism: visibility, space and masquerade

Some of the essential gender dynamics of *Foxfire* are laid down in the first three sequences of the film when we see Legs's rooftop visit to Maddy, Rita's assault by the Viscounts and her humiliation by Mr Buttinger. The first sequence suggests empowerment. Even as the male gang takes possession of the street, Legs shows her capacity to escape their gaze and establish a festive, female solidarity with Maddy that is all the more enjoyable for being unseen by others. Rita's assault is similarly invisible to adult society but shows her objectified and victimised by the male group. The classroom scene is similar yet different: it also involves humiliation but is public. Buttinger makes Rita come to the blackboard to solve a maths problem. As she hesitates, he suggests that she should spend more time studying and less in front of the mirror. She is pinned by the mocking, complicit looks of the male teacher and pupils, and tied to a negative stereotype of superficiality and intellectual inadequacy. These scenes are all taken from Oates's novel but, as we might expect in a film, especially one by Cantet, much emphasis is placed on visuality and spatial dynamics.

We might note, firstly, how the exercise of male power shifts in nature as it moves between public and private (or hidden) spaces, with a more symbolic violence done to women in the former, more visible domain and a more physical oppression being exercised in the latter. We might also note, however, that female empowerment arises in spaces beyond men's control and away from their controlling gaze like Maddy's bedroom or the rooftop from which Legs looks down on the gang. Yet, probing further, we also note the presence of the dissenting and unseen gaze of some of the young women in the classroom scene. As Rita is humiliated and Mr Buttinger invites the class to align their look with his mocking gaze, the camera picks out Maddy's downturned eyes and Legs's brief but angry sideways glance along the row where Maddy and Rita sit. Maddy's shame at Rita's shaming is at once an acknowledgement of her own part in what has taken place and an expression of solidarity or at least understanding. Legs's look is different: neither sharing shame nor partaking in Rita's humiliation, it expresses active dissent. Within the overall distribution of publicness and visibility, it points to a potential for silent, public disagreement, precisely because women's looks are granted no social weight and their agency is discounted. This potential is one that the film soon develops.

When the girls take their revenge on Buttinger by writing about his abuse of young women on his car, they place him in the situation in which he had placed Rita, making him an object of public spectacle and shame. At the same time, they claim an agency that is made possible and magnified by their own invisibility as a source of action. As the increasingly anxious teacher drives home, we see the girls watching him, apparently doing nothing even as they orientate the gazes of the townsfolk. Next day in the school, when the now isolated man is turned upon by the class, the girls look on, smiling but again apparently inactive. The triumphant Goldie (Claire

Mazerolle) says, 'it's like we killed him'. Legs adds, comparing them to the male gang, 'They can't touch us. We're not like those assholes, the Viscounts, with their stupid pennants and jackets. We don't need that. We're invisible.' This sense of being an unseen force, powerful and untouchable precisely because it is not recognised, continues as they tattoo themselves with a flame, the Foxfire insignia, on the back of their shoulders. A symbol of the intensity of their solidarity, the flame marks a belonging that is hidden from public view. The sense of empowerment grows as, taking advantage of darkness, another aid to invisibility, the girls paint bright red flames on some buildings and one of the school windows. The next day in school, as the flame is admired and discussed, the girls exchange a complicit look. The Viscounts suspect a male gang from another school, public agency, in their eyes, being a male monopoly.

The girl's manipulation of publicness and visibility takes a different form in the sequence where they humiliate Uncle Wirtz. A respectable businessman when outside his shop or in the public part of it, Wirtz turns into a sexual harasser in the backroom or when the blinds are down, a duplicity that encapsulates the two faces of male power in the film. When he wants Maddy to perform fellatio on him, the girls of Foxfire burst in and confront him. Knocked to the ground, his ageing, flabby body made a spectacle, he finds himself the object of a hostile, mocking female gaze. The girls know he will not report the event. While Buttinger was humiliated by his harassment being forced into public view, Wirtz is driven to silence by the fear of a similar shaming. The girls now seem to have reversed the dynamics of the early classroom episode where Rita was pinned by the gaze of others: they have taken control of the visual field while remaining unseen. But this new-found invincibility is clearly utopian: when its source becomes visible, it will be challenged by official and unofficial instances of male power.

Matters come to a head with the confrontation with the Viscounts on the school steps. The sequence condenses some of the power relations that we have observed up till then. Firstly, through their public harassment of Violet, the boys bring what had hitherto been a hidden oppression into full view. Secondly, when the girls of Foxfire spring to Violet's defence, they assert the gang's collective power but lose the invisibility that had been their main weapon. Thirdly, when Legs defeats the boys by holding a knife to their leader's throat, she carries out another public shaming but exposes herself and the other girls to the gaze of official power in the guise of the head-teacher. While the gang's subsequent theft of a car is a utopian prolongation of their empowerment, it can only postpone the moment when they will be brought to book. The courtroom scene will restore the gendered status quo.

Cantet is drawn to formal scenes. The meeting between management and union representatives in *Ressources humaines*, the closing job interview in *L'Emploi du temps*, the disciplinary hearing in *Entre les murs*: these are all moments when we see people forced to play the scripted role that the context allocates to them with little say as individuals. The trial in *Foxfire* is another such scene where the context and its power relations make themselves graphically felt. The scene is quite short but long enough to show the girls' initial sense of invulnerability crushed. We see only one witness, Legs's father (Brandon McGibbon). Dressed in a suit for the event, he talks of having lost control over Legs and notes how things might have been different had he remarried when her mother died. Legs challenges his version of their relationship, denouncing him as a drunk. The judge asks whether she is sexually promiscuous and 'mixes herself with drugs'. When the father sits with his eyes cast down, the judge comments, 'that is answer enough'. The girls are back where they started. Just as, in the initial classroom scene, Rita was defined by a masculine gaze and negative gender stereotypes, Legs finds herself forced into the role of the delinquent girl in thrall to men. She is convicted but, being a minor, is given no maximum sentence. If she behaves badly, she can be kept inside until she is eighteen. Maddy, the narrator, comments, 'We thought we were untouchable, invisible, invincible but we were wrong.' The girls' rebellion has shown their capacity for agency and self-reinvention but also underscored that power relations cannot simply be disregarded. They will need to change course.

In the first part of the film, the girls are drawn to liminal and private areas (rooftops, bedrooms, alleys) or nocturnal spaces. If one way that they evade the controlling gaze of others is to be unremarkable, this is another route: to gather where they escape surveillance. After Legs's imprisonment and release, it is this latter strategy that they will follow and radicalise. Unable to live as they wish in the town, they lay claim to their own space by renting the isolated house. In theory at least, they can now make their own rules. However, as we noted earlier, they still need money and, with too few of them employed, have to turn to extortion and kidnapping to achieve it.

Both the extortion and kidnapping involve elements of masquerade whereby the girls adopt images of glamour (to entrap men) or respectability (to win acceptance from the Kelloggs). In the film's exploration of the dynamics of visibility and power, masquerade represents a new variant. In her famous 1929 article, 'Womanliness as masquerade', Joan Rivière analyses the behaviour of an intellectually brilliant woman who behaves in an exaggeratedly feminine way, flirting with men, after her lectures. For Rivière, the woman is driven to produce this mask of excessive femininity because she has occupied the normatively masculine role of public intellectual mastery and must placate men observing her. The radical conclusion that Rivière draws from this is not simply that this particular woman's femininity is an inessential performance, but that *all* femininity is a masquerade developed to reassure men (Heath, 1986). Discussion of womanliness as masquerade has been of clear importance to cinematic theories of spectatorship and notably to two important interventions by Mary-Anne Doane, later gathered together as successive chapters of the same book (Doane, 1991). In her first intervention, Doane tended to view the masquerade positively. Noting that important accounts of spectatorship, such as that developed by Laura Mulvey, seemed to position women, in their to-be-looked-at-ness, on the side of the image, or the object, thus denying them any distance from representations, she suggested that the masquerade opened up a more promising possibility. To the degree that women could *knowingly* put on an image, they could hold it at a critical distance and assume a more active role (1991: 25–6). Doane was less sanguine in her second piece. While she retained the idea that the masquerade opens a gap between women and their image and problematises any sense of essential gender identities, she also noted that it places femininity in an essentially reactive and subordinated position. Women take on the masquerade because of the presumption of male dominance. Masculinity as a naturalised position of domination may be a charade. It is nonetheless real in its effects (1991: 37–8).

The use of the masquerade in *Foxfire* is not entirely like that described by Rivière. The young women do not adopt an excessive femininity in order to compensate for a previously exercised masculine power. Rather, they adopt a feminine mask as a way to exercise direct power over men. On the first occasion they do so, Rita appears as a vamp to lure a mature man from a diner. In some ways, this might appear to endorse a familiar gender stereotype that emphasises the duplicity of women who make active use of their sexuality. What is different here is that the role is so quickly shed that it does not adhere to Rita. What is instead emphasised is the gang's collective agency and self-conscious control of the image. The same occurs in more bravura form when Violet carries out her sting operation in the hotel. When she goes into the hotel room with the man, she is an image of feminine glamour, in an elegant, pale pink, off-the-shoulder dress with a frilly petticoat. When a waiter brings a bottle of champagne to the door, she retreats into the bathroom. She takes confident stock of herself in the mirror and, beginning a transformation, removes her earrings. By the time the man opens the bathroom door, she has changed persona. The front of her dress is undone, her mascara smeared and her hair unkempt. She cries, says that she is a runaway, the police will be looking for her, and she wants to go home. The man protests that he never meant to touch her and gives her the contents of his wallet. She joins the other girls in their car, again smiling and self-confident, but now enjoying the success of her contribution to the group, a validation in the eyes of others that operates at the level of material deeds rather than appearances. Of course, the vamp and the *ingénue* are two established stereotypes, their very complementarity underscoring the limited roles available to young women as either fallen or in need of protection. However, Violet's command of both roles, her ability to shift from one to another in the space of seconds, and then shed both, opens up a space of self-conscious agency. Doane's rethinking of the masquerade reminds us that it works on patriarchal terrain and that the agency it gives women is a paradoxical one that leaves structures of domination in place. *Foxfire*'s use of it is similar yet different: the girls play roles not of their making to gain access to the money that men control. Their agency not only leaves structures of domination untouched but depends on them for its effectiveness. But, the difference here is that the existence of the gang interjects a female group (an on-screen audience) between the individual woman and the patriarchal society of Rivière's original account in a way that profoundly changes the dynamics: because of the group, the girls can be proud of what they have done while the men are silenced by their shame. As elsewhere in Cantet, the group plays a key intermediary role between the individual and broader society. If the individual is always exposed to the look of others, here that look is a validating one that allows the young women to keep broader social pressures at bay.

A similar analysis could be applied to the scenes in which Legs and Violet seek to convince the rich Kelloggs that they are respectable young women. Legs wears frumpy clothes that sustain her performance as one of the deserving poor. She insists that she could accept support for the studies she is undertaking to improve herself but not charity. Violet plays a similar part. While still undoubtedly attractive, she is much more demure, with a simple, elegant dress buttoned up to the neck. To pass muster in wealthy company, the young women must play the roles expected of their class and gender. If they thereby seem to be leaving stereotypes unchallenged, the fact that they are *performing* effectively detaches them from their roles and frees them for other possibilities. This management of the visual field represents a tactical advance from the earlier part of the film where they naively felt they could pass unseen and escape the roles allotted to them in a male-dominated society. They have now realised that, given the asymmetry of the forces in play, a more effective freedom can be achieved through the manipulation of appearances. This, in a very different context, was also the lesson of *L'Emploi du temps*, a film whose unemployed management consultant could only achieve a degree of autonomy by *seeming* to fulfil dominant social expectations.

The self-conscious masquerade is not the only way that *Foxfire* works against gender stereotyping. More generally, across the length of the film, the girls have no fixed appearances. If, during its earlier parts, they tend to wear everyday dresses that do not draw attention to themselves, later they shift between more androgynous apparel and the exaggerated femininity they don for sting operations. When in their house, for example, they are more likely to be seen in denim shorts or jeans and shirts or T-shirts. Goldie, the most butch of them, wears dungarees. When she digs gravel, Legs dresses like the men on the same job, as does the black girl with her. Once, she visits Marianne Kellogg, in the absence of the latter's parents, wearing trousers, a T-shirt and an open shirt, an androgynous figure in contrast to Marianne in her flowery frock. She tries on a fancy hat belonging to Mrs Kellogg (Briony Glassco), before putting on one of the father's and pursuing Marianne around the bedroom, saying 'Daddy's going to get you', finally cornering her and planting a kiss on her lips. The moment is left hanging there, its homoerotic element at most a subtext of a film where female bonding is nonetheless a constant. Yet, what it confirms is the more general pattern by which the film destabilises gender boundaries and challenges – not simply norms of gendered appearance, but the sense that appearances can be relied upon at all.

This destabilisation of appearances is condensed in moments of mirroring (and non-mirroring). There is a filmic cliche whereby a character expresses self-questioning by standing in front of a mirror and asking who they are. *Foxfire* gives this cliche a double twist. In its moments of apparently faithful reflection, as when Violet stands in front of the mirror in the hotel room, or when Legs looks at her demure self in the mirror in the Kelloggs' bathroom, the characters are implicitly saying 'this only appears to be me'. Just as significant, however, are the repeated moments of what one might call non-mirroring. The first occurs when the girls, on the outside, look through the window of Legs's house at the father's girlfriend as she dances seductively for him. The composition of the shot might suggest that they wanted to be like the woman inside. Instead, as their mockery makes clear, this is precisely what they do not want. Something similar happens during the Hallowe'en sequence when they look through the window at the suburban housewife. The glass becomes a meeting point as the image of those outside meets with the reflected interior on its surface. Yet, rather than producing a mirroring, this encounter only serves to emphasise the distance separating the girls outside, in their witch disguises, from the domestication inside. The non-mirroring continues shortly afterwards when the young women move onto the main street and look at a shop window full of dummies wearing elegant, decorative clothing. Again, rather than the glass being a place of reflection or frustrated desire, it becomes a plane of separation, as the girls, still in their witches' gowns, manifestly fail to mirror the feminine images inside. Ramming home the point, Legs daubs '$$ = shit = death' on the window, clearly showing her scorn for the models of femininity on offer from the burgeoning mass consumption of the 1950s. Later, when Marianne Kellogg visits the juvenile detention centre, with other smartly dressed young women, there is another lovely example of non-mirroring. The inmates' choir, which includes

Legs, lines up to sing a hymn for their visitors. There is a shot that places the two groups opposite each other, but the inmates, in their bluish-grey shirts and trousers, do anything but reflect the decorative young women opposite them, in their pastel shades, hats, frocks and white gloves. In these different examples, it is not so much a case of a non-conformist image of femininity existing opposite a conformist one and failing to match up to it. It is more a case of femininity itself being split between a version that exists at the level of appearances, constantly seeking approval from other eyes, and another version that cannot or will not exist on that plane.

As if to confirm that point, the film's probing of stereotypes of femininity does not only involve appearances. It embraces behaviours: the girl's refusal of victimhood; their ability to respond physically to aggressive or abusive men; Legs's defiance in the school and court-room; the gang's desire for economic independence and access to the consumer economy (cars, beer, a fridge, a house) that does not rely on men; and their purchase and use of a gun. Because the girls refuse to be judged on the level of the image, they necessarily express themselves through actions. Tellingly too, their moments of joyous solidarity all involve festive, bodily proximity. Rather than being exposed to a distancing, judgemental gaze, they come together to dance, eat, sleep or sing: moments of shared being, not of being seen.

The gang's dilemma, however, is how to sustain these utopian moments and produce a durable challenge to the gendered order when so much is stacked against them. In a typical Cantetian way, their desires are repeatedly brought into a collision with the real. If their first, more naive aspirations were to exert a hidden power, they quickly discovered that they had made themselves targets and that gendered domination could not be challenged on such a broad front. Their modified, more modest utopia was to be enacted away from mainstream society, in their rented house. Yet, it still came up against obstacles, some internal, some external. The brute need for money would force them back into engagement with the broader society and another collision with the law. The failure of their ransom demand would remind them of the difficulty of bending others' wills to any project, with Mr Kellogg's stubborn refusal to co-operate or even eat making them face what one might call the friction of the real in directly embodied form. Yet, their venture would also be laid low from within, torn by the same tension between old attitudes and radical idealism that lay behind another failed separatist utopia in Cantet's *Les Sanguinaires*. These tensions were already there in latent form at the time of the attack on the clothes-shop window. While others set to with obvious glee, Rita looked at the clothes with obvious longing. It is no surprise when, later in the film, she fails to break with her boyfriend, as the gang's rules dictate, and is expelled, with newcomers to the gang like VV being zealous in defence of group discipline. Legs is frustrated in turn when not everyone shares her idealistic belief in universal sisterhood. She was devastated when assaulted by another woman inmate in the detention centre and is upset again when the gang vote against admitting the black girl, with Goldie showing herself the most outspokenly opposed. While Rita cannot shed certain traditional aspects of femininity, Goldie shows the hold of long-standing prejudices.

A pre- or post- political film?

One of the reasons that Cantet deliberately inscribed a certain chronological indeterminacy into his film through choices at the level of the music, style or narrative organisation was to make it easier to connect to our present moment. Tellingly, the book's author suggested that the kind of raw sexual oppression seen in her novel (and in the film), is just as current today as it once was, even if, in the age of the internet, it had taken new forms.[2] Cantet also pointed to the broader contemporary relevance of the film. While he had been interested in the parallels between the girls' invisible or clandestine struggles and the Weather Underground group and their decision to disappear from view and radicalise their struggle at the end of the 1960s, he also saw the link to contemporary protest network, Anonymous, and its use of anonymity in its struggle against State power and powerful organisations (Mangeot, 2012: 14). He also noted how, when wondering if an anti-Communist, anti-union rant from Mr Kellogg was parodic, he had been reassured by how much it resembled Mitt Romney's speeches during his 2012 campaign for the American presidency.[3]

2 Oates made these comments in a newspaper piece (Atkinson, 2012a).
3 For the Romney comparison, see Atkinson (2012b).

It would seem that *Foxfire* was not *only* about feminism. Nor was it simply relevant to the 1950s.

In relation to its gender politics, *Foxfire* seems above all to be a pre-feminist film. If we consider that the overt commencement of second wave feminism in the United States can be dated to around 1963 – the year of publication of the influential Presidential Report on the Status of Women and of Betty Friedan's legendary book, *The Feminine Mystique* – then the film's mid-1950s action is most definitely from a pre-feminist period. The gang in the film have neither a broader movement nor an elaborated feminist discourse that they can tie into. Theirs is a politics that they have to assemble on the hoof. But it is precisely this sense of building from scratch that makes the film so relevant to the current moment, where the need for a politics is so keenly felt yet available models seem conspicuously lacking.

On this same score, it is worth noting that the situation established by the girls in their shared house resembles a primitive communism (Mangeot, 2012: 15). As they pool resources at the start of their adventure, some regret how little they can put in. Legs comments, 'we just contribute what we can, when we can'. This little phrase bears clear echoes of Marx's encapsulation of a realised communism in his legendary saying, 'from each according to his ability, to each according to his needs'. But, it also resonates in a contemporary context within which a range of important European thinkers (Badiou, Rancière, Žižek) have once more started to posit what might be called the communist 'hypothesis' (Douzinas and Žižek, 2010). In this, as in other areas, *Foxfire* seems very current.

Yet the film also seems to be about a finished political sequence. It is surely no accident that the gang's rebellion seems to shadow the political trajectory of the twentieth-century left in some of its key aspects and phases. The progression from the initial euphoria of burgeoning solidarity to a need to confront obstacles and face repression could surely be mapped onto other historical experiences with relative ease. Similarly, the group's discovery that, despite their desire for a clean break with the past, they bear received attitudes within themselves, is a familiar difficulty faced by radical movements. The related decision to 'purge' Rita for backsliding and Maddy's own choice to leave the gang bear echoes of other purges and schisms. More specifically, as noticed by Cantet himself, when he evoked the Weather Underground, the way the girls drift into something akin to terrorism (the kidnapping and shooting) bears clear echoes of the evolution of elements of the post-1968 left, not simply in the USA, but also in countries like Germany and Italy, where high-profile kidnappings took place. As in Foxfire's case, those ultimately sterile actions signalled the exhaustion of an idealism that had failed to effect wider change and, in its frustration, tried to force events. To the extent that we accept these echoes – and they seem clear enough – we might suggest that Cantet's film is about a completed political phase and its ultimate failure.

We might note however that, although the film's time-frame *precedes* second wave feminism, it anticipates it in at least two ways. Firstly, although the gang wishes to reach out to all its 'oppressed sisters', it has to confront its own racial exclusions just as feminism was challenged by black feminists for its failure to address differences among women. Secondly, the group is divided between the separatists (notably VV and Goldie) and those less able or willing to break with men (Rita, Violet): this split clearly echoes debates within feminism.

The sense that Foxfire's experience parallels that of others before (or after) them is reinforced by the comments of the old priest whom Legs knows and who compares the girls' trajectory to his own and that of other revolutionary movements. He stresses that the oppressed need to make their own rules, as in 1776 (the American Revolution), 1789 (the French Revolution), 1848 (European Revolutions) and 1917 (the Russian Revolution). He also notes how inspired he and his comrades had felt in 1917 but laments that all that people are now allowed to talk about is happiness. He clearly represents historical memory but, rather than enabling the girls to locate their experience as part of an *ongoing* process, he seems to invite them to draw parallels between it and other *completed* revolutionary moments. In this view, history is less about continuous progress than about periodic interruptions to the dominant order, each of which leaves a trace that may be picked up by future generations in their moments of rebellion. This is perhaps the sense of the Foxfire symbol and particularly the tattoo that the girls have inscribed on their shoulders at the start of their adventure. The flame evokes the intensity of the shared experience of rebellion. It is, by its nature, something short-lived. But, when worked into a tattoo, it survives as a memory, as something that marks those who have been touched by it, reminding them that the status quo is not all that there is or the limit of the possible.

It is perhaps this sense of an intermittent politics that best allows us to make sense of the film and explain how it can show a rebellion that is at once pre- and post-political and bites upon the current moment despite its apparent pastness. It now seems clear that the political phase represented by the twentieth century left has come to an end. Yet, with the emergence of groups like Anonymous and Occupy, a new phase *may* be beginning, one anxious not to repeat the errors of the past and consequently still searching for a clearly defined project. With its ability to condense elements of both a finished phase and one that has to start afresh and find its own forms, *Foxfire* is absolutely current.

Conclusion

As we have seen, *Foxfire* has many of the signature elements of a Cantet film while still being able to open itself up to other voices in a typically Cantetian way. Yet, one equally typical characteristic that we have not yet considered is how the film denies us a stable position from which to view it. Part of this relates of course to its complex temporality, the sense of the finished and the newly beginning that is embedded in its politics, but also in the way it moves between the pastness of Maddy's account and the immediacy of what is unfolding. This sense of distance and immediacy also comes through in the visual style, with its tension between classicism and rawness, and in the musical score, with its ability to bridge and blur past and the present. We are never quite sure where we stand in relation to the story. Nor are we entirely certain where to position ourselves in relation to its characters. If the film challenges male spectators, not simply by foregrounding the material and institutional oppressions of a male-dominated society, but also by refusing them any positive male identificatory figures (unless we count the old priest), it does not necessarily offer any straightforwardly positive place from which women can view. While the young women's revolt appears absolutely justified, some of the forms it takes make less easy watching. We are drawn to Legs's principles and courage but also see how the same things may lead to intransigence. The young women provide an admirable example of solidarity but their venture fails, not before the group itself has split. If the film is easier viewing for women than men, it nonetheless asks them to think hard about their position with respect to what they have seen.

Rather than leave us with something glibly conservative (all attempts to improve the world inevitably lead to tyranny) or glibly progressive (a feel-good story of women's revolt), *Foxfire* concludes with indeterminacy, leaving us with both a sense of a social order that must be challenged and deep doubts about the form such a challenge might take if it is not to repeat past errors. *Entre les murs* conveyed its own sense of indeterminacy by having multiple endings. *Foxfire* does something similar. Should we hold onto the gang's defeat and dissolution (ending one), Maddy and Rita's memory that something happened that changed their lives (ending two), or the possibility that Legs may have carried on her struggle elsewhere (ending three)? Should we focus on the pastness of the story and the sense that it encapsulates a completed and ultimately failed political phase? Or should we concentrate instead on the sense of a present unfolding and of something new being invented? The film refuses to leave us in any comfortable place.

References

Atkinson, N. (2012a), 'Joyce Carol Oates on bringing Foxfire back to the big screen', *National Post*, 10 September, http://arts.nationalpost. com/2012/09/10/joyce-carol-oates-on-bringing-foxfire-back-to-the-big-screen/ (accessed 13 April 2014).

Atkinson, N. (2012b), 'Laurent Cantet & cast bring "a particular kind of energy" to Foxfire', *National Post*, 11 September, http://arts.nationalpost. com/2012/09/11/laurent-cantet-cast-bring-a-particular-kind-of-energy-to-fox%EF%AC%81re (accessed 13 April 2014).

Doane, M.-A. (1991), *Femmes Fatales: Feminism, Film Theory and Psychoanalysis*, New York and London, Routledge.

Douzinas, C. and Žižek, S. (2010), *The Idea of Communism*, London, Verso.

Heath, S. (1986), 'Joan Rivière and the masquerade', in V. Burgin, J. Donald, and C. Kaplan, eds., *Formations of Fantasy*, London and New York, Routledge, 45–61.

Jameson, F. (1991), *Postmodernism; or, The Cultural Logic of Late Capitalism*, London, New York, Verso.

Mangeot, P. (2012), 'Entretien avec Laurent Cantet', in the *Foxfire* press-book, downloadable at www.hautetcourt.com/film/fiche/191, 6–19 (accessed 11 April 2014).

Melinard, M. (2013), 'Laurent Cantet: Foxfire "montre les bienfaits de la résistance"', *L'Humanité*, 2 January, www.humanite.fr/culture/laurent-cantet-foxfire-montre-les-bienfaits-de-la-512011; and 'Laurent Cantet: "Foxfire assume l'idée d'être un film classique"', 2 January, www.humanite.fr/culture/laurent-cantet-foxfire-assume-l-idee-d-etre-un-fil-512013 (accessed 9 April 2014).

Oates, J. C. (1994), *Foxfire: Confessions of a Girl Gang*, London and New York, Plume (Penguin).

Rigoulet, L. (2011), 'On était sur le tournage de *Foxfire* de Laurent Cantet', *Télérama*, 24 September, www.telerama.fr/cinema/on-etait-sur-le-tournage-de-foxfire-de-laurent-cantet,73097.php (accessed 12 April 2014).

Shumway. D. (1999), 'Rock 'n' roll sound tracks and the production of nostalgia', *Cinema Journal*, 38:2, 36–51.

Stam, R. (2004), 'Introduction: The theory and practice of film adaptation', in R. Stam and A. Raengo, eds, *A Companion to Literature and Film*, Malden MA, Blackwell, 1–52.

Conclusion

What makes Cantet such an important director? It is not the relatively small though growing number of his films. It is more to do with his capacity to be absolutely of his time, not in the superficial sense of latching onto current events but in a much deeper sense of probing the dynamics of his period, the changes it is marked by, the subjectivities it generates and the conflicts that lie beneath its surface. Across a series of important films, Cantet has investigated the contemporary world and its fault-lines. If one sought to define what his films were about, one might say workplace oppressions, the blind spots of the French Republican school, sex tourism, or gendered oppression and resistance to it. But the power of his film-making lies in the way his films resist any such convenient encapsulation. Each Cantet film is better seen as an open-ended investigation of something much broader than its ostensible theme. When he goes into the workplace, it is to probe contemporary class differences, shifting modes of social organisation and the emergence of new forms of oppression. When he engages with sex tourism, he is not interested in such a specific topic but instead uses it to investigate the profoundly dysfunctional and oppressive relationships embedded in globalised consumption. When he tells us the story of a girl gang in 1950s America, he is certainly interested in patriarchal oppression and proto-feminist resistance, but also looks outwards to probe the more general political lessons of the past and the emergent possibilities of the present.

Is Cantet a political director? If by political one means aligned with a particular movement or committed to a particular doctrine, clearly not. If, however, one gives political a broader meaning, then he certainly is. To begin with, his films are always about power, not in an abstract or general sense, but as it expresses itself in the concrete, embodied encounter between individuals and groups, the collision of looks and the unevenness of space. Secondly, his films always probe the tension between radical or conservative utopias and the frictions of the real: they test out values and beliefs. Like the school-teacher in *Entre les murs*, they probe and question. They force their characters to rethink their place in the world but also challenge their audience and ultimately their director to ponder their position with regards to what they are seeing. They offer no easy answers, but in their probing and questioning and their attention to power, they are surely political.

Looking at the films as a group, one is struck by a certain pessimism running through them. From the failed utopian community of *Les Sanguinaires*, through the impossible escape of *L'Emploi du temps*, to the abortive rebellion of *Foxfire*, they show the desire for freedom or revolution curtailed by the resistances of the real, not only as found in the encounter with others but also in the embodied habits of the self. Were the films simply pessimistic, one would be tempted to label them critical rather than more positively political, able to sound out social fault-lines beyond and inside the individual, but unable to show how the world might change. But, their dissection of the mechanisms of power is always balanced by their recognition of resistances. Their characters are never simply products of their social environment but always partially detached from it and able to reflect, rebel and surprise. If the films remind us why it is so hard to effect change, they also open a gap between people and their social role that is enough to show that the social order is not immutable.

Is Cantet an auteur? Certainly, as long as one immediately recognises the very specific nature of his authorship. As discussed in this book, there are features that run through his films. They always produce a very particular combination of the melodramatic and the coldly distanced, drawing us into the often familial dramas of the characters, making us feel their shame (or refusal of it), but also forcing us to stand back and take stock of what we are seeing and our reaction to it. They all operate at the intersection of the individual, group and broader society, in what one might call a concentric organisation, as long as one immediately adds that no one level is self-enclosed and that the social is always already inside the individual. This interaction of individuals, groups and broader frames is certainly expressed in dialogue but is often translated visually. In true melodramatic fash-ion too, the thrust of a Cantet film is more to do with what is forced into view by the encounter of looks and the passage of characters through what only appears to be frictionless space than with any-thing available on the surface. All these things (and more) combine to create a strong authorial signature. Yet, there is also something remarkably self-effacing about Cantet's directorial voice, as we saw in his very particular use of non-professional actors. While others turn to amateurs for their malleability or cinematic innocence, Cantet recognises their expertise in their social experience and allows their voices to shape his film and challenge his position. The power of his film-making lies in this paradoxically self-effacing assertiveness of his voice. His films bear his mark but are always open to other voices, whether of his amateur performers or those whose books he adapts. He achieves a real polyphony.

We live at a time when inequalities are growing ever deeper, when there is no shared oppositional project to create meaningful alterna-tives or even name oppressions, and when the voices of the disem-powered struggle to be heard. With its unwavering attention to power dynamics, commitment to the equality of voices and (melodramatic) determination to restore eloquence to the social terrain, Cantet's cin-ema speaks precisely to this moment. If it shows that individuals are never self-enclosed or self-sustaining, it cannot offer any stable col-lective belonging as an alternative. Instead, a cinema of questioning, not answers, it forces us to ask where we belong and where we stand. 'Elle est où, ta place?', that archetypal Cantetian question, could stand as an epigraph to the whole work.

Afterword. Returning to Cuba

Between *Entre les murs* and *Foxfire*, Cantet took part, along with six other well-known directors including Benicio del Toro, Julio Medém, Gaspar Noé and Elia Suleiman, in the portmanteau film *7 Days in Havana*, sponsored by Havana Club, the rum-makers. Each director was allocated a day of the week, with Sunday falling to Cantet. The celebrated Cuban writer Leon Padura was granted a co-ordinating role and, with his wife Lucía López Coll, co-wrote some of the episodes. However, only a few recurring characters and shared locations held together what was a loosely articulated work. Cantet took the inspiration for his episode from a chance encounter on a previous trip to Cuba, a country he had visited both while scouting for locations for *Vers le sud* and to run a cinema workshop. The meeting was with Nathalia Amore, a Santera, or priestess of the syncretic Santería religion, with its fusion of Yoruba spiritual traditions and Catholicism. When Cantet met her, Nathalia was involved in supervising the construction of a shrine to Oshun, a figure with African roots but also associated with the *Virgén de la caridad del cobre*, Cuba's Catholic patroness. Cantet enlisted Nathalia as Marta, his heroine; borrowed her story; shortened its time-frame to a day; used the cast of neighbours that she assembled for him; and, after the habitual period of workshopping, shot 'La fuente' ('The Fountain'), his contribution to the collective production.

The film's day begins as Marta opens her door and wakes up the other inhabitants of the building by shouting loudly up the stairs. As they assemble before her, she tells them that she has dreamt that she must build a fountain in honour of Oshun in her apartment. She also wants the room repainted in yellow, Oshun's colour; a wall removed to create more space; and a new dress for herself. The neighbours look at her quizzically but quickly rally. Some know where to find bricks, others where to get some paint. A woman measures Marta for the dress. Some men set about knocking down the wall. The bricks are brought in by wheelbarrow. The lovely Brazilian yellow paint they wanted has gone, but they can have some of the bright orange paint used to prevent corrosion on boats. There was no water in the house the night before so the tanks are empty. But a group of young men ferry in water from the sea in buckets. With everyone pitching in, the job is done and the dream realised. As they all assemble for a celebratory party, an old woman sings Schubert's 'Ave Maria' before everyone joins in a traditional Afro-Cuban song, the dancing bodies overflowing the frame. Changing the mood sharply, the penultimate shot shows the dozing Marta as she leans against her newly built fountain. As a solitary violin plays 'Ave Maria' again, the final shot shows her tired old face before tilting down her arm to finish on her hand in the water.

We are seeing an unfamiliar variation on a classic Cantet scenario. As the story begins, and despite the Cuban setting, we think we are in familiar territory. An individual's utopian imagination is to be confronted by the look of the group and the resistances of the real. Instead, our expectations are confounded as the group come together and, through collective endeavour and improvisation, turn the utopian dream into a reality. In some ways, the little film seems to announce the un-theorised communism that we saw in *Foxfire*. Given the Cuban context, we might think it was a tribute to the regime. The film's communal house and reference to the island's patroness are a clear invitation to read it as an allegory of the nation and its functioning. Yet, the collective success we see is one that operates at the level of mucking in and making do, and says as much about the difficulties faced by the society as its successes. In any case, the typically Cantetian double-ending (the celebration, the isolated consciousness) blocks any easy triumphalist narrative. What one retains in the end is the film's implicit reflexivity and its radical egalitarianism. The improvisation and collective endeavour that it celebrates are a key part of Cantet's own film-making. Its openness to the experience of ordinary Cubans is also typically Cantetian. As the director himself noted in the press kit, this is 'a film that allows you to see faces you never see in cinema, to hear voices you never hear. And which above all will give a voice to those who are so rarely heard."[1]

At time of writing, Cantet is in post-production of his latest film: another Cuban venture, *Return to Ithaca*. The film was co-written by Cantet and Padura. Unfolding on a Havana rooftop, it tells the story of a man's return to Cuba after many years of exile, and his encounter with his old friends. We know very little of the film at this early stage. We can already see, however, that it bears Cantet's signature, the rediscovery by someone of a place that they think they know being a recurrent device in his films. But we can also be confident that Cantet's voice will be self-effacing enough to allow Padura's experience of Cuba to express itself in what will certainly be a polyphonic work.

1 The press kit can be downloaded here: www.wildbunch.biz/films/7_days_in_ Havana (accessed 1 September 2014).

Filmography

Note: The dates refer to the year of release rather than the year of production.

Tous à la manif (1994), 27 mins, colour

Production company: Sérénade Productions
Producers: Vincent Dietschy, Bénédicte Mellac
Screenplay: Laurent Cantet
Photography: Pierre Milon
Editing: Muriel Wolfers
Principal actors: John Bertin (Serge), Michel Brun (Jean-Pierre)

Jeux de Plage (1995), 27 mins, colour

Production company: Sérénade Productions.
Producers: Vincent Dietschy, Bénédicte Mellac, Géraldine Michelot
Screenplay: Laurent Cantet
Photography: Pierre Milon, Catherine Pujol
Editing: Thomas Bardinet
Principal actors: Jean Lespert (Denis), Djallil Lespert (Eric), Julia Minguet (Marion), Isabelle Bels (Denis's wife)[1]

Les Sanguinaires (1998), 68 mins, colour

Production company: Haut et Court, La Sept Arte
Producers: Caroline Benjo, Carole Scotta, Simon Arnal-Szlovak
Screenplay: Laurent Cantet with Gilles Marchand
Photography: Pierre Milon

---

1 In *Jeux de Plage* and *Les Sanguinaires*, Jalil Lespert's name is listed in the credits as Djallil Lespert, a variant spelling.

Editing: Robin Campillo
Principal actors: Frédéric Pierrot (François), Catherine Baugué (Catherine), Marc Adjadj (Pierre), Djallil Lespert (Stéphane)

Ressources humaines (*Human Resources*) (2000), 100 mins, colour

Production company: La Sept Arte, Haut et Court
Producers: Caroline Benjo and Carole Scotta
Screenplay: Laurent Cantet, Gilles Marchand
Photography: Matthieu Poirot Delpech, Claire Caroff
Editing: Robin Campillo, Stéphanie Léger
Principal actors: Jalil Lespert (Frank), Jean-Claude Vallod (Frank's father), Chantal Barré (Frank's mother), Lucien Longueville (factory manager), Danielle Mélador (Mme Arnoux), Pascal Sémard (Human Resources manager), Didier Emile-Woldemard (Alain)

L'Emploi du temps (*Time Out*) (2001), 132 mins, colour

Production company: Haut et Court, Arte France Cinéma, Rhône-Alpes Cinéma, Havas Images.
Producer: Caroline Benjo
Screenplay: Laurent Cantet, Robin Campillo
Photography: Pierre Milon
Editing: Robin Campillo, Stéphanie Léger
Principal actors: Aurélien Recoing (Vincent), Karin Viard (Muriel), Serge Livrozet (Jean Michel), Jean-Pierre Mangeot (Vincent's father), Monique Mangeot (Vincent's mother), Nicolas Kalsch (Julien), Marie Cantet (Alice), Félix Cantet (Félix), Maxime Sassier (Nono), Nigel Palmer (Jeffrey), Didier Perez (Philippe), Nicolas Beauvais (Fred)

Vers le sud (*Heading South*) (2006), 107 mins, colour

Production company: Haut et Court, Les Films Séville, France 3 Cinéma, StudioCanal
Producers: Caroline Benjo, Carole Scotta, Simon Arnal-Szlovak
Screenplay: Laurent Cantet and Robin Campillo
Photography: Pierre Milon
Editing: Robin Campillo, Stéphanie Léger
Principal actors: Charlotte Rampling (Ellen), Karen Young (Brenda), Louise Portal (Sue), Ménothy César (Legba), Lys Ambroise (Albert), Jackenson Pierre Olmo Diaz (Eddy), Paul Wilfried (Neptune), Anotte Saint-Ford (the colonel's mistress), Marie-Laurence Hérard (the woman at the airport).

Entre les murs (*The Class*) (2008), 130 mins, colour

Production company: Haut et Court, France 2 Cinéma.
Producers: Carole Scotta, Caroline Benjo, Simon Arnal, Barbara Letellier
Screenplay: Laurent Cantet, Robin Campillo, François Bégaudeau
Photography: Pierre Milon
Editing: Robin Campillo, Stéphanie Léger
Principal actors: François Bégaudeau (François), Franck Keita (Souleymane), Henriette Kasaruhanda (Henriette), Carl Nanor (Carl), Esmeralda Ouertani (Esmeralda), Rachel Régulier (Khoumba), Wei Huang (Wei), Frédéric Faujas (Fred), Fatoumata Kanté (Souleymane's mother).

7 Days in Havana (*7 jours à la Havane*) (2012), 124 mins, colour[2]

Production company: Full House Films (Paris) and Havana Club International
Producer: Didar Domehri
Screenplay: Laurent Cantet
Photography: Daniel Aranyó, Diego Dussuel
Editing: Alejandro Rodríguez
Principal actors: Nathalia Amore (Marta), Othello Rensoli (Barbalao), Pedro (Andrès Vidal), Manolo (Alexis Vidal), María Martínez González (female neighbour).

Foxfire: Confessions of a Girl Gang (*Foxfire: confessions d'un gang de filles*) (2012), 138 mins, colour

Production company: Haut et Court, The Film Farm, France 2 Cinéma
Producers: Carole Scotta, Caroline Benjo, Simon Arnal, Barbara Letellier, Simone Urdl, Jennifer Weiss
Screenplay: Laurent Cantet and Robin Campillo
Photography: Pierre Milon
Editing: Robin Campillo and Stéphanie Léger
Principal actors: Raven Adamson (Legs Sadovsky), Katie Coseni (Maddy), Madeleine Bisson (Rita), Claire Mazerolle (Goldie), Rachel Nyhuus (Violet), Lindsay Rolland-Mills (VV), Brandon McGibbon (Ab Sadovsky), Ian Matthews (Mr Buttinger), Uncle Wirtz (Ron Gabriel), Tamara Hope (Marianne Kellogg), Rick Roberts (Mr Kellogg), Briony Glassco (Mrs Kellogg)

---

2 I only give credits for the Sunday 'La fuente' section of the film, the part directed by Cantet, which lasts for approximately 18 mins 30 secs.

Further reading

Up till now, the only book-length study of Cantet has been in French. There have been relatively few academic articles or book chapters on his work. Some are listed below. Others can be found in the references for individual chapters of this volume. There have, however, been a good number of high-quality articles addressed to the general public in periodicals such as *Les Cahiers du cinéma, Les inRocks, Positif* or *Télérama*. Film reviews in newspapers like *L'Humanité, Le Monde* and *Libération* are also worth consulting, as are the interviews that Cantet has given in these and similar publications. There are a growing number of online interviews, by far the most important of which is the one Cantet gave to Pascal Mérigeau: Mérigeau, P. (2013), 'La Master Class de Laurent Cantet', *Forum des images*, 17 January, www. forumdesimages.fr/les-rencontres/toutes-les-rencontres/la-master-class-de-laurent-cantet (accessed 17 September 2014).

Bégaudeau, F., Cantet, L. and Campillo, R. (2008), *Le Scénario du film 'Entre les murs,'* Paris, Gallimard.

The script of *Entre les murs* with commentary from Bégaudeau, Cantet and Campillo. Gives precious insights into how and why the film changes during shooting and editing.

Berlant, L. (2011), *Cruel Optimism*, Durham, NC and London, Duke University Press.

A wide-ranging and stimulating book with a chapter analysing *Ressources humaines* and *L'Emploi du temps* in terms of contemporary precariousness.

Burdeau, E. and Thirion, A. (2008), 'Entretien avec Laurent Cantet', *Cahiers du cinéma*, 637 (September), 10–18.

An interview published when *Entre les murs* was released but which ranges much wider and provides precious insights into Cantet's development and 'method'.

Higbee, W. (2004), 'Elle est où, ta place?': The social-realist melodramas of Laurent Cantet: *Ressources humaines* (2000) and *Emploi du temps* (2001)', *French Cultural Studies*, 15:3, 235–50.

Very good on the two films discussed as social melodramas. Particularly interesting on their gendered dimension.

Lebtahi, Y. and Roussel-Gillet, I. (2005), *Pour une méthode d'investigation du cinéma de Laurent Cantet: Les déplacés, vertiges de soi*, Paris, L'Harmattan.

An informative book that discusses Cantet's films up to and including *Vers le sud*. An important source.

O'Shaughnessy, M. (2007), *The New Face of Political Cinema*, Oxford, Berghahn.

Contains analyses of only two Cantet films but helps situates his filmmaking within broader trends in French cinema.

Williams, J. (2013), *Space and Being in Contemporary French Cinema*, Manchester and New York, Manchester University Press.

Incudes a fine chapter on the use of space in Cantet's films with some excellent close analysis.

Index

1950s, the 7, 22, 153–60, 164,
    172, 175, 180
    see also Jameson, Fredric
1968
    politics of 75, 176
    and radical film 10, 24, 34
7 Days in Havana (2012), 7,
    183–5, 188

adaptation 6–7, 11–12, 59,
    96–107, 129–32, 153–4,
    160, 161–5
amateur actors, use of 1, 6–11, 21,
    25, 26, 32, 34, 41, 47, 96,
    124, 128, 132–3, 182, 183
    see also workshopping
authorship 1–2, 4, 7, 11–13, 132,
    164, 181
    and Cantet's method 2, 6–13,
    26, 30, 132–3, 153–4, 190
    see also adaptation; Bakhtin,
    Mikhail; polyphony

Badiou, Alain 51, 175
Bakhtin, Mikhail 11–12, 126,
    131–5, 149, 164
    see also polyphony

Bauman, Zygmunt (and liquid
    modernity) 74–6, 79, 86
Beauvoir, Simone de 119–20
Bégaudeau, François 6, 124–6,
    128–35, 145, 188, 189
Benjo, Caroline 4, 186–8
Boltanski, Luc and Chiapello,
    Eve 74–6, 84
Bourdieu, Pierre 38–40,
    68, 126
    and cultural capital 137
    on education 136–9, 143,
    147, 152
    and *habitus* 39–40, 68
    and symbolic violence 136, 147
Brooks, Peter (on
    melodrama) 23–5

Campillo, Robin 3, 5, 6, 129–30,
    132, 153, 162, 186–9
Chiapello, Eve, *see* Boltanski,
    Luc and Chiapello, Eve
commitment 2–3, 7–8, 12, 48–9,
    88, 182
communism 175, 184
consumption 2, 46, 71, 75, 110,
    118–21, 172, 180

Dardenne, Jean-Pierre and
    Dardenne, Luc 8–9, 11, 25
Dardot, Pierre and Laval,
    Christian 84–5
debt (as governance) 80–4, 105

education 15, 32, 37–8, 60, 129
    pupil-centred 125, 127, 140, 151
    Republican 124–5, 127–8,
        135–7, 140, 149–51
    see also Bourdieu, Pierre
L'Emploi du temps (2001), 5–6,
    13–14, 18, 57–60, 70, 71–88,
    96, 119, 181, 187, 189–90
Entre les murs (2008) 6–10, 13,
    17, 19, 57, 68, 124–51, 153,
    178, 187–8, 190
L'Esquive Abdellatif Kechiche,
    2003) 149–50

family 5, 15–16, 20, 22, 35, 44–5,
    60–1, 70, 72, 77, 79–80, 82,
    85, 87, 107, 115, 119, 140, 142
    and the family romance,
        12–14, 26
    see also Freud, Sigmund;
        Oedipal drama;
        primal scene
Fassbinder, Rainer Werner 22–3
feminism 122, 154, 175, 180
    and post-feminism 120–1
    second wave 120, 175–6
Fordism (exit from) 56, 58,
    69–72, 74–6, 81, 87, 119
Foucault, Michel 79, 81
*Foxfire: Confessions of a Girl
    Gang* (2012) 7, 13, 122,
    153–78, 181, 188

Freud, Sigmund 13–16
    see also family:and the family
        romance; Oedipal drama;
        primal scene

gaze
    female 37, 166–7, 170
    male 165–6
    of others 16–17, 20–1, 27, 43,
        76, 79–80, 108, 167–8, 173
    tourist 19, 106–9
    see also spectator (the
        position of)
glass (as plane of encounter) 37,
    78–9, 107, 159, 172
    see also windows
globalisation 2, 24, 47, 49, 56,
    86, 96, 102, 114, 180
groups, *see* individuals and
    groups

Haut et Court (production
    company) 4, 126, 186–8
hooks, bell 110, 118

IDHEC 3, 5
individuals and groups 12, 16–18,
    26, 30–1, 34–5, 41, 47–51,
    53–4, 57, 59, 67, 86, 88, 111,
    134–5, 165, 170–1, 181–2, 184
integration (and exclusion) 70,
    124–5, 141–2, 143, 145–6

Jameson, Fredric (on the 1950s
    and post-modernism)
    154–5, 160
Jeux de plage (1995) 3, 13, 30–1,
    41–6, 52, 54, 119, 186

La Chair du maître (2000),
    see Laferrière, Dany
Laferrière, Dany 6, 96, 98–107,
    110, 111, 116, 121–2, 129
Laval, Christian, *see* Dardot,
    Pierre and Laval, Christian
Lazzarato, Maurizio (on
    debt and neo-liberal
    governance) 81–4
Lespert, Jalil (Djallil) 41–2, 47,
    51, 57, 68, 186–7
Looks, *see* gaze

Marchand, Gilles 3–4, 47,
    186–7
masculinity 53, 139, 169
masquerade (femininity as)
    169–71
melodrama 12, 21–6, 30–1, 36,
    42–4, 57–67, 79, 87–8, 101,
    115, 181–2
    see also Brooks, Peter; text of
    muteness
mise en scène 22, 53, 54, 116
music
    references to 107, 110, 140
    use of 83, 102, 155–8, 160, 164,
    174, 177

neo-colonialism 7, 27, 54, 100,
    105, 110–13, 117, 121–2
neo-liberalism 81, 83–5, 87, 121

Oates, Joyce Carol 7, 153,
    161–6, 174
Oedipal drama 13–15, 20, 24, 25,
    30, 43, 51–4, 57–8
    see also Freud, Sigmund

Padura, Leon 7, 183, 185
Plato 125, 130–1, 149, 150
    and the Socratic teacher
    146–7, 149
polyphony 11–12, 101, 129, 131, 135,
    150, 164–5, 182, 185
    see also Bakhtin, Mikhail
primal scene 15–16, 23, 45,
    111–12, 144
    see also Freud, Sigmund;
    family:and the family
    romance

Rampling, Charlotte 1, 6,
    96, 120
Rancière, Jacques 38–40, 68–9,
    126, 148
    and Jacotot (the ignorant
    schoolteacher) 147–9
realism 6, 12, 21, 24–6, 65
Recoing, Aurélien 6, 84
Ressources humaines (2000) 1,
    4–6, 9, 13–18, 20, 23, 27, 33
    (fn. 3), 44, 53, 56–71, 74–6,
    79, 81–2, 86–8, 96, 116, 119,
    187, 189–90
Return to Ithaca 3, 185
Romand affair 5, 59–60, 78, 87

Sanguinaires, Les (1998) 4, 30–1,
    46–54, 77, 85, 86, 96, 174,
    181, 186
sans-papiers, les 7–8, 145–6
Sartre, Jean-Paul 16–17, 120
Scotta, Carole 4, 186–8
Sérénade (production company)
    3–4, 186
sex tourism 97, 113–14, 180

shame 12, 16–18, 24, 44–6, 53–4,
78, 112, 117, 131, 134–5, 164–6,
170, 181
age-related 54, 119–20
class-related 16, 53, 63, 66
refused 86–7, 113
Sirk, Douglas 22–3, 25
space 18–21, 35–6, 49–50, 108–9,
113, 190
and non-places 72, 78
openness to outside of 19,
35, 113
and power 19–20, 62, 78,
144–5, 159, 168
and spatial barriers 20, 36,
62, 76, 79, 107, 109
and thresholds 19, 30, 108–9,
123, 159
spectator (position of) 9, 27,
45–6, 67, 87–8, 108, 122,
164, 169, 177–8
Stam, Robert (on adaptation)
99–100, 102, 105–6, 164

text of muteness 23–5, 62,
67–9, 104
see also Brooks, Peter;
melodrama

Tous à la manif (1994) 1, 3–4, 13,
30–44, 46, 49, 52–3, 56,
68, 108, 186

utopia 12, 18, 30, 38, 45, 48,
50–1, 52, 60, 64, 67, 70,
72–3, 76, 83, 98–9, 110–11,
114, 135, 161, 165, 167–8,
173–4, 181, 184

Vers le sud (2004) 1, 6–7, 11, 13,
18–20, 23, 27, 46, 54, 57,
96–122, 129–30, 146, 154,
183, 187, 190

windows (as planes of
encounter) 18, 20, 23, 37,
78–9, 108, 144, 172
see also glass
work (and workers) 5, 8, 10,
15–16, 20–1, 23, 24, 33,
36–8, 42, 48, 53, 56–88,
97, 109, 135, 137, 180
and the thirty-five hour week
legislation 5, 58, 67, 87
workshopping 6–8, 32,
132, 183